# SINGAPORE SWING

## JOHN MALATHRONAS

summersdale

SINGAPORE SWING

Summersdale Publishers Ltd
46 West Street
Chichester
West Sussex
PO19 1RP
UK

www.summersdale.com

Printed and bound in Great Britain

ISBN: 1-84024-594-8
ISBN 13: 978-1-84024-594-3

'Fashionista' by Jimmy James © Made Records.
Extract reprinted by permission

# SINGAPORE SWING

## SWING

JOHN MALATHRONAS

*For Karen*

# ACKNOWLEDGEMENTS

I am indebted first and foremost to the people I met during all my trips who have helped to put a human face to a city that still remains exotic and fascinating.

In no particular order many thanks to Richard Lim, Dave CTS, Keanesy and Benjamin Sim for the memories, Tom Hayhurst for the laughs, MJ Chow, Sunkist, Uranium, AK47 and Wisely for being such wonderful hosts, Doris at the Chinatown Hotel for bearing with me, Jeanette Ejlersen for being herself, Stephanie Huysamen for organising so many things from South Africa, Clarence Tay at Mango Travel for helping however he can and everyone at Banyan Tree Resort, Bintan. I am particularly indebted to my knowledgeable guides, Razeen and Geraldine; I recommend their Singapore Walks unreservedly.

Special thanks to the Reverend Shi Miaodao with whom I hope to continue corresponding and to Alex Au for his wit, intelligence and friendship plus his extensive guidance in the minefield that is Singaporean censorship. If you are buying this in Singapore, thank him for that; if not, then I am to blame.

Finally, thanks to Sarah Herman for all the extra hours she spent poring over the manuscript and to Jennifer Barclay for commissioning this book before it was written; I hope I have not betrayed her trust.

*But on her Land's End throned, see Cingapùr*
*Where the wide sea road shrinks to narrow way;*
*Thence curves the coast to Conchin's shore*
*And lastly trends Aurora-ward its lay.*

Canto X, 'Os Lusíadas', Luís de Camões

# CONTENTS

# PART ONE:
# IN SINGAPORE
# WITH A SLING

# CHAPTER ONE

# THE BUDDHA'S MESSAGE IS ETERNAL

A long, long time ago the pious monk Xuán Zàng undertook a long journey to procure the Buddhist sutras and enlighten the people of China. After a long and eventful expedition, Xuán Zàng and his three omnipotent followers – Monkey, the simian god, Friar Sand, the incarnation of a river spirit, and Pigsie, a creature half man, half pig – reached their destination. Two of the Buddha's most dutiful disciples, tall, thin Ananda and short, stout Kasyapa, were guarding the sacred scrolls.

'Oh, Devout Ones,' cried Xuán Zàng, 'we have arrived from afar, full of spiritual hunger for the key to Enlightenment. Please grant us the knowledge of the holy scrolls.'

Xuán Zàng waited in vain. Ananda and Kasyapa stood motionless in front of him.

'Oh, Sage Ones,' cried Monkey with annoyance in his voice, 'we have suffered many privations to come here. Please reward us with the Light of Knowledge.'

Friar Sand stretched himself in a huff, preparing for battle. Pigsie, impatient as ever, made a move to reach the trunks behind the two disciples.

Ananda stood firm, obstructed him and broke his silence.

'The Buddha's Knowledge does not come cheap, oh honourable pilgrims.'

Pigsie was astounded. 'They want their palms greased,' he squealed. 'They want us to bribe them with gold!'

Kasyapa was the next to speak. 'Do you lot know the cost of copying papyri nowadays? The scribes have formed a guild and demand ever higher wages.'

Monkey was well and truly incensed. 'Call yourselves Keepers of His Bidding? *Pah*!'

Xuán Zàng was angry. 'The Buddha *himself* sent us here,' he bellowed, 'and I will tell him of your profiteering.'

Ananda and Kasyapa smiled enigmatically.

'So be it,' they said. 'You can have the scriptures. They are in those three crates over there. Go back to your land and spread His Message.'

Xuán Zàng, Monkey, Friar Sand and Pigsie cast incredulous looks at each other. This was easier than they thought. The invocation of the Buddha's name must have alarmed those greedy con men.

The four pilgrims loaded the 8,048 hallowed books on their dragon-horse and flew away hastily in case the two custodians changed their minds. After a few hours, they dismounted to rest under a sacred Bodhi tree. Plus, of course, they were curious to begin reading the Word of the Buddha.

Xuán Zàng carefully unrolled one of the scrolls and shook with indignation.

'It's blank!' he shouted.

He opened another bundle. It was also full of blank scrolls.

'They have given us nothing,' cried Monkey.

'The swines!' cried Pigsie in an unfortunate turn of phrase.

'The Buddha will hear of this!' said Friar Sand shaking with fury.

The four friends were despondent. They had failed in their mission. In desperation, Xuán Zàng prayed to the Buddha who immediately appeared in front of him.

Monkey opened his mouth to complain but the deity silenced him with a gesture.

'I know what happened,' said the All-Knowing One. 'You gave nothing and received nothing in return. Empty hands, empty scrolls. My disciples have been told: the sutras can not be given away lightly.'

The pilgrims lowered their heads awkwardly.

'But we don't have any money to give them, All-Powerful One,' cried Monkey.

The Buddha pointed at Xuán Zàng's golden begging bowl. 'Ananda and Kasyapa will accept this for payment, I'm sure.'

The four friends fell quiet. They never expected the Buddha to stoop so low as to demand money for a spiritual treasure.

The Enlightened One broke the pervading silence.

'Oh dutiful pilgrims,' he said. 'Let me reveal this to you: you carry the right load.'

The pilgrims looked up in surprise.

'These empty scrolls are the real wordless sutra. *They* truly lead to Enlightenment.'

'But –' started Monkey.

'But the rabble in your ignorant, distant land will not comprehend. They will require words. They will ask you how long you bargained for, how much you eventually paid, and whether you got a good deal.'

'So –' started Xuán Zàng.

'So it is to convince *them* that you have to pay,' said the Buddha. 'For this is the society you live in: they understand only the value of material exchanges.'

- | -

'*Man's brown wallet OUTRAM PARK 20:00 6/1*'

The text messages flash on the black-and-green phosphorescent screen above the taximeter and linger there casually. My sleepy eyes follow them with the fascination of a toddler who is only just beginning to manage focusing in the middle distance.

'In Singapore, first time, is it?' asks the driver.

'No. Second time,' I reply, 'but last time was seventeen years ago.'

The driver nods. He is a tall, lanky Chinese with a Fu Manchu moustache who is sticking to the speed limit with Confucian commitment. I long him to get on with it, for it is almost morning and I've had no sleep tonight. *Their* night. What is it now, my day? Or is it also *my* night 12 hours later?

'Long time, *lah*. Changi not there then, *leh*?'

I try to think back in time. I look at the super-duper ECP Expressway we are on, driving into central Singapore in a night as thick as it is sultry.

'No, I've been driven this way before,' I say. 'It was Changi airport I arrived at then.' The driver doesn't object. Maybe he agrees, maybe he thinks he should not antagonise a client.

'*JP Gaultier black bag DHOBY GHAUT 10:35 7/1*'

'Place different now, *ah*?'

I don't reply to that. My sensory perception has been dulled after watching five films back-to-back on my in-flight video screen. My mind is full of plots and moving images. Maybe that's why I am concentrating on the message display; bright and beaming, it is the closest to a surrogate TV.

'*Blue jacket ORCHARD ROAD 9:00 7/1*'

'What are these messages?' I ask in return.

'Thing passenger lost.'

'In the taxis?'

I shouldn't have asked, for it all made sense immediately: a blue jacket had been left behind in a taxi to Orchard Road at 9 a.m. on 7 January.

'Lost thing – you return,' replies my driver in that staggered oriental singsong. 'Taxi company pay commission *lai dat*.'

I wouldn't expect less from Singapore's drivers and taxi companies. There is always something novel to admire in the city-state: tough on crime, tough on the causes of crime, tough on the temptations to crime.

We are approaching the centre and the night, always dense and hefty but never drab or gloomy, has begun to give way to a strange radiance of film-noir cinematic artificiality as structures appear etched against a bottleglass-green pre-dawn sky. I look at my right as we drive across the bridge over Marina Bay. By the Singapore River the skyscrapers of the Central Business District flash through momentarily, unreal and unnatural, wearing their windows like twinkling chain mail. If there exists any beauty in this vision, it is not the Creator's; it is the elegance of geometric lines and curves fashioning a horizon shaped by Man as master of the jungle's anarchy. This is a vantage point for a great photo: deservedly unreachable because we are in the middle of a motorway and – as its essence is human and ephemeral – appropriately transient, since the grand view lasts for only several seconds before my taxi swerves down the bridge incline into Prince Edward Street.

*'Man's brown wallet OUTRAM PARK 20:00 6/1'*

Looping back to the first message? Just as well, since we've arrived in Chinatown. The sunlight is now seeping through and the lack of people on the pavement exposes the lack of street detritus for which Singapore is famous. I stare at the freshly painted, two- and three-storey shophouse façades of Neil Road trying to recollect my first impression all those years ago.

*It's even cleaner than I remember it.*

I shudder as I recall my sleepy shock at Changi Airport, when I realised that I was smuggling one half-depleted pack of chewing gum through customs into this most masticophobic of states. What awaited me if they had found out? Fine, flogging or imprisonment? Perchance all three?

'Hotel Pacific, *lah*,' the driver announces.

About time.

I get out and the smell of warm, wet asphalt hits my nostrils at once. I pay the fare – plus the trauma of the airport supplement – and cart my luggage on its rollers to the hotel door. By then, the sun has truly come up: Singapore lies just one degree above the equator and any suspicion of dawn or dusk lasts less than the drive from Changi Airport into town.

The big, fat Chinese receptionist inside the hotel is not too happy to see me – I seem to have disturbed his sleep. Yes, they had a reservation on my name but no, no indication that I'd be coming so early. 'We have room after eleven,' he says.

I'm cross: 'But I made a phone call specially to warn you about this. I said I was prepared to pay extra if need be.'

The receptionist doesn't appear to register and his eyelids, as sleepy and droopy as mine, hardly budge. 'No room until eleven,' he repeats.

I take a big breath and count to ten. Should I take a stroll around the empty streets for a few hours and watch the traffic turn from brisk to hectic? I notice an ominous sign on the wall written in that inimitable oriental singular: 'No guest in room after midnight. $40 surcharge', which clearly means that you could bring in a girl if you play by the rules and make a house payment. Aha, that's why the hotel was exceptionally cheap.

The receptionist mistakes my slow-mo thinking as an indication that I am about to go. 'I give you room to sleep. You move to new room when you wake up,' he proposes. 'Passport, please?'

I am about to relent but the seasoned traveller within me flashes a yellow card. 'Can I see the room first?' I ask.

The receptionist takes me outside the hotel and down a back alley where a smaller, unobtrusive door slides sideways to reveal a low-ceilinged corridor. Five rooms open up on my right; there is just a mouldy wall on my left and the asymmetry brings a jailhouse to mind. Or, as I step into the cell-like, windowless, oppressive atmosphere of the first room, a brothel. These are quarters rented by the hour to hookers and their clients.

'No thanks, I'll go,' I tell the receptionist whose ready acquiescence confirms my original impression: I am not welcome here. I roll my suitcase to the street outside. There are four different hotels I can see from where I'm standing; Keong Saik Road is not what we would call residential. Two of them look prohibitively grand, so I cross the street to the Chinatown Hotel which looks the least expensive. As I approach the entrance, the doors open automatically and a steely breeze of air conditioning punches me in the chest. My mood mellows; over at Hotel Pacific any cooling had been entrusted to the doubtful performance of a noisy fan. Before the Chinese girl at reception smiles at me, I have seen the writing behind her and assessed it approvingly: 'Absolutely no guest in room after midnight'.

This will do.

I don't know of any people who've been to Singapore and don't like it. The ones who scoff at its well-reported intolerance for everything that interferes with its *harmonie communitaire* – like chewing gum, litter or Western pluralist democracy – have never been there. Despite what my *Guardian*-reading brain dictates, my heart commands me otherwise: I love this place. OK, sometimes too much order can drive you suicidal, but I make an exception for Singapore. It leads an existence unencumbered by the indigence of its neighbours, and it is a paragon of true multiculturalism in an area of religious and ethnic monolithicism. This is a city-state just a little smaller than the Isle of Wight and yet it has four official languages. Although three-quarters Chinese, there is a large Malay minority, a significant Indian and Arab population and a European expat circle. This is a country with Friday mosque worshippers mingling shoulder-to-shoulder with the six-o'clock pilgrims to Hindi shrines dotted among the Buddhist temples. Jews assemble in synagogues on Saturdays to be followed next day by Christians attending mass in Anglican and Catholic churches. A so-called multi-faith celebration in Britain normally calls for a rabbi, a mullah and a bishop. In Singapore the official commemoration of the Indian Ocean tsunami disaster involved an assembly of no less than nine religions representing Hindus, Christians, Jews, Muslims, Sikhs, Taoists, Buddhists, Bahá'ís and, lest we forget them, Zoroastrians.

Those nine faiths and four official languages notwithstanding, the social texture, the look-and-feel, or better the heart and soul of the state, are Chinese. Languages such as Hokkien, Cantonese, Hakka and Hainanese were spoken widely by the emigrants who left the southern provinces of China in pursuit of the British dream; yes, there was one, once, that of the self-made trader, half a century before the American version fired the imagination of the world's ambitious underprivileged.

In place of all these dialects we now have Mandarin, a compulsory subject for Singapore's Chinese schoolchildren, where 'z' is considered a vowel and words mean different things depending on whether your voice is high, high and rising higher, falling, or falling and then rising. British administrators who were sent to South East Asia were forced to learn a local language – yes, I was surprised, too, when I read this – but in order to be considered for Mandarin, they had to pass a musical test: you can't learn this language, if you are tone deaf. It is the idiom of the old, centralising Beijing civil servants and it is its unifying grace that kept the Chinese community in Singapore ultimately cohesive.

Such cohesion is relative since the Peranakan, the Chinese/Malays, speak Malay, the second official language that has given us such words as 'amok', 'gong', 'rattan', 'orang-utan' and, believe it or not, the word 'compound' (as in 'enclosed space') from the original *kampong* (village) in one of the great imperial mishearings. More markedly, it has defined three major words in the West, all three via the Portuguese. Firstly it provided us with the name of Nippon, the Land of the Rising Sun, as 'Japan', it comes from the Malay *Japang* itself stemming from the Chinese *jih pun,* meaning 'sunrise'. The second major word is 'Mandarin' itself, from the Malay *mantri* which means 'a minister of state'. The Portuguese confused it with their own *mandar* – as in 'mandate' – and bequeathed us a word for the most popular language on the planet – plus the name of a small fruit whose colour reminded them of the Chinese officials' robes. Finally, the Malays with their *teh,* gave as 'tea'. Europeans who imported their tea from South East Asia call it tea (the English), *tee* (the Germans), *té* (the Spaniards) or *thé* (the French). Those nations who acquired it via the land route from China use the Mandarin form *ch'a*: the Turks say *çay,* the Greeks *tsai,* the Russians *chai.* The Portuguese call it *cha,* too, so you may correctly deduct that they traded directly from the Chinese – which they did, in Macau. Tea was arguably *the* major item of trade in the late eighteenth century and the struggle for the monopoly of this commodity effectively created Singapore.

But let's not jump too far ahead but only a bit further north from the centre to Serangoon Road, where people from the subcontinent communicate in Telegu, Punjabi, Hindi, Bengali and Tamil. As befits the geographical location of Singapore, its third official language is Tamil, whose speakers dominate the south of the Indian cone. This language has given us first and foremost 'curry', from the Tamil *kari* meaning 'sauce for rice'; 'pariah' from *paraiyan* meaning 'drummer', the occupation of members of the lowest caste during festivals in south India; 'cheroot' from *curuttu* (roll); and 'catamaran' from *kattu-maran* (tied wood). Tamil is a language with three genders (masculine, feminine and non-human) and an ancient script that doesn't let you write down the spoken idiom in full unless extra, sacred, Grantha characters are employed. As a result, spoken Tamil and written Tamil have been diverging for centuries, and the older, ancient version is of no use for any English loanwords, like *hamburger* or *computer,* because it can't express them in written form.

Ah, English at last. We have arrived at the fourth and final official language – the instrument of empire, the unifier of unifiers and the ultimate constant in the narrow, loud alleys of the Babel that was Singapore. Now everyone speaks English: not because they're educated (they are), not because they want to tap the tourist trade (they do), but because – from my humble taxi driver to *The Straits Times* newspaper editor – speaking English is a question of survival. Singaporean children must leave school proficient in two languages: one is English and the other is the language of their ethnic group. For the children who fail such exams – the 'gone cases' – a study in the dreaded ITE, the Institute of Technical Education, beckons. It's considered so second rate that its initials are colloquially referred to as 'It's The End'.

- 2 -

I wake up from my jetlag slumber at some indeterminate evening hour, shower and leave to reconnoitre the area. The hotel receptionist takes my key chirpily. 'What happened to your arm?' she asks.

I glance at my left arm which is hanging in a sling from my shoulder. Clad in just a T-shirt, I can hardly hide it under my coat like I could in wintry London.

'I have torn two tendons,' I mumble and decide not to name them explicitly, although I could. 'I can't lift it more than this.' I try to raise my arm – and true to my word it comes up to just below my nipple and stops. 'See?'

'How did you do it?' she goes on.

*Ahem.*

'Long story,' I reply and see myself out.

Outside the heat isn't as oppressive as I had feared. Singapore is unchangingly hot and sticky with temperatures steady and ranging between 23°–35°C. What *does* change is precipitation with not just one but two monsoon seasons. Even during the so-called dry season, however, the average monthly rainfall is twice or three times that of London. The only difference is that the water comes all down in a pelter rather than over a 24/7 shower like we are used to in England.

I'm hungry, so I'm in the right place: Chinatown, or rather what has been left of it after continuous redevelopment. There are only two great civilisations the world has borne where dining has been elevated to an art beyond mere bodily satiation: the French and the Chinese. Both cultures eat for the sake of eating, the means of sustenance having become ends in themselves. Their art reflects this: the two great foodie films of all time have been the Chinese *Eat Drink Man Woman* and the French *La Grande Bouffe*. In fact, I dare you to find me a French film where there is no lunch or dinner sequence – you'll have to resort to the 1895 experiments of the pioneering Lumière brothers for that. And even they, after filming workers leaving a factory in *La Sortie des Usines Lumière*, and a train entering a station in *L'Arrivée d'un Train en Gare de La Ciotat*, what did they film next? *Repas de Bébé*: I rest my case.

As befits such a culture, it sometimes seems that all Singapore is about is food. Every hawker stall in the streets offers its own speciality dish: from translucent aromatic marine delicacies at a stall on Mosque Street to the day-glo green of a wheatgrass and aloe vera shake on a Trengganu kiosk. Men and women around me are gobbling up food: sat down, standing up, leaning against a wall, walking rapidly alone, strolling slowly arm in arm. Some are even eating for charity under a banner: 'Meals for Tidal Waves Asia

Victims'. I feel a warm glow when I realise that I can satisfy a pressing bodily function and help the destitute at the same time, but the menu puts a dampener on my appetite: Pig's tail noodle? Grass jelly with tadpole? Tripe and tendons? I have seen many weird things eaten across the Channel but the Chinese beat the French in devouring disgusting life forms hands down. I decide that boiled pig gut and sliced jellyfish had better be left to the connoisseurs. As for fried carrot cake – it sounds worse that anything the Scots could have concocted.

I move away from the hawkers and back to the sound and vision show that is every weekend night in central Chinatown. I walk under a sign for the Cantonese Opera *The Patriotic Princess* performed in aid of a 'Moral Home for the Disabled' – and that 'moral' has me pondering a lot. This is an old red-light district; the Chinese name for Banda Street means 'End of the Foreign Brothels' for here is where the Japanese girls, the Karayuki-sans, were based. I glance at a large hand-painted movie poster opposite that advertises *Blue Velvet*, warning us that the film has a 'matured' theme. (Is this how they fooled the censors? Did they think it was about cheese?) I stroll past closed shops with names out of a Jules Verne literary fantasy: Onn Fat Hong Tea Merchant; Hai Loo Store; Wong Loy Kee Aquarium – do you keep the fish as pets or as victuals?

I finally stop by the Samsui women's restaurant on Smith Street which boasts the best ginger chicken in town. The Samsui were Cantonese and Hakka women who lived together around Chin Chew street. Their distinctive red head coverings have become iconic: sloping and flat, they look like upside-down open books. The sole purpose in life of the Samsui was to work and send money to their families on the mainland. Some of them were married but most opted for spinsterhood having assumed the role of breadwinner: not only as housekeepers and wet-nurses, but also as stevedores and construction workers. Theirs was a one-way ticket to the poor quarters in Chinatown; starvation wages killed any hopes of return. As they turned older and infirm, the only luxury they permitted themselves was their traditionally cooked chicken during the Chinese New Year. This was a whole chicken, steamed with ginger for a fixed duration at a specific temperature so that it maintained its fragrance and flavour. It is still the dish of choice in the Smith Street restaurant: it is served already shredded, and you eat it by dipping a piece in ginger sauce and wrapping it in lettuce.

I walk upstairs and an old, wrinkled, diminutive Chinese waitress moving more slowly and stiffly than a legless man on crutches leads me to a table. I sit on an exquisitely carved low wooden stool in the shape of a bongo drum under the whirl of a ceiling fan and open the menu that resembles a pharmaceutical catalogue. As in every other society – from a medieval witch's brew to a Jewish mother's chicken broth – the healing power of female cooking is part of Chinese whimsy. The Samsui women were famous for their herbal, healing soups, so every dish on the menu comes with claims of its medicinal value. Everything is double-boiled: the *ling zhi* and pork soup, the *waisan* and ginseng chicken broth, the steamed pork with salted fish. I have no idea what a *tien chee* is or whether it is vegetable, animal or mineral, but it is supposed to be good for my blood circulation. The ginger chicken itself is associated with the relief of wind; well, I did mention that it was a dish served to old women.

The waitress looks at my sling and gives me a golden-toothed grin. She points at the double-boiled American ginseng with San-Yu soup and then at my arm. Thinking that, hey, two billion Chinese can't be wrong, I agree, praying that the dish does not include any reptilian parts. Her choice returns to haunt me in a soup with half an eel in it – at least I hope it's not a snake – complete with scales and bones. If after this my arm does not improve, I'll sue the chef.

A Chinese family of eight that comprises three generations – from a grandma to a pre-teen boy – is dining at a round, shiny wooden table opposite me. My gaze lingers on the grandmother, the Great Matriarch, who sits there, immobile and inscrutable. I don't know how old she is but, like most Chinese grandmothers, she looks as if she knew Confucius in person. Her expression is blank and she appears physically embalmed; I wonder whether those sweat beads on her brow are natural formalin secretions. She is impervious to the activity of the rest of her clan who are flapping animatedly to reach every small dish and sauce plate around the table. The most agile is the father who chopsticks his way assiduously, picking up the optimum amount of spinach and ginger for his rice bowl to balance the yin and the yang of the flavours. Bless.

There is a non-functioning pendulum clock on the wall surrounded by a number of old sepia photographs. They are all personal: a couple at their wedding; a family of thirteen flanking the gaunt bodies of their barely smiling grandparents; a youth looking forward with that vacant look only teenagers can perfect. They look like snippets out of any household's empire album but, although the clothes are all Western, the faces are Chinese. The father opposite exchanges glances with me, bows in recognition of our mutual, investigative stare and follows my gaze to the pictures on the wall. He examines the photos, shrugs his shoulders and immediately chokes on his fish. He receives a mighty slap on the back from the embalmed grandmother – who sure moved fast there – but in vain. He never recovers from his cough, still clearing his throat half an hour later, as he pays for the bill. Just before he leaves, he gives me a second, accusing look to make me feel guilty for his predicament.

The old waitress comes to me and asks: 'Good?'

I look at my half-eaten eel and lie: 'Good'.

'Bill?'

'Erm, no I'm still eating.' Strange, that. I thought the Chinese were more respectful of other people's prandial enjoyment.

Maybe not, for as soon as I finish and put the spoon down, she smiles and asks me '*Bill*?' again. I look around. I am the only one left. It is probably closing time. The streets outside are heaving, but these old Samsui ladies must need their sleep. 'OK,' I reply.

It is only when she brings me a Tiger beer instead of the tab that I realise what she *really* meant to say.

Right. Before I proceed any further: this is first and last time I will allude to oriental rhotacism, that indistinction between the 'r' and the 'l' on which so many cheap jokes have been based and not just those that play with elections and erections. The liquid 'r' sound is an odd one and spans a continuum – from the strangled uvular 'r' of the French to the trilling 'r' of the Italians, it glides into the wide, open-mouthed 'l' of the Brazilians and the dry, lockjaw 'l' pronunciation of the

English. In fact, European languages do invert up their 'l's and 'r's. Did you know that our Elisabeth is the Hungarians' Erszébet? Ever compared Spanish with Portuguese where the colour white is not *blanco* but *branco* and silver is not *plata* but *prata?* Did you know that African languages invert the 'r' to 'l' too? In Zulu a 'teacher' has been mutated into a *utishala* and the South African capital Pretoria into *iPitoli*. As for Malay, no prizes for guessing which nationality is meant by *ingris*. So we've had our fun, that's it – although if I come across a Chinese who has adopted a name like 'Rory', I might be tempted to return to the subject.

# CHAPTER TWO

# THE IMMORTAL

Tung Pin came from a clan of officials; his grandfather had been master of ceremonies at the Emperor's palace and his father district prefect. But, unlike them, the young man was torn between following the family tradition and the realm of religion and philosophy.

One night, Tung Pin arrived at an inn in the capital, where an old Taoist priest impressed him with his ability to compose poems without any effort.

'Who are you, Master?' asked Tung Pin, certain in his belief that the priest was a *hsien*, a supernatural apparition.

'I am the Master Yün Fang,' the Taoist revealed himself. 'I live upon the Crane Ridge and hold the secret of Immortality.'

Tung Pin's blood raced in his veins.

'Will you show me the Way, Master?' he asked.

'Why would you want to know the Way?' asked Yün Fang.

'So that I can help others,' Tung Pin replied without hesitation.

The priest smiled. 'Follow me,' he said and beckoned with his finger. Tung Pin accompanied him to his room where the priest brought a pot of millet to the boil. Tired as he was, Tung Pin fell asleep on a cushion leaning on the wall.

When he woke up, it was next morning and Yün Fang had gone. Dispirited by the apparent rejection, Tung Pin decided to listen to his father's advice and follow in his footsteps. He studied for two years and passed the triennial Mandarins' examination, coming top of the list. He started his career as a junior civil servant but rapidly gained promotion to the Censorate and eventually reached the position of privy counsellor in a dizzying upward advancement. He married a wife born into a family of wealth and authority. She bore him two sons who became important scions of society themselves. Eventually, Tung Pin became prime minister and wielded unqualified power. Unfortunately, such power corrupted him and he began to ask – nay, *demand* – bribes and commissions from everyone and for everything. It was only a matter of time before he was accused and tried for corruption. The outcome was dire: his home and all his possessions were confiscated, he was separated from his wife and children and was banished beyond ten thousand *li*. As he was crossing a snowy mountain range to reach a desolate corner of the empire, his horse refused to gallop on, and he was left stranded, a sad, solitary outcast on an untrodden path.

Someone touched him.

Tung Pin opened his eyes. He was still in the inn next to the Taoist Master, leaning on the cushion against the wall.

'One lifetime passes, and the millet simmers still uncooked,' laughed Yün Fang. 'Do you still want to become Immortal?'

Tung Pin swallowed hard. 'More than ever, Master,' he replied and looked at the pot. 'Is that *it*?' he asked.

'No my boy,' replied the Master. 'There is no magic potion. You only become Immortal through your deeds.'

## - 3 -

There are some cities in the world that are the creation of a single man with singular vision: Alexandria, Constantinople, St Petersburg. But Alexander, St Constantine and Peter the Great were powerful potentates whose word was law and whose will was limitless. That Singapore is the brainchild of a thirty-year-old company administrator named Raffles begs comparison; that it was established against the will and sometimes open hostility of the board of the East India Company, the British government and the Dutch Crown defies logic – or rather says a lot about Sir Thomas Stamford Raffles himself. I mean, the guy has been able to wipe out from posterity the memory of his other middle name – Bingley.

As befits someone with such an international reputation, Raffles was born a few days out of Jamaica on board a four-gunner ship escorting a convoy bound for England. It was 1781: the year of the British army surrender in Yorktown that sealed the fate of the American colonies in their War of Independence; the symbolic year when Britain turned her gaze away from the west and started focusing east.

Raffles entered the offices of the East India Company in Leadenhall Street at the age of 14 as a general dogsbody. For the next ten years he worked assiduously and educated himself at home. An admiring biographer compared his time as a clerk with that of the legendary Chinese sage Che Yuan who worked hard all day and studied at night under the glint of the fireflies. A more apt comparison would be with a moth attracted by the torch of success: Raffles networked like a bee, latching on to his boss through whom he met people well above his station in life. It was not long before Raffles attracted the amorous attentions of a surgeon's widow, Mrs Olivia Fancourt, ten years older than him, but well-connected. After gaining so much social capital, it was hardly surprising that Raffles was chosen in 1805 to accompany the governor of the new settlement of Penang as his assistant. He married Olivia a month before they embarked on the trip that kick-started his dizzying career. He was just 24 years old.

In Penang, Raffles was both diligent and lucky: he learned Malay and made a very important friend, Dr John Leyden, a medic and orientalist who fell for the charms of Olivia. There is little doubt that Raffles cultivated Leyden's passion: there exist numerous romantic letters between Leyden and Olivia that can not have escaped the attention of such a clever operator like young Raffles. The reason for such encouragement is clear. Leyden was a close friend of the most powerful man outside the British Isles: Governor General of India, Lord Minto. If there is a moral there, I fail to find it.

Leyden had translated the *Malay Annals*, a compendium of the legendary history of the Malay people. One of the earliest such fables involved Sang Nila Utama, the young Raja of Palembang. He was sailing from the island of Bintan to hunt on the forested outcrops that dot the archipelago when he landed on the island of Temasek. There, he came momentarily face to face with a majestic, wild animal he hadn't seen before in his maritime kingdom and guessed that it must be that famed lion of the songs and the myths and the epic poems. Believing the encounter to have supernatural significance, he founded a city which he called Lion (*Singa*) City (*Pura*) and built a palace up on a hill by the river. His harem used to bathe by the spring at the bottom which is why he prohibited access to the area; the locals called it the Forbidden Hill. This taboo was entrenched further when Nila Utama himself died and was buried at the top.

While Raffles was learning Malay and, no doubt, entertaining himself with the *Annals*, Lord Minto in Calcutta was agonising with a specific brief. The Low Countries had just been annexed by Napoleon: the French could not be allowed to outflank India through the colonies of Holland. Britain captured the Dutch colony of Cape Town, an important shelter-and-provisions point on the way to the subcontinent. Malacca in Malaya capitulated not long afterwards. By 1810, the only threat to the subcontinent's trade were the Dutch outposts in Java. But before Minto could act, he needed intelligence: how would Holland's colonial subjects react? What would the independent sultanates do? It was there that Leyden's friendship proved crucial: on a trip to Calcutta he told Minto of that man Raffles, who had learned Malay and was on personal terms with various Malay sultans. Minto sent for the ambitious under-secretary, and Raffles grabbed the opportunity with both hands. He arrived in Calcutta in June 1810 – wisely leaving his wife behind.

Minto and Raffles got on like a *kampong* on fire and planned the invasion of Java together. The naval convoy was assembled in the summer of 1811. On the way to Java, the fleet passed by an island bemired by swamps, populated by fishermen and belonging to Mahmud Shah III, Sultan of Johore-Riau.

Raffles knew it from Leyden's legends: it was called Singapura.

My sling has been attracting looks making me nervous, sheepish, diffident. It's been two days already and I haven't yet ventured far; I've been reading a Raffles biography in bed. I have discovered some licensed brothels at the other end of Keong Saik Road, but I've not been accosted. Prostitutes in Singapore are subject to continuous health tests – I wouldn't be surprised if they had their vaginas barcoded – and are forbidden to walk the streets. On top of that, the ladies of the night are, let's say, *mature* and their clients visibly of the Viagra generation, so any activity stops around 10 p.m. Out of curiosity, I peek into one of the open doors; from a poster the sitting, smiling, silent women are holding, I deduce that oral sex is on offer with a condom only. This is highly risqué; Singapore's puritan penal code criminalises 'carnal intercourse against the order of nature' – which includes oral and anal sex even between husband and wife.

True to type there is an Indian corner shop nearby, where I make friends with several members of the Tamil family who own it (and keep it open long after the sex action in the area has dwindled). I get slowly addicted to aloe vera juice with pulp bits; conceived in Japan and manufactured in Malaysia, this is like nothing I've drunk before as the aloe chunks seem to retain the coolness of the fridge long after I have opened the can. During my forays there, Rita, one of the owners, conveys to me her knowledge of the neighbourhood, some of which I've already passed on to you.

At her recommendation, I sit down for lunch at the seafood restaurant opposite and ask for king prawns. 'Are they shelled?' I ask repeatedly, as I don't want to wipe my hands in heaps of wafer-thin napkins. 'O' course, shell,' comes the reply, but I should know better for in Singapore the final 'd' has long been swallowed out of existence; as the poster above my head reminds me, the Japanese miracle drink Amachazuru offers a 'Balance Blood Pressure'. Even when that tricky 'd' is used, it's used incorrectly: signs inform me that shops are 'opened' or 'close'. So my giant king prawns come in their shells and, since I am a messy eater, my T-shirt gets speckled with blackbean sauce. But all is forgiven, because the waitress provides me with a bowl with lemons to wash my hands in; it is so large I could use it for my laundry. For that thoughtful gesture, I forget any missing, ingested consonants and tuck in.

The furthest I've been so far has been to the Pearl Centre, a working-class shopping mall on the way to Outram Park metro station (or MRT as they call it here). Half of the shops sell mobile phones or accessories and the other half are a mixed bunch. There are food stalls outside offering dim sum or curry puffs, barbecued pork slices or exotic fruit. There is a Western-style bakery where every individual sandwich is wrapped and rewrapped in cellophane. If you follow the sign, 'More Shop Inside', you can find an Internet Café where everyone is playing *Doom*, a 'New Million Years Hairdressing Salon' (a mistranslation of 'millennium' if ever I've seen one) and an 'Erotica Adult Toys Store'. *Huh?* This is a country where even *Playboy* is banned. I come closer and read the warning: 'We do not sell medications, porno VCD, DVD or magazines'. Phew! My world is the right way up again.

Too many people are staring at my arm. Ill at ease, I start making my way back to my hotel. At Duxton Park, I sit on a bench and chase away a flock of mynah birds. South East Asia is colonised by those feathered punks with chocolatey bodies, white underwings, distinctive orange beaks and a lot of attitude. Mynahs are one of the great survivors of our planet: they are intelligent enough to walk on the edge of the tarmac waiting for insect roadkill, sufficiently ferocious to drive away kingfishers and small animals from their nests, and so massively hungry that they can devastate miles of vineyards and acres of fruit orchards. I bet they'd be proud to learn that they have been assigned to the Extreme Threat Category for exotic species in Australia and thrilled that they've been nominated among the World's Top 100 invaders by the World Conservation Union. Frankly, if we left it all to Darwin, there would only be three animal species left in the long run to keep us company: cats, rats and mynah birds. Thankfully, they prefer hot climates, like British lager louts. Unsurprisingly, they are a nuisance in Singapore, nesting as they do in their hundreds on houses and high-rise flats.

Look, the mynahs are coming back already; they have classified me under 'harmless'. I stand up ready to chase them away again but then I take a big breath and clench my teeth. Is this what I am going to do all day? Have I used the sling as an excuse to shy away from this Sphinx of a city?

The Java campaign was a success; Lord Minto thanked the young Raffles by appointing him lieutenant governor. He was to preside over the island for the next five years and, although it was Singapore that has provided him with posthumous claims of greatness, it was his governship in Java that provided him with esteem during his lifetime. It is a mark of Raffles' inquisitiveness that, even though the Dutch had been in

Java for decades, it was he who made the discovery of the great Buddhist temple of Borobudur. He also wrote a book, *The History of Java*, and, this being the age of Elgin and his marbles, he compulsively stockpiled specimens to send back to England: archaeological, botanical, anthropological. His discoveries provided tremendous novelty value for London's high society, and he became a celebrity *in absentia* among London's learned circles.

But not in the offices of the Honourable Company.

Raffles' careerism did not endear him to his colleagues or, indeed, his superiors. The governor of Penang was miffed because his ex-secretary had jumped over his head and reported directly to Calcutta; Raffles' military attaché in Java fell out with him and accused him of profiteering in a land auction (he was cleared after an enquiry); Minto retired and the new head in Calcutta – the later Marquess of Hastings – looked upon Raffles as a maverick, which, of course, he was. On a personal level, life bit hard as it is bound to do in the tropics: Leyden died and Olivia followed suit; Raffles buried them side by side in Batavia. The world also changed: Napoleon was defeated and the now liberated Dutch demanded their possessions back.

Global politics is a grandmaster chess tournament: having decided to hold on to strategic Cape Town, the British government wasn't going to start a further quarrel with the Dutch. Despite what its name loudly declared, the East India Company appeared not be interested in possessions, well, east of India. In March 1816, Raffles left Java with 200 packed cases of artefacts, specimens and manuscripts. His successor had the specific task of ensuring that Dutch rule – and its ensuing monopolistic trade power – was restored.

Back in London, Raffles became the darling of the salon

set, being an expert in all things Malay and Javanese. He became a close friend of Princess Charlotte and Queen Caroline and was knighted by the Prince Regent. There is a portrait of him by George Joseph in the National Portrait Gallery dating from this period: it's a study in scarlet with black, brown and pink shadings – only Raffles' eyes, tinted in sapphire blue, pierce through the broad-brush crimson haze. He is wearing a black, high-collared Regency shirt with a white tie, as dandyish as Beau Brummell on a first date and as foppish as Lord Byron at high table. He is sitting down, a document in his hand, his right elbow resting on a desk with a red file rushed-shut on a bunch of papers. Leaning on the table at the back, half unseen, is a bevelled illustration of a Buddha in the style of the Borobudur original. Raffles stares at us rather clumsily, much like many people appear on their passport photos: awkward, self-conscious, rather clueless. What strikes you most about the man is how handsome he is, despite his solemnity: fashionably wigless, with a full head of black unruly hair, sparkling eyes and features sprightly and symmetric, he looks not unlike Roger Daltrey of the Who in their sixties incarnation.

Before I go inside Outram Park metro station, I check the prohibition signs. 'No Smoking: Fine $1000'; 'No Eating and Drinking: Fine $500'; 'No Flammable Goods: Fine $5000'. And finally, a red circle with an oblique stroke over what looks like a thorny hand-grenade: 'No Durians' without a penalty proclaimed; this is a sign to put on the frighteners by association.

Durians are fruit, in case you are wondering, and be thankful we don't have them in Europe – they don't travel well. (They don't travel, full stop: airlines have banned them). They are the ultimate in olfactory abominations – had Moses been born in the vicinity, he would certainly have appended another prohibition in Leviticus. Like all horrible comestibles, they are an 'acquired taste' which means they smell and taste like shit. No, really. So why do people eat them? Because their yellow, custard-like flesh tastes like *sweet* shit. Yes, durians have extreme cult appeal. Some fans keep them until maggots rush out from within; only then do they cut them open, certain that their sugar is concentrated, and proceed to eat the overripe sweet flesh, picking out the creepy crawlies in the process. Other devotees gather below the tall durian trees every year waiting for their cherished fruit to fall. As durians are shaped like large, heavy melons with spikes, several deaths occur annually after the odd plunging fruit slices open the head of an impatient aficionado. I wonder if they can carry dead bodies in the metro. It's certainly not prohibited, and they'll smell better than the durians.

The MRT station may be shiny and glistening like Tom Cruise's dentition, but the transactions leave a lot to be desired: this is the only transport system in the world where you queue at the ticket machines *on the way out* as well. Unless you pay good money for a permanent plastic ticket, you have to use a disposable one every time and, in the interests of recycling, you pay one dollar deposit which you reclaim by returning the ticket in the exit station. Then there is the pricing itself which is a function of distance. You choose the destinations, you pay accordingly, and you get your plastic ticket. If you make a mistake, tough: your ticket is only valid for the selected destination. I presume there is some fine to be inflicted for changing your mind while on transit.

The lines (red, green and purple) are imaginatively named North-South, East-West and North-East, and each station is given not just a name but – this being the twenty-first century – an alphanumeric code, too. Outram Park is on the North-East Line so it's given a code of NE3. NE-*three?*

I approach the information window.

'Excuse me,' I say pointing at my map. 'Look. First station: Harbour Front, NE1. Second station: Outram Park, NE3. What happened to NE2?'

The officer looks at me as if I'm carrying a durian.

'No NE2,' he said. 'No exist.'

'Is it a secret station?' I ask.

The officer makes a face like a cat that chewed a wasp. I look at my map again. There were other missing stations.

'Look here!' I persist. 'There are missing stations everywhere! NE10 Potong Pasir, next station NE12 Serangoon. What happened to NE11'?

'No NE11,' answers the official, plainly annoyed.

'I know there is no NE11,' I retort. 'What I'm asking is what happened to it.'

'Nothing happen,' he repeats. 'No exist.'

Ah, the mysteries of the East.

- 4 -

I get off the metro at Raffles Place and immediately lose my bearings. It is like being parachuted into the middle of Broadgate with office blocks, hotels and shopping arcades as far as the eye can see – which isn't far at all since the surrounding skyscrapers have elevated the horizon to neck-stretching heights. The only architectural anomaly in the pedestrianised plaza is the MRT station itself, a chalky fusion of a sultan's palace and an English cenotaph surrounded by a so-very-Home-Counties lawn. I try to guess where north might be, but the sun isn't helping: when Singapore gets overcast – which is almost every day – shadows disappear and everything is bathed in a dull, carceral grey. I seek a map inside the station, but the only guidance comes in the form of more prohibition signs ('No Skateboarding'). I glance at my city plan: useless – no glimpse of sun, no shadow, no street to guide me by. Which way was the train headed to? It's lost among the zigzag of escalators to reach the top.

I try asking some people for directions but they are not interested in my plight. Unshaven, in shorts and sandals, I am under-dressed and look peculiar. Appearance is all in oriental cultures: as late as the early 1990s, long hair was not tolerated and some backpackers entering South East Asia were in danger of being given a forced haircut, even in laid-back Thailand. Long hair meant hippies; hippies meant drugs; they, as every traveller knows, lead to the death penalty in this part of the world.

Singapore has a policy of zero tolerance for drugs, which adds to its reputation as a draconian, disciplinarian dystopia: for instance, the Misuse of Drugs Act carries a mandatory death sentence for anyone found guilty of trafficking in more than 15 grams of heroin. Yet arguing against such statutes would be tantamount to trying to persuade Germans that Holocaust denial should not be a crime: this is a city where hundreds of thousands suffered in the opium dens of Chinatown. I visited one of them, at 26 Pagoda Street. It dates from the 1840s and offered a two-in-one: you paid for and got to enjoy both your pipe and your girl at the same time. The British authorities didn't just tolerate opium distribution; they had a monopoly on the drug whose Chinese characters signify longevity and happiness. It was anything but: 80 per cent of all rickshaw pullers were addicted and emaciated their bodies to an early death. Opium dens were abolished after World War Two, but in one of those twists so common in Singapore public life, the addicts weren't forced to turn cold turkey and obtained their drugs discreetly well into the sixties.

I look as if I have just emerged from such a den, as I try to approach a European-looking gentleman in a three-piece suit and a laptop case. To my consternation, he doesn't slow down but shrugs his shoulders gallically and ignores me in his rush: out of all refusals his hurt more. I feel as if I have to relearn to walk in public, for, as befits the Central Business District, it's busy, busy, busy. Everyone is in a hurry and if you turn unexpectedly, somebody's bound to charge into you. My sling seem to attract knocks: passers-by stare at it in Darwinian critique, perplexed by the *ang moh* who should have known better than to go travelling since he's so demonstrably a cripple. They miss no opportunity to underline the message by colliding against my arm as hard as they can. Only by trial and error and doubling up on my own trail a couple of times do I end up outside the Fullerton, one of the most distinctive city hotels, next to a life-size street sculpture of a huddle of men in formal Western suits and ties holding umbrellas. They are identical to the business clientele which has been frequenting the Fullerton since 1999 when it was converted into a hotel. During my first visit so many years ago, this neoclassical building with its tall Doric columns standing on a thick, rusticated base housed the Central Post Office. I have to admit that hotelhood becomes it.

It is here, on the other side of Cavenagh Bridge that lies in front of the Fullerton that the Chinese bumboats used to anchor, side by side with the double-ended Indian *tongkangs* and the squat, flat-bottomed *twakow* vessels easily distinguished by the red and green eyes which were superstitiously painted on their bows. The town was truly an entrepôt, an *Emporio Rafflesi*: goods were brought in, exchanged and then resold. I try to imagine the worn, musty smell of foodstuffs like beef, flour, wheat and wine; the cold inorganic odours of iron, lead and copper; the pungency of spices such as pepper, mace and nutmeg; the blunt aroma of camphor; the stench of hides and gutta-percha; the disorienting fragrance of coffee, tea and opium. I take a big breath, but only petrol fumes scorch my nostrils.

My eyes focus horizontally in the distance. I can make out the clocktower of the Victoria Theatre.

*There, the Padang…*

The self-anointed 'Grandest Society of Merchants in the Universe' didn't know what to do with Raffles. Punching above his weight in terms of breeding, he was consorting with royalty. Still in his thirties, he was over-promoted and in the directors' eyes hugely overrated: although his administration in Java had been popular locally, he had cost the company good money.

In the end, Raffles was promoted downwards. He was sent as lieutenant governor to Bencoolen, by far the least fashionable and most pestilential of the Asian settlements – even its position at the rear end of Sumatra lends itself be dubbed as the 'arsehole of the archipelago'. Before Raffles left, he handed a memorandum to the chairman of the board, George Canning, the later Foreign Secretary and future prime minister. In its pages Raffles was advocating a new colony on one of those islands he had passed on the way to invading Java at the tip of the Malay peninsula. Canning agreed and authorised him to check the Dutch influence in the region. What exactly the unwritten terms were is still a matter of contention, yet Raffles was clear: '*I left England under the full impression that I was not only Lieutenant-Governor of Bencoolen but in fact Political Agent for the Malay States.*' But then, he would say that, wouldn't he?

Before he left, Raffles married again and took his second wife, Sophia – descended from good, landed Irish stock – to Sumatra where he made his other big discovery after Borobudur. During one of his expeditions to the interior, he came across the largest flower on earth that now bears his name: *Rafflesia*. But this was not one to collect for a posy to Sophia. This plant blooms only once every ten years or so, with a flower a yard across and a nectary that can hold a gallon and a half. Furthermore, it smells strongly of decomposing carrion to attract pollinating flies. What with the durians and all, the aromatically-challenged Indonesian rainforest must be hell for sniffer dogs.

I cross Elgin Bridge to the north side of the river, dominated by the Padang, a grassy emptiness of a sports ground for rugby and cricket. This must be the most expensive field in the world, standing as it is on a prime development site. Hey, isn't this the city where everything has its price? But no, Singapore needs the Padang because the memory of Empire and descent from Raffles is the historical glue that holds its disparate communities together. Sometimes one must be thankful for petty patriotism, manufactured or not; it may be the last refuge of the scoundrel, but it also acts as a scarecrow to the sly land speculator. Maybe the Buddha was mistaken: there are some things that money is not allowed to buy, even in Singapore.

A small pavilion housing the Singapore Cricket Club is dwarfed by the soaring Raffles City skytowers behind it. The rugby goalposts are zoned in such a way that Jonny Wilkinson could score a conversion across the road straight into the Supreme Court cupola. This was the last of the great neoclassical colonial buildings, completed in 1939, right at the twilight of the Empire. Japanese propagandists criticising British imperialism liked to point out that the Supreme Court and Changi Prison were the finest buildings in all Malaya. They were not far off the mark: the Supreme Court is an elegant, domed building with a beautiful triangular pediment, *The Allegory of Justice,* standing on six Corinthian columns.

The Corinthian motif continues next door at City Hall, with its long, colonnaded portico. Its dramatic entrance at the top of a long flight of steps lends itself to occasion and it is no surprise that it is in this building that the biggest events in Singapore's history have taken place. This is where Lord Mountbatten accepted the Japanese surrender in 1945 and where Singapore was granted self-government in 1959. More poignantly it is here where it finally broke off from Malaysia on 9 August 1965, Singapore's National Day. At the time, no one thought that a city with no hinterland, not enough water, no agriculture and no factories could be a viable state. In retrospect, this was all bunk from backward-looking analysts who had fetishised manufacturing and heavy industry. Singapore made its income from trade and services and attracted investment by being a model of efficient administration in an area where having both hands on the till is as natural as having noodles with your lunch.

I take a picture of Raffles' statue in Singapore that stands tall outside the Victoria Theatre on the other side of the Supreme Court. His arms are folded like a master engineer surveying a greenfield site. He looks much older than his portrait with a thin, resolute face, a receding hairline, and a commanding erect poise. He is dwarfed by the clock tower rising behind him on top of the theatre, over a double series of Italianate windows. No one but me stops by the statue or pauses to admire the building itself.

If the East India Company directors thought that Raffles' ardour would suffocate in the fetid backwater of Sumatra they couldn't have been more wrong. The first thing he did was to emancipate the slaves in Bencoolen against the wishes of the Honourable Company. The board were indignant: why should a commercial enterprise be in the vanguard of this new morality? Would they now have to *pay* those slaves for working? What a dent in the profits *that* would make!

But the real preoccupation of Raffles was with the Dutch who were set on expanding their influence, claiming every cove and cape for themselves and putting pressure on the sultanates not to engage in commerce with the British. Something had to be done and, in 1818, Hastings invited his Bencoolen governor to Calcutta where they met for the first time. They got on well in person, but the Governor General was a stickler for procedure: before Raffles made any move, London had to be consulted. Raffles knew that the company board and the British government were wary of antagonising the Dutch. Despite this, he managed to convince a reluctant Hastings to provide him with troops from Penang in order to found a settlement, ideally on the Riau Islands to the south of Singapore. Hastings insisted though, that if the Dutch had already established an outpost, Raffles was to avoid any conflict.

When Raffles arrived in Penang he heard the bad news from Governor Bannerman: the Dutch had claimed the Riau Islands, anticipating the British move. Bannerman, who disliked Raffles immensely, and even more so his proposition that a competitor colony be established, refused to lend him any troops. Raffles couldn't wait, as things were unfolding rapidly – well, for 1818 – so he tricked the Penang governor into sending a convoy to the South Seas, which is how South East Asia is generally known throughout the area, ostensibly to reconnoitre the territory. The assembled fleet left but, on Raffles' instruction, anchored out of sight of the port until he set sail to meet them clandestinely. Once aboard the *Indiana,* commandeered by Captain James Pearl, Raffles cheekily dispatched a message to Bannerman alleging that, ultimately, '*he thought better to direct the reconnaissance in person*'. By the way, it was this same captain who in 1822 purchased a plantation on the hill that bears his name today, and it is that same hill that has passed on his name to the Pearl Centre by Outram Park, with its plethora of mobile phone shops and the sex shop that isn't.

The convoy made a beeline for Singapore, where Raffles landed at 4 p.m. on what is now North Boat Quay – about a hundred yards up from the site he surveys from the forecourt of the Victoria Theatre. A second statue and a small plaque, yellowed by damp, commemorate the occasion:

> On this historic site Sir Thomas Stamford Raffles first landed in Singapore on 28 January 1819 and with genius and perception changed the destiny of Singapore from an obscure fishing village to a great seaport and modern metropolis.

Raffles' action was a coup in many respects. His ideas were revolutionary and their reverberations are still felt today. Singapore was a free-port-to-be where no customs duty would be levied. Situated bang in the middle of the route from India to China, among money-grabbing authoritarian sultanates and monopolistic Dutch administrations, Singapore's laissez-faire radiance became a beacon for entrepreneurs.

It was also a more conventional coup, because Raffles manipulated a complicated political situation to his advantage. The throne of the sultanate of Johore-Riau was in dispute: the old sultan, Mahmud Shah III, had died leaving two sons, the elder of whom, Hussein, was by right his successor. However, he was abroad when the Sultan died, so Hussein's younger brother ascended the throne. The pragmatic Dutch had come to terms with the status quo and supported the usurper. But then came Raffles who recognised the exiled first-born as the rightful heir. During a meeting on the island of Penyengat, he provided Hussein with protection guarantees against outside interference. Hussein – who must have thought he was dreaming – quickly agreed. Raffles also closed a deal with the Temenggong, the local warlord – and real ruler of the island – who paid tribute to the Sultan and without whose cooperation any deal with Hussein was pointless. In return for protection and a pension, they granted the East India Company full settlement and administration rights. Even in 1819, the fortunes of the island and mainland Malaya had started to diverge.

Raffles' latitude far extended anything London or Calcutta had authorised. He knew the dangers well: that the Dutch might attack Singapore; that the Sultan of Johore might try to trounce his brother once and for all; that the company board might accuse him of subordination; and that the British government would be furious. His action was a gigantic bluff: in this victorious, post-Napoleonic climate, he simply didn't think anyone would dare rise against Britain.

- 5 -

There's English and there's Singlish – and there are signs to remind me of the way the old imperial language has been adapted to the magical world of the East; there be dragons and there be new words: 'leisureplex' and 'merlion' hit me within two minutes of each other. A sign by a building site uses the impersonal passive: 'Inconvenience caused is regretted'. No one here regrets anything in the active voice for that would mean losing face.

There's 'Wellness' now in front of me in this New Age Singlish. It is a large reflexology centre with a smiling Chinese woman in a doctor's white apron touting for business. She looks at my arm and the sling and waves me in. I follow her call, admiring the *wa* of the ambience where innocuous pastels of beech beige and pomegranate pink predominate. The spacious chamber looks mostly empty even though there are half a dozen clients being, no, not massaged, but *rejuvenated, revitalised, reinvigorated*. Slow synth music soothes the subconscious: did Brian Eno ever cut a record *Music for Spas*?

My host, who introduces herself as Lillian, gives me a price menu. She is silent, because talking and haggling disturbs the Tao of Therapy. She points at my shoulder suggesting a massage, but my tendons need time to mend and fuse. I vacillate between an ear-candling session, which '*restores neural functions as it allows the oxygen to travel through the cleaned passageways of the ears and enter the brain*', and a reflexology session which is really a foot massage. Reasoning that my grey cells have already been smoked to extinction by various chemicals, I opt for half an hour of the latter. Lillian finds her voice and finally speaks with only the faintest hint of disapproval: 'We advise forty minutes.'

I check. It's ten dollars more. I smile and say no, trying to match her detached, polite manner. It's easy; I know how to refuse.

I lie on a reclining armchair and take off my sandals. I close my eyes while Lillian washes and talcums my feet in a ritual as old as submissiveness itself. When she rests them on a small cushion and starts pinching my toe tips, I enter metatarsal heaven: '*This little piggy went to market/this little piggy stayed home.*' She pinches every toe following its contour and pressing hard against the phalange bones. '*This little piggy had roast beef/this little piggy had none.*' I'm secretly afraid I might start giggling, since I'm very ticklish, but I needn't have worried.

'*This little piggy cried wee, wee, wee, all the way home!*'

'OUCH!' I scream.

Lillian smiles angelically. She points at my nose. 'Sinus,' she says, or rather I guess. And yes, I suffer from bouts of rhinitis. I tell myself that this New Age nonsense is in reality Old Age nonsense, having been part of Chinese medicine for thousands of years.

I sneeze violently. 'Slow on the nose bit,' I blurt out.

She points at the open window. 'No nose,' she says. 'Dust from construction.'

As if to underline her sentence, the merciless sound of a drill fills the room with un-Enoesque unpleasantry, and twenty Chinese collectively wince at this sudden breaking of harmony in the ether. My masseuse looks up outraged and walks to the only woman not dressed in a medical apron who fans herself by the till. They talk sotto voce and the woman disappears through an inside door. She reappears with a wrestler build-alike and leads him hurriedly through the exit. I wouldn't like to be in the drill operator's flip-flops when they meet him.

Lillian makes a move mid-foot and I jump.

'Shoulder,' she says and points at my sling.

As she works her way in a small semicircle, starting between the fourth and fifth toe and ending at the edge of my foot's arch, I feel pins and needles on my two rotator tendons. The bottom of my heel hurts a bit. I look at the explanatory leaflet – it is my sciatic nerve. 'Bad posture?' Lillian offers in return. And so on to eyes, brain, lymphs, kidneys, pancreas – all my insides are being stroked through my soles. Dammit, if this really is working, I can't wait till she reaches the penis reflex.

The drill stops and everyone breathes in. The wrestler and the till woman return and smile at the patients. Well, she does; he grunts. We can now distinguish those sustained synth notes again. Not that there was any chord change since the drill started, mind you.

I close my eyes and enter a dream state of pleasure. There is the odd pain here and there, which never goes above four out of ten, but it disappears under Lillian's considered pummelling. The muscles above my cuneiforms hurt particularly badly. They correspond to my lungs and my chest and yes, I have the odd allergic wheeze. I take a deep breath in the wet, Singaporean weather as Eno changes two chords dramatically in the space of ten seconds. I surrender to the comforting, sonic warble, for this is what ambient muzak demands: total passivity. This is music for meditation to offload your brain: don't try any knee-jerk tap against the beat. (What beat?) Don't follow melodic lines – they don't exist. This is minimalist musical nirvana and in the circumstances it's perfect; I like its hypnotic rumble, though I'd never download the MP3.

Lillian has now finished one foot and is massaging my calf to half way below the knee; then she bursts out laughing. I feel awkward and so does she because she stands up until her throaty chortle subsides. Then she sits down again and starts symmetrically on the toes of the other. But then she stops as if she'd forgotten something, picks up both my feet and raises them.

'You feel this lighter?' she asks and points at the foot she's been working on. I do and tell her so. She starts laughing again, this time uncontrollably. I bet she's discovered something embarrassing about me. I try to remember: when was the last time I checked myself at the clinic?

Lillian catches my eye and beams like an enlightened bodhisattva. Such a strange job, massaging people's feet. Does she enjoy it? Would she rather be a proper nurse? Does she get paid enough? Why did she laugh before? I look at her smiling eyes whose sole purpose are to keep me relaxed and I can't tell. It is not that oriental expressions are inscrutable. It is that orientals try not to break the mutual harmony by allowing you to scrute them.

Raffles left Singapore on 7 February 1819, having founded in ten days one of the most important British colonies, and returned to Penang to confront a fuming Bannerman who had heard the astonishing news. Soon after, an official Dutch protest arrived: since Johore was a dependency of Malacca and Singapore belonged to Johore, Singapore was obviously Dutch.

It was then that Raffles knew his bluff had paid off: the mere fact that the Dutch were protesting diplomatically and had not gone to capture the British outpost straight away was excellent news. Nowhere more so than among the expat box-wallahs of Calcutta. Money talks and in this case it crowed dithyrambically about the opportunities opened up by the founding of a British port halfway between Canton and Calcutta. Hastings was astonished at the audacity of the manoeuvre but took note of the commercial reaction in India. He wrote a cagey letter, on one hand praising Raffles' initiative and confirming the engagement with the 'legitimate' heir to the throne, but at the same time regretting the measure itself since it might incur a collision with the Dutch. He also wrote a flaming missive to Bannerman ordering him to send troops immediately.

Raffles returned to Singapore on 31 May 1819. In less than four months, the fishing village had become a small town of 5,000 people who had moved to this tax haven. Raffles and his friend, William Farquhar, who had been left behind to oversee the settlement's development, roughly delineated the various neighbourhoods of the city: to this day they remain the same. The secure north side of the river was to be the government and European settlement – this is where today we find the City Hall, the Victoria Theatre, the Padang and the Christian churches. Further north, where Sultan

Hussein and his court resided, would emerge as the Muslim area, still very much alive today. The south side of the river would be left to the Chinese whose junks could find shelter inside the river mouth in the North and South Boat Quays; since the cargo was being unloaded there, the commercial area was established in what nowadays is termed the Central Business District (CBD). The only hill in view would be the army headquarters, Fort Canning, in use until World War Two. The locals still had the memory of Forbidden Hill and were afraid to climb it, until Farquhar fired off a huge cannon from the top and announced that he had dispersed the ghosts. The dispersal was terminal: as I approach the river by Coleman Bridge and look at the bottom of the hill, I notice that the spring where the Raja's harem used to bathe has metamorphosed into the River Valley Swimming Pool. Nice touch.

Raffles wasn't to return to the colony he established until three years later. When he disembarked at Singapore on 10 October 1822, the population had risen to 10,000 souls and the value of its trade was greater than Penang and Malacca put together. But the more the colony flourished, the more Raffles was being chastised by life: he received an official rebuke from the company and the court as the legal status of Singapore was still the subject of Anglo-Dutch negotiations; he fell out with Farquhar and sacked him; his supporter in Calcutta, Hastings, retired under a cloud, accused of malversation; and his royal friend and ally, Princess Charlotte, died during childbirth. Closer to home and to the heart, Raffles' employers extracted their revenge by proxy: his three children succumbed to the treacherous climate of Bencoolen and Raffles himself started having a series of strong headaches we now suspect to have been the beginnings of a brain tumour.

I am suspicious of the claim, quoted in some travel guides as 'fact', that biographers have been coy and that it was really tertiary syphilis, considering that his wife never showed any symptoms.

Raffles left Singapore for the third and final time on 9 June 1823 at the age of 42. Three years had transformed '*a haunt of pirates to the abode of enterprise, security and opulence*'. He only had three years more to live, three years he was to spend in the company's displeasure and, it seems, those of the gods, too. When the couple finally left Bencoolen on 2 February 1824, a devastating fire broke out on their ship. Raffles lost all his possessions: his manuscripts and memoirs, his valuables, his maps, his natural history drawings – all gone.

When Raffles eventually reached Plymouth, he heard some good news at last: the status of Singapore had been settled with the Treaty of London between Great Britain and Holland. The Equator divided their spheres of influence: Bencoolen was surrendered to the Dutch, but Singapore and Penang remained British while Malacca was returned to Britain. The three ports became collectively known as the Straits Settlements; they led to the colonisation of the whole of Malaya and served as a springboard to China: Hong Kong would be ceded within a generation.

Raffles waited for compensation for his losses during the fire and a pension from the company. In the meantime, he issued a subscription to buy a plot of land above Regent's Park and house the tropical animals he'd brought back from Java and Sumatra. They became the first residents of the London Zoological Gardens which he co-founded with Sir Humphrey Davy (of the miners' lamp fame). Raffles was elected as London Zoo's first president and, if you visit the Lion House, you can see his bust outside.

- 6 -

A glowering, grey sky shrouds the colonial buildings, a fit setting for the war memorials on the opposite side of the Padang. A small stone-paved path leads to the first marble column facing City Hall, dedicated to 'Our Glorious Dead'. Each of the five steps is inscribed with a Great War year: 1914, all the way to 1918. Its foundation stone, laid on 15 November 1920, was attended by George Clemenceau, and its unveiling, on 31 March 1922, was made by the Duke of Windsor. *'We are met here to do honour to the men who, in common with many others from all parts of our great Empire, died that we as an Empire might live,'* said the Duke. Within two decades another, Asian, empire would take over Singapore and shatter the image of Britannia forever. And, like the city itself, which has had to learn how to live in cramped conditions, the memorial has been recycled: a second inscription is unveiled when you look at the cenotaph from the other side. Conveniently, the ground slopes down, allowing for seven steps at the back inscribed each with a year from World War Two, a war that was not observed from afar but was felt and suffered for in the city itself.

The paved promenade in front has a space-age view: two huge constructions that look like two giant metallic flies' eyes dominate the landscape. This is the Esplanade – Theatres on the Bay, Sydney Opera House wannabes that lack the grace of the Australian original, though I'm sure the acoustics are no less than perfect. New states in search of self-definition want to be patted in the back for their cultural credentials and Singapore, like Sydney, has opted for a showcase edifice devoted to Western culture: opera and symphonies, ballet and theatre. From another angle the flies' eyes remind me of two monstrous durians that have fallen gracelessly out of the sky. Prince Charles is right about modern architecture in one respect: when it fails, it fails with great aplomb.

The Esplanade development, completed in the mid-nineties when the Asian 'tigers' seemed to grow and grow with no upper limit, appears curiously lifeless today, and pales in comparison with, say, Raffles Place. The restaurants – Chinese, Thai, Italian – have the plastic atmosphere of fast food joints with the obligatory cockroach running on the odd, well-polished floor. The setting is spectacular, but the menus look routine and the seats appear cheap. Through the glass panes, the Embassy Restaurant – recommended in older guides – is closed 'until further notice'. So, there is a limit to expansion and a frontier to the dream, as everyone found out in the Asian market meltdown of 1997. Although it suffered much, much less than the rest of them – Singapore's economy actually expanded by 0.4 per cent during that period – even this most dynamic of the 'tigers' had to count its teeth and lick its wounds.

Lick its wounds like Raffles...

Despite his colossal historical status the man Raffles must have been unbearable. He was too much of a lone wolf and had argued and offended everyone in his whirlwind path: from the Dutch and English Crowns to the East India Company Board and from his military attaché in Java to his old friend Farquhar. It is in this life we pay for our sins, not any other, and Raffles' behaviour came back to haunt him in the final act.

In April 1826, a few years after he had arrived back in London, he received two letters from the company. The first was, in modern terms, a job appraisal which can be summarised as, 'your actions were wrong, risky and uncondoned but with the benefit of hindsight we forgive you since Singapore ended up a success'. The second was a thunderbolt. Not only did the board refuse to compensate him for his losses, not only did they not issue him a pension, but they asked for their money back. Hastings had let him draw his salary during the years he spent in London between Java and Sumatra but without explicit authorisation. Now Accounts Receivable – the bane of us all – demanded this amount back (with interest), along with the expenses Raffles claimed in founding Singapore. To cap it all, the company demanded reimbursement for his *precipitate and unauthorised emancipation of the company's slaves.'*

The bitterness must have broken Raffles. Three months later, on 5 July 1826, one day short of his forty-fifth birthday, he collapsed at the bottom of the stairs in his country house near Edgware. An autopsy found that he died of a stroke brought upon by a brain tumour. The funeral at St Mary's Church in Hendon was private and sparsely attended. Raffles had a knack of making enemies even posthumously: the parish priest turned down all requests for any commemorative plaque until his own death 50 years later, because of the deceased's *'unchristian and thoughtless actions in Java and Bencoolen'*. By that, the good servant of God meant the slaves' manumission.

It was thus that Raffles' bodily whereabouts were lost and forgotten; only in 1914 were his remains rediscovered, and an inscription was hung above his burial vault. History, of course, keeps its own pantheon that exists independently of human pettiness: within eight years of Raffles' death, a statue had been commissioned by his considerable fanbase and placed in the north isle of Westminster Abbey.

Raffles's only surviving daughter, Emma, lived until the age of 19. His widow, Sophia, settled with the company on a much reduced amount within seven months of Raffles's death and wrote a memoir of his life which she published in 1830. She died in their Edgware estate in 1858 at the age of 72; hardly an age reached by a syphilitic.

Today, London Zoo survives, bigger and grander, at the same site in Regent's Park. Nineteen species of Rafflesia have been identified, and there is a specimen at Kew Gardens that attracts scores of nose-pinching visitors every time it deigns to bloom. The temple of Borobudur is a Unesco World Heritage site, Indonesia's most popular tourist attraction.

And Singapore is a thriving metropolis of four million people.

# CHAPTER THREE

# ON INNS AND VALUABLES

The Innkeeper was watching Master Sushan intently. He had invited the Master and his retinue to dine in his establishment. He had provided him with his best rice wine, served him on his best porcelain and offered him a set of golden chopsticks. This was no ordinary inn: it was well known among people living up to ten thousand *li* away and all government messengers carrying imperial documents had commended its luxurious ambience. Old terracotta statues adorned every corner; calligraphy masterpieces hung from the walls; and the tablecloths were made of the best quality silk.

The Innkeeper craved a morsel of the philosophical insight Master Sushan possessed; the only thing he longed for in return for his hospitality was an enlightened *koan* from the lips of the Master. In vain did he hover around the sage and his two closest disciples; they were eating and drinking slowly and quietly, as if meditating before, during and after every mouthful. He tried to draw the Master into conversation by asking him if everything was alright, or whether he was happy with the food? the wine? the service? – yet Sushan would only smile and nod imperceptibly with his head.

The Innkeeper's frustration grew and grew so that eventually he dared sit down at the table with them and ask them the question that had been lingering in his mind.

'Forgive my impertinence, Oh, Master,' he said, 'please enlighten your poor servant whose belief in your wisdom is beyond compare. I have surrounded myself with beautiful objects but I still don't know: what is the most valuable thing in the world?'

As if on cue, a disciple spoke.

'The most valuable thing in the world is the throne of the Emperor, for he who possesses it controls the known world,' he said.

The other disciple took up the thread.

'The most valuable thing in the world is the teaching of the Buddha, for he who possesses it controls the known and unknown world,' he said.

At last, Master Sushan opened his mouth.

'The most valuable thing in the world is the head of a dead cat,' he declared.

The Innkeeper and the two disciples looked at each other in bafflement.

'Why is this, Oh Master?' they asked.

'Because,' Master Sushan replied, 'no one can name its price.'

- 7 -

It's hard to get away from that man Raffles. Like his cat burglar namesake, he is invisible but ubiquitous: that skyscraper is Raffles Tower extending skywards from Raffles City shopping centre; this is Raffles Avenue leading into

Stamford Road; the first parallel up is Raffles Boulevard. My sling and I are getting used to walking around being stared at. Today's venture is one notch up from yesterday's colonial stroll: I still feel uncomfortable going to any nightspot, but I'm hoping that a late afternoon visit to an upmarket bar will help. I need to get over my people fright, because I'll end up agoraphobic.

I have reached the Marina Mandarin Hotel, although in Singapore it is sometimes difficult to tell where a mall starts and where a hotel begins. I've always wondered how Oxford and Cambridge undergraduates react to having tourists wander about outside their residences, looking in while the students are burning their toast. The experience must be similar to that in some of the five-star hotels in Singapore where you have casual shoppers pushing buttons in the lift just as you are trying to get to your room for a shower. The Marina Mandarin at least can claim a world first: it is the only hotel after which a flower has been named. It is an orchid, called *Dendrobium Marina Mandarin* and its appearance is as complicated to describe as the hotel's floor plan.

Although naming an orchid after a hotel is a first, the ease with which these flowers breed and mutate has led to an explosion of silly names. If you don't believe me, go to the National Orchid Garden in Singapore and look around by the crane fountain: you will be dazzled by a sprinkling of Golden Showers, small yellow orchids named in a long-disappeared, innocent past. These very gardens only recently bred an orchid called *Dendrobium Jackie Chan* and, lest we forget our sporting heroes, a local supporter created the *Holttumara Singapore Netball Team*.

I was over at the National Orchid Garden earlier because I love their glamour. I am not alone: they have been admired by Ancient Greek philosophers and Chinese emperors, and similarly Singapore's fondness for flamboyant flora goes back a long way. Its national flower is, itself, a purple orchid: the all year bloomer *Vanda Miss Joaquim*, chosen in a 1981 competition by Singapore's Ministry of Culture as part of an overall strategy to foster and bolster national pride and identity. It is sort of 'native' to Singapore, having been cultivated in the garden of an Armenian lady, Miss Agnes Joaquim, back in 1893. Pleased immensely by her hybrid she duly registered it in Sander's List, the *Who's Who* of orchids, and entered it in several competitions, winning in the Rarest Flower category at the 1899 Singapore Flower Show. That was the peak of her success with the *Vanda,* since she died, unmarried, a few months later. One century on, like so many low-rise dwellings, her garden and her house on Narcis Street have been demolished to provide space for a shopping mall.

I don't know who first thought about it, but give the guy some kudos: orchid breeding is now used for political flattery. My jaw dropped when I walked into the VIP Orchid Garden and came across the lavender-like *Dendrobium Margaret Thatcher* (withered), named during the British prime minister's visit to the gardens in April 1985. At least she saw her orchid bloom; this is more than can be said for Princess Diana: her sparkling white jasmine-like hybrid with a pink centre was named in her memory a month after she died. There is the orchid de rigueur for Nelson Mandela (golden brown) but there is also an orange/mocha *Dendrobium* for Prince Norodom Sihanouk of Cambodia and a white, pink and yellow *Mokara* for Bertie Ahern. Still, it is the *Vanda Tsolmon*, dedicated to the wife of the Mongolian prime minister, that delivers the ultimate political snub: its shrubs are refusing to flower.

Ah, orchids are great fun. Now, where am I?

Let's see. There is the old imperial NAAFI, the Britannia Club, built in the Spanish style. Like many older buildings in Singapore it is closed and under scaffolding; is it being demolished or renovated? A sign proudly shows the Health and Safety statistics: so many accident-free hours achieved in many more total man-hours toiled. The total number of fatal accidents is zero, although, confusingly, the fatalities seem to have a positive annual rate: an alarming 1.95, no units given. I consign the inexplicable to oriental mystique.

There it is – I've reached my destination, the most famous watering hole in South East Asia.

It is through grand establishments like the Savoy in London, the Ritz in Paris or the Copacabana Palace in Rio de Janeiro that a bourgeois narrative and perspective can be reconstituted; their mere presence helps define a city in the same way the city provides them with uniqueness in return. They are the catwalk on which celebrities sashay; their rooms and bars are the canvas for the creation of legends; and their past, peppered with showbiz anecdotes, provides the glamour. They may be the *Hello!* magazine alternatives to academic historical discourse, but it is there that the spirit of a metropolis chooses to dwell. They *are* the city and *of the city* at the same time, as much alive as museums are dead. So if you want to experience the Singapore of old, come to the Raffles Hotel, as imperial a relic as the Privy Council and as English as bad weather.

Surprisingly for such a colonial icon, the Raffles was a venture by four Armenians, the Sarkies brothers. They purchased a bungalow on Beach Road whose previous ownership history reflects the waxing and waning of fortunes in the raw capitalist atmosphere of the free port. It was originally built by the Dares, a well-known Singaporean-Anglo family who owned one of the four original ship chandlers' firms. There exists a wonderful memoir by George Dare, one of the teenage boys in the family. He used to go off shooting pigeon and wild pig *'in the jungly swamps beyond the race course and the Hindoo cremation ground'* – today's Toa Payoh – where he was unsettled by stray dogs devouring three partly burned corpses *'slightly grilled and smelling horribly'*. After rats, controlled by Farquhar who paid one *wang* per corpse, and centipedes that fell from the atap roofs, stray dogs were the biggest nuisance in Singapore. On one occasion, a pack of them attacked the boy's pony on the Esplanade and threw him down *'dreadfully shaken and stunned'*. Because of such incidents, the first three days of every month were set aside for convict labourers to catch dogs.

Yet even they weren't as dangerous as the tigers who roamed the island. The main casualties were plantation workers who had to work in the outskirts of the jungle: in the 1840s they averaged a casualty a day. Pitfalls, cages with those captured strays as bait and shooting parties decimated the man-eaters, but it took until the dawn of the new century to clear the island completely. Funnily enough, it is then that the most celebrated tiger story pops up for posterity – at Raffles.

It was the proverbial hot and steamy night in August 1902 when the drinking *tuans* in the Raffles Bar and Billiard Room noticed an unwelcome guest – unwelcome not because of its low breeding, but because of its fearsome character: crouching under the billiard table was an adult Bengal tiger. A tiger in the city? Why, it must have swam the Straits of Johore and stridden through the jungle, before it decided to chum it up with the punters in the bar. (*'Who's that, old boy?' 'A tiger, M'lud.' 'Have we been introduced?'*) A crack shot was summoned and the impertinent tiger soon became a trophy as well as providing a cracker of a tale that still delights tourists, combining as it does the stereotypes of imperial derring-do and English sangfroid. The truth is not as dramatic. The billiard room was a pavilion outside the main Raffles Hotel and, like any floodable structure near the waterfront, it stood on four-foot brick pillars to survive the monsoon. The tiger had escaped from a travelling circus and was as tame as can be. Scared and hungry, it found shelter underneath the billiard room, hiding among the stilts. An Indian servant spotted the animal staring through the low veranda railings and informed the management. They, in turn, brought in Mr C. M. Phillips, the schoolmaster at Raffles Institution next door, who shot the beast into legend with his Lee-Enfield rifle. When measured, the animal was found to be 7 feet 8 inches long and 3 feet 4 inches tall.

But back to the Dares: their business went under and their Beach Road house was sold to the Yemeni trader, Syed Mohammed bin Ahmed Alsagoff, a member of a wealthy Arab family who came to Singapore and made his fortune through coconut and lemon grass plantations in what is now Geylang Serai. He also branched into shipping with the Singapore Steaming Company and bought the *Jeddah*, the ship whose voyage in August 1880 caused a sensation as big as that of the *Titanic* some thirty years later.

The *Jeddah*, under Captain Joseph Clark, set sail from Singapore to Saudi Arabia carrying 953 Muslim pilgrims for the hajj. She found herself in the centre of a hurricane in the Arabian Gulf, and started to leak while her boilers became incapacitated. What happened next shocked the merchant navy: Captain Clark and his crew panicked. Leaving the passengers to their fate, they lowered the lifeboats and abandoned ship ignominiously. They were picked up by another vessel, the *Scindia*, and cabled Singapore that the

*Jeddah* had foundered. No one would know what had transpired, had the steamer *Antenor* not appeared in time to tow the *Jeddah* expertly to the safety of Aden much to the shock of Captain Clark who had arrived there the day before. The resulting court of inquiry heavily censured Clark, but it was the first officer, 28-year-old Austin Williams, who became the inspiration for Joseph Conrad's *Lord Jim*. Unlike the central character of the novel, Williams – the *real* Lord Jim – did not find redemption among wild tribes in Borneo but worked humbly as a ship chandler in Singapore, living at 32 Barker Road in Bukit Timah, near the present Methodist church. He died of a fall in 1916 and is buried at Bidadari cemetery next to his only son who predeceased him.

The Sarkies brothers bought the bungalow from Alsagoff and extended it with two wings that offered 20 rooms in total. On 1 December 1887 the Raffles Hotel opened for the first time and one of its first guests was Rudyard Kipling, who came up with a double-edged verdict: *'Providence conducted me… to a place called Raffles Hotel where the food is excellent and the rooms are bad.'* The principles of marketing being immutable through time and space, the Sarkies Brothers cleverly curtailed the quote to: *'Feed at Raffles where the food is excellent.'*

The current three-storey building with its grand, colonial façade, its filigree railings and the double-sloping roof with its red Mediterranean tiles stems from a major rebuild in 1899, when structures were still being erected for show as much as for function. A special inauguration dinner for 500 prepared by a French chef was held in November in the new Marble Dining Room. The band of the King's Own Regiment entertained the guests who marvelled at the electric ceiling fans, a modern gadget that put the punkah-wallahs out of a job. The Raffles was the first building in the region to be wired for electricity and, as it stood at the seafront sparkling in the Asian humid night, it doubled as a fairy lighthouse for the approaching Chinese junks. This is difficult to imagine today, since protracted land reclamation has ensured that the Raffles is nowhere near the water's edge, the town having devoured the sea like a dragon; nevertheless, the hotel's private generator secured its burgeoning reputation. London's *The Sphere* newspaper called it '*the Savoy of Singapore*' and a 1905 brochure could already claim amongst its guests such notables as HIH Grand Duke Cyril Vladimirovich of Russia, HSH Prince Adalbert of Germany and HIH Prince Kan'in of Japan. Admit it, even Z-list royalty sounds impressive.

The next thirty years were the golden era of the hotel whose advertising slogan was breathtakingly self-aggrandising: '*When at the Raffles, why not see Singapore?*' Somerset Maugham wrote his short stories in the Palm Court, sitting under the aroma of the white frangipani and the shade of the purple bougainvillaea. Noel Coward was snubbed by the posh colonial society who thought him '*rowdy and perhaps on the common side*'. He returned the compliment with interest: '*After meeting the best people [here], now I know why there is such a shortage of servants in London.*' Hermann Hesse detailed his short sojourn in the book *Journey to the East*, writing with his typical Teutonic sourness: '*We stay expensive but very good at Raffles Hotel. The food is as bad as everywhere.*' Standards must have slipped since Kipling's time.

The last remaining Sarkies brother was forced to sell the hotel when he embarked upon a costly renovation project during the 1929 crash and the ensuing world rubber slump. At least it remained a hotel; its main rival, the Grand Hotel d'Europe was demolished altogether to become the Supreme Court. Under new management, the Raffles had a last, brief gasp of grandeur in the late thirties before World War Two which occasioned more apocryphal stories. Guests were casually informed not to worry about Japanese air raids, for the building had its own early warning system. Little did they know that it consisted of an aged engineer who looked up in the sky to spot any enemy planes and blew a whistle should he detect any. During the occupation the staff had to learn Japanese and master the exotic flavours of beef sukiyaki and chicken teriyaki, but they held their own. They emptied the cellars into the Singapore sewers before the invading army could get their hands on the expensive wines and liquors and buried the silverware underneath the Palm Court, so that they wouldn't have to serve the Japanese in style.

The Raffles went through another major renovation in the 1990s and is currently capitalising on its reputation as '*the last caravanserai east of Islamabad*' having acquired a memorabilia shop, a shopping arcade and many more bars. But along with the facelift came the facelessness; it now belongs to Raffles Hotels & Resorts, a generic brand name for several luxury hotels in places such as Phnom Penh (Raffles Hotel Le Royal), Beverly Hills (Raffles L'Ermitage) and, believe it or not, Hamburg (Raffles Hotel Vier Jahreszeiten). Raffles Hotels & Resorts are in turn owned by Raffles International Ltd which is the hotel management arm of Raffles Holdings Ltd, a lodgings-and-resorts conglomerate listed on the Singapore Stock Exchange. Finally, Raffles Holdings is a subsidiary of CapitaLand, one of the largest multinationals in Asia, headquartered in Singapore and specialising in the hospitality industry, real estate and assorted financial services.

If this is not the story of the city itself, I don't know what is.

- 8 -

Today's Raffles Hotel has brushed off any signs of overt snobbishness. It is certainly expensive, it is unfailingly upmarket, but it welcomes everyone and since it appears on every travel guide, there is a steady stream of tourists ordering their Singapore Slings, the hotel's most famous export.

I am sipping mine in a gazebo in the Palm Court, still an oasis of floral luxuriance in the traffic-choked city, and my ears prick up. The bartender has just told me something I can't believe. He is a short and agile thirty-something Malay, affable, courteous and perfectly spoken, but at the same time cool and detached; he resembles more a stately butler than a high-class barista. He enunciates every word precisely and separately as if a slow, invisible autocue has been laid out in front of him.

'Yes, Sir – the recipe for a Singapore Sling was written down by an anonymous guest back in 1936,' he replies assuming the mien of a travel guide. 'It was he who first described the cocktail. It was being drunk in the plantations.'

I look at my glass. It is an aggressive pinky red, more befitting the dress of a Hungarian milkmaid.

'It was also considered a ladies' drink because of its colour.'

I gulp more of the fruity concoction; like any good cocktail, it doesn't hit you right away.

'Ngiam Tong Boon hid the recipe in a safe.'

*Ngiam Tong Boon?*

'The barman who invented the cocktail.' He uses the fingers of both hands to draw imaginary quotation marks around the spoken 'invented' and then goes on pouring lager into a frosted glass for the Australian couple next to me.

'Oh, it's a secret! Is this why you poured the drink out of a plastic bucket?' I ask.

The hidden sting in my question makes the bartender shadow-flinch: 'No, Sir. Every morning we prepare the Slings afresh and store them in sterile containers because we don't have the time to prepare them from scratch.'

I am not so easily convinced.

'On a good day we might be asked for 2,000 Singapore Slings. They must all taste the same,' he maintains. 'And no, Sir, it's not a secret any more.'

He hands me a beer mat with the recipe.

'Last time I was here, I'm sure they prepared it in front of me,' I say.

*Last time…*

When I first visited South East Asia as a poor, scruffy backpacker on a Round-the-World ticket, the Raffles Hotel was one of the reasons I budgeted a few nights in Singapore. As soon as I had found a room in the backpacker turf that Bencoolen Street used to be, I walked into the lobby in reverence and decided to splash my daily budget on a slowly-slurped Singapore Sling in the Writers' Bar. It was just before noon and I was the only tourist – correction, I was the only *obvious* tourist: young, short-trousered, T-shirted and Duran Duran-haired (I cut it shorter in Penang, fearful of the Thai border barbers). Everybody else – and there was a very sparse crowd – was older, well-groomed, mostly male, smelling of Old Spice. There were no pairs; everyone was sipping a solitary drink, sitting as far away from each other as is possible like repulsed magnetic filaments of the same polarity. What I remember most vividly was the silence: a London Underground mind-your-own-business silence. People had not come to this bar to be sociable. They had come to be transported to the past.

That's where I'll take you now.

I can still see her standing there. She just curled her index finger at me like Elizabeth Taylor in *Cleopatra* and commanded me over to buy her a drink.

No, I jest. The truth is, and I am embarrassed to admit it, I spilled her drink as I was passing by, like a Little Boy Lost. I was, after all, a wide-eyed backpacker whose vision might have been 20/20 but only within the tunnel of his own existence. And she was not 100 per cent in the clear, either: she was sitting down, holding her drink carelessly at my waist level away from her face, so far away it was contributory negligence, Your Honour.

'I'm sorry,' I said. I was young and timid and maybe I was afraid they might chuck me out. Oh, the humiliation – being escorted out of Raffles in disgrace.

'You can buy me another,' she said commandingly.

It was then I had a good look at the woman I would remember as Edith. Truth is, I have forgotten her name but she looked like everyone's aunt – thin and old, dressed in a tight white dress that emphasised the lack of curves in her body. She looked old and frail, but her voice was a deep mezzo-soprano that would easily belt out the Habanera from *Carmen*. She was the whitest woman I had ever seen, as if recently exsanguinated by a vampire; maybe there were some suppressed oriental genes in her make-up that had emerged in her life's twilight. I have forgotten her name – did she ever tell me? – but I remember our conversation in detail: it's etched permanently into my brain, like a plastic bag unwittingly burnt on a kitchen hob.

'A gin and tonic,' she continued. 'With an *orange* slice, please. Can't stand lemon. Too acidic.'

Yes, I bought her one; there went my eating budget for another day, but I was captivated. There are people who never have to work for a living not because they have been born with a silver spoon in their mouths, but because everyone else wants to feed them with one. They are the people we simply want to take care of because they are either attractive or helpless and at her age she was both. She was attractive in the way only a woman late in life can be: by being demanding in her femininity and by playing pushy with her incapacity.

By the time I arrived back with her drink, she'd wiped her dress dry with a personalised Raffles napkin.

'Thank you,' she said, 'you are a real gentleman. Chin-chin.'

Her pronouncement had a barely perceptible but calming authority in the bar whose atmosphere had been disturbed by the Duranie look-alike who had spilled the lady's drink. It was not as if muted conversation restarted after total silence, no; it was a subtle change in the air – as if the thoughts of the punters could again be allowed to wander off and their eyes left to focus at infinity.

'So what do you do?' she asked.

'I am on a Round-the-World trip,' I said. 'I've just come from Indonesia and I'm making my way up to Thailand.'

She gave me an uncomprehending look, as if she was asking herself why anyone in his right mind would ever think of going to Thailand.

'And you?' I asked boldly in return.

'I live here,' she said. Her accent was courtly – and I have the Edwardian court in mind.

'In Singapore?' I asked.

She stared at me with her tiny, blue eyes still as lively as they must have been in the zenith of her youth. I felt it was then she realised that it was a lowly backpacker who had bought her the drink; it was obvious that she did not approve but had to make conversation out of politeness.

'No,' she said. 'At Raffles.'

I said nothing, weighing the implications of that admission.

'It's gone downhill, I know. But where else do you stay in Singapore? And where else do you go? KL? Penang? Or,' – and I swear I saw horror in her eyes – 'India?'

I shrugged my shoulders and tried to say something but wasn't quick enough.

'And don't say Surrey,' she answered her own question. 'Don't talk to me about Surrey – the chill…'

She shimmied a bout of shivering.

'Do you know that there is an original billiards table – in the Tiffin Bar – from 1900?' she said. 'It was underneath that table – the very same – they shot a tiger – a real Sumatran tiger – it had swam across the straits from Johore.'

She sat upright and leaned forward.

'Damn right, they did – don't believe anything else – anything else they tell you. I knew the guy – the guy who shot it – and he told me the story – as it happened – under the billiards table. That was a time when the name Raffles *meant* something – a time when everyone knew their positions in life. The Chinese did the cooking and the cleaning – the Malays, they tended the gardens – and the Tamils, they were the porters and the guards.

Never seen a better man in a uniform than our Tamils – beautiful, manly, tall, with thicker moustaches than any Sikh you can find. The manager was never English – he was always someone from the continent. No Englishman, you understand, would deign to serve other Englishmen in Singapore – this was not a job to go for in the colonies. Best left to some Continental chap – Italian I think – or Swiss – I knew a few, all gentlemen – though they could not really manage the hotel, as in *manage*. They couldn't hire and fire – jobs were inherited. When someone retired – this cleaner or that cook – his village would send you a replacement. If you didn't get on with someone – and you sacked him – the village would send you someone even less – what's the word, *employable* – and you were stuck with him. The manager just had to make things work – he had to make all these people with no common work ethic – what's the word, *function*'.

She shifted position in her low rattan chair and put her glass down, exhausted by her long diatribe.

'You are not English,' she said, focusing her eyes intently on me with a squint. 'There is Italian in you, I dare say.'

'Greek,' I corrected her. 'I was born in Athens.'

She lay back. 'Athens. *Athens*. The owners of the hotel used to be Armenian – would you believe it? They sold it after the crash – that's when my family lost everything. The rubber prices tumbled,' she made a gesture with her hand as if to pick up something from the floor, 'and that was it. Might as well have set the farm on fire ourselves. Have you been to the Black and White Houses? In Alexandra? No? You should go – they are still *the* address in town – every living room had a grand piano, maybe two. It was a struggle to keep them in tune, you know: the damp, the heat – but mostly the damp. Even when in tune, they didn't sound like the pianos in Europe. When I first played on a piano back in England, I jumped – the clarity, the crispness – it was like a church bell ringing at night. Here the keys sound like gongs – there is a resonance, a density, something that rebounds off the wall – like an echo – until it is consumed by the damp. Like all of us, I dare say.'

She sucked on the flesh of the orange slice.

'Don't knock the damp – the heat and the damp do wonders for my arthritis – but once you've heard the sound of a piano in England, you don't want to hear one here. You know, there are many people in the Black and White Houses – and not all Europeans who'd willingly pay double and triple for a piano that would make that crisp sound you take as granted in England – or Greece, I suppose.'

She took another sip from the cocktail glass and picked up the thread again.

'Double and triple, I say. In Singapore, you learn to appreciate the good things in life – especially my generation who saw war. Have you been to Kranji? No? You should go. I will never talk to the Japanese. You see them everywhere – some even stay here, at the Raffles. The only ones who take to the rickshaws nowadays – Europeans never would. We are too conscious of our past – afraid to be perceived as colonial. The Chinese never hated us, the English – but three years of the Japanese – they rounded them up and killed them, you know. They took them away to the beaches – and shot them – and waited for the tides to carry them away.'

She looked me straight in the eye.

'They have a long memory the Chinese – those ancestors of theirs – they speak to every generation. Have you been to the National Museum? No? You should go. You will then see: Singapore was as English as Essex. Still is – don't be fooled.'

'You were here during the war?' I asked.

She half-ignored my question.

'When the Royal Navy arrived – during the Liberation – the Japanese let us go from the camp. But go where? We had nothing – we had to beg for food from our servants. They took good care of us then – like we took good care of them before. But you can imagine – the indignity. On the morning the Japs surrendered there was bread for all of us – baked by the Royal Navy. Oh, the taste of that bread! Now you've never tasted such bread in England – or in Greece, I dare say.'

She sighed.

'It's here in Singapore you discover the simplest of pleasures – like well-baked bread or the proper sound of a baby grand.'

And with a tiny lowering of the jaw and a faint gesture, she dismissed me.

'Time for tiffin,' she declaimed.

I am halfway through my second cocktail when I ask the barman to take a picture of me. 'I'm in Singapore, with a sling, having a Singapore Sling. Couldn't make it up if I wanted to,' I tell him.

*This is it! I can laugh about it.*

The joke sweeps the bar like a Mexican wave. Two German girls chuckle; they have ordered one Sling between them and make it last for an hour, whereas the giggling

English girl opposite has downed one by herself. Next to me, the backpacker couple laugh in that loud manner only Australians have perfected.

'There is another famous Raffles cocktail, Sir,' says the barman. 'Invented by Ngiam Tong Boon, himself: the Million Dollar Cocktail.'

'Does it cost as much?' I ask in jest.

The barman grins with the familiar condescension of someone who has heard the same witticism one million times. 'For you, $16 only – but that's before tax,' he says. 'It appears in a book by Maugham,' he adds as a further incentive.

He's right, it does. The Million Dollar Cocktail crops up in *The Letter*, one of Maugham's short stories made famous in the 1940 film of the same name starring Bette Davis. I'm getting nicely sloshed, I have travelled far, and I am not going to miss out on such a literary encounter. Especially if it is freshly made.

'Let us all know how it tastes,' say the Australians, probably hoping I'll offer them a sip. Well, no, we haven't been *that* friendly.

I try the brown concoction placed in front of me, sweet-and-sour, like, like…

'It tastes like fruity real ale,' is my verdict.

The Australians laugh loudly again. I wonder if sometimes they unconsciously expect that empty gullies and baking deserts will swallow the sounds of their mirth, bless them. They certainly scared off the mynahs and that's no mean feat. The barman on the other hand appears shocked – whether it was my opinion or the racket of the Australians, I can not tell. Without saying a further word, he shows me a mat with a recipe which, of course, contains no traces of beer.

'It's probably the sweetness of the Sling lingering on,' I say trying to make excuses, but they're all in vain: from that point on, I am ostracised by the bar staff, who never speak to me again.

Only when I leave them a tolerable tip, does the barman manage a dutiful, 'Thank you, Sir'.

# CHAPTER FOUR

# THE FAVOURITE

*F*u means Luck; *Fu* means Favour; *Fu* means Goodwill.

*Fu* is what Mi-zi Xia got in abundance when, as a beautiful slim, smooth youth, he appeared in front of the King of Wei. The passion of the King for him knew no bounds; in the courtier's lashing tongue, 'he was as affectionate and familiar with Mi-zi as a man would be with his wife'. Sometimes it seemed that Mi-zi's pleasure and wellbeing were more important than matters of state and this troubled greatly the King of Wei's mandarins. But while other sages whisperingly denounced the King's all-consuming passion, the Chief Mandarin smiled cryptically and said: 'Wait.'

One day, when the Chief Mandarin was accompanying the King and Mi-zi on a stroll in the Forbidden Orchard, the youth picked up a ripe peach from a tree. Impetuously, he bit into the orange-pink flesh without offering it first to the King. The Chief Mandarin seized the opportunity and cleared his throat with an eloquent cough. Mi-zi understood the implication at once and turned around, offering half of the peach to the King. He, in turn, beamed and accepted the fruit with a celestial smile. 'Oh, Mi-zi,' he said, 'in truth you do love me sincerely. You have forgotten your craving and your hunger in order to please me. Blessed shall be our days together.'

The King's entourage looked warily at the Chief Mandarin who whispered: 'Wait.'

The days passed and the youth's radiance turned into a man's athletic blossom. The King was still taken in by Mi-zi and everyone lived happily – until, that is, Mi-zi's mother fell ill. In his rush to be at her bedside unhindered by sentries and unmolested by highwaymen, Mi-zi secretly used the King's carriage. Word got to the Chief Mandarin who leapt at the news: unauthorised use of the royal carriage was punishable by amputation of both legs. But when the King of Wei heard of the deed, he murmured approvingly: 'What a son to his mother! In order to be at her deathbed he didn't care about the sanctions. By heavens, this is true filial piety! Blessed shall be our days together.'

The King's courtiers were assembled excitedly outside the Great Reception Hall. When the Chief Mandarin told the congregation of the ruler's reaction, their looks hung dispiritedly in the air. 'Wait,' said the Chief Mandarin exuding confidence and detached wisdom.

The years passed and the good life took its toll on Mi-zi. He turned portly; his hairline receded; his face turned red from the over consumption of rice wine. While he steadily lost his looks, his *Fu* with the King diminished until there was none left. One spring morning when the snows from the mountains had melted, Mi-zi decided to go fishing, as he normally did that time of year, and made his way to the King's private pond. The warden routinely informed the Chief Mandarin that Mi-zi had caught three of the Emperor's own plump carp. But this time the Chief Mandarin was quick to denounce Mi-zi's misdemeanour; using the King's private pond was punishable by banishment – never mind that Mi-zi had fished there every spring for years.

The ruler's reaction was swift: 'I believe anything you say against that scoundrel,' he cried. 'Once he offered me a half-eaten peach! Remember? Another time he tried to steal my carriage! Remember? Ungrateful knave – to hell with him.'

The Chief Mandarin left the Great Reception Hall beaming. He conveyed the long-awaited news to a relieved assembly of courtiers: 'It is my duty to announce to you that henceforth Mi-zi shall be banished from the Kingdom,' he said and, shaking his head, he added: 'The scales on the dragon's back are smooth downwards, but they are sharp upwards: when you ride the dragon, you can only fall.'

- 9 -

The most unlikely place for a gay bar in Singapore must be on the first floor of a corner building overlooking a busy Chinatown junction, but that's where you'll find Backstage. In the most crowded pedestrian part of a city where sexual coyness reigns supreme, a huge rainbow flag is flying brazenly over the evening crowd. I swallow hard. It's taken me ages, but I'm out on a Friday night.

A small sign leads me up a stairway adorned with old movie and theatre posters all individually framed. Some of them are familiar: Jack Lemmon in drag in *Gentlemen Prefer Blondes*, the lithography of the little girl's face in *Les Miserables*, the intertwined arms in *Blood Brothers*; and some are lost in thespian mist: The Andrews Sisters in *Over There*, *Copacabana* starring Gary Wilmott, *Company* by Stephen Sondheim. In the bar itself, the air con is set on max as if coolness could be measured by degrees Fahrenheit. The young barman is the first peroxide-blonde Chinese I've ever met; in the bar's dim darkness his hair is as strong a light source as the individual table lamps – perhaps more so. It's 10 p.m. and Backstage is at its fullest. This must be the place to come before hitting the Singapore clubs, and I must confess that I am secretly curious about the nightlife of a city with the rip-roaring reputation of a sleepy Siberian settlement.

'Go to Club Taboo,' says the peroxide blonde whose name is David ('like Beckham', he informs me). 'Most popular.'

I am concerned it might be too late. 'Should I leave soon?'

'Still early. Normally go there after midnight.'

Wow, an all-nighter, I tell myself as I open the balcony door. The hot, humid air hits me straight away. Singapore is a sauna in reverse with the sweat-inducing chamber on the outside and the cool relief to be found in the air-conditioned rooms inside. I sip my vodka and tonic next to the rainbow flag while observing the multitudes below. The male-only crowd around me is composed equally of gregarious Westerners and giggling Asians. The Westerners are mostly old, English, and uninterested in me. The Asians are much, much younger and they are staring at me unabashed, their pert eyes examining my face and the direction of my gaze. I daren't look at any of them directly for longer than a nanosecond because I fear I will embolden them too much. I'm also feeling uncomfortable, because I've left my sling behind and I am keeping my left arm stuck lifelessly in my jeans pocket. *Will they notice?* I keep wondering. I gulp my drink quickly, overwhelmed by my new surroundings and self-conscious in an environment that should be familiar but turns out to be mildly oppressive.

As soon as I put my empty glass down, David is there immediately to take an order. I look out for the CCTV.

'Another one?' he asks me.

I point at an advertisement for the Chingay Parade. Is that Gay Pride?

He shakes his head. 'No, Chinese festival. The "gay" bit accident. Pride different. We celebrate Pride. Out there.'

*Out there* is a scene so colourful it belongs to a Gilbert and Sullivan production. The low-rise terraced shophouses are bedaubed with deep, vivid pigments: paprika red, mustard yellow, sage green, date brown, berry blue. They stand on five-foot covered walkways, as decreed by Raffles himself, very practical in those frequent downpours. The fascias are a mixture of the colonial and oriental: there are pilasters and there are louvres, but they are painted in contrasting colour combinations that would have made even a Victoriana collector faint. The combined decorative effect is mildly psychedelic; there are good reasons for the ban on psychotropic substances in Singapore, and one of them is for your own protection against chromatic overkill.

I turn my gaze to the diner opposite which is closing. The lone waitress picks up the plastic chairs and stacks them by the kitchen. She lifts every round table with an audible grumph and walks awkwardly. Her centre of gravity is highly precarious as her arms form a twenty-past-eight arrangement on the round table boards. I grab sight of a middle-aged Chinese couple looking up and I detect some curiosity in their glances. They catch my eye and instantly look away, as if they had peeped through a keyhole and come up against a depravity.

David interrupts my reverie.

'Pride not advertised. We must be discreet.'

I point at the big rainbow flag hanging over the Chinatown masses. 'You call that discreet?'

David shrugs his shoulders. 'A rainbow? Why no rainbow? Even children love rainbow. Nobody say "rainbow flag minus one colour, gay". I did no' say that. You did no' say that.'

I kind of see the mindset behind relaxation of the Confucian leash; no persecution in turn for invisibility. It's like being in an eternal Clintonian limbo: don't ask, don't tell. Toleration rather than tolerance is always the first step out of the shadows.

'And you are happy with that?' I ask.

'Yes. We have club, sauna, bar and they leave us alone. And every year we have biggest gay party in Asia: Nation, on Sentosa Island.' And picking up my empty glass, he repeats: 'Another one?'

Yes, I do need another vodka and tonic. I need to get to terms with the imponderable. A thriving gay scene in Singapore? This is a country that still uses flogging for petty offences like scrawling graffiti on walls. This is a country with more mundane rules and regulations than the army and navy manuals combined. More to the point, it is a country that explicitly criminalises sex between males.

The heat outside is getting oppressive so I follow David to the bar and I pick up a gay map of ultra-conservative, Muslim Malaysia – plus one of Singapore. I look in and find Backstage, the bar I'm in. What is this mark on the map opposite us? An escort? A *male* escort?

David hands me a glossy magazine along with my vodka. 'This is *Manazine*. It is gay,' David explains matter-of-factly. 'Before you buy it like a newspaper. But now MDA say: subscription only or free in gay bar.'

MDA stands for the Media Development Authority, a powerful organisation that can close magazines and fine editors.

Its Censorship Review Committee was last convened in April 2002 and its report was typically vague. Publications and society's values should walk hand in hand and the press should be a follower, not a leader. Free speech depended on the cultural, economic and political set-up of a society and the parameters of expression regarding race, religion, violence, sexual content, nudity, homosexuality and coarse language had to be set considering Singaporean community values. (And who sets a marker for those values? No prizes for guessing.) So, although the 'promotion of homosexuality' – such Thatcherite wording – was to be prohibited, a more flexible approach would be put in place when dealing with homosexual themes and greater leeway would be allowed for adults to access non-exploitative content. In short, a discreet gay scene was to be allowed.

'My friend there likes you.'

I crash down back to the present. David is pointing mischievously at a guy leaning against the bar. He is more Malay-looking than the rest of the patrons and his string vest loosely covers a well-defined torso. As I turn, he looks towards us, sees me staring, sees David giggling and makes a shooting sign with his finger. Then he points at his mouth and blows to cool down the imaginary barrel.

I laugh, give him the thumbs up and make a mental note to exchange phone numbers when I leave. Tonight I really want to check out those clubs.

- 10 -

I leave Backstage at midnight and follow the South Bridge Road down to the end. It's a Saturday night and yet all is quiet. The damp air should magnify the flip and flop of every sandal's footstep; yet, in a city where open footwear is de rigeur, I hear none: I am the only one walking the street. This is a major road but there are few cars and they are gliding around mutely like dolphins in the deep. I long for the drivers to rev the engines up and accelerate until the traffic lights where they can drop two gears in succession to make some ear-splitting noise. Are orientals as in love with the motor car as Westerners? Maybe yes, maybe not; maybe this is the love that dares not count its cost: import prices on this congested island can be triple those in the United States or Europe. But even so, those who have cars don't seem to enjoy them. *Give it some gas, remind me I'm in a city that's alive.*

Yet the street is stirring in a different way: it is hypervisual. The light-polluted sky appears verdigris like an ancient Greek discoloured bronze. Flashing neon signs make up for what the night lacks in sound and the occasional strobe illuminates a laminated glass door from the inside. So, there *are* people within those soundproofed clubs. But the whirr of the air conditioning units is more boisterous than the timid hum emanating from Tantric Bar – another rainbow flag poised over a main traffic artery – and it doesn't even have a door to shut. This area was a nutmeg plantation until the 1850s; I bet it was more noisy then. Is anyone out now or shall I go back to my hotel?

I suddenly notice the silent line of clubbers a few minutes ahead and pinch myself. A *queue*? And by the rate this one is moving, it looks like twenty minutes or so to the scary bouncer with the pencil 'tache.

The guy next to me must have arrived at the same conclusion, because he's lighting up.

'Cigarette?' he offers me.

I take a good look at him. Another *ang moh*, but tall, taller than me, much more corpulent and with a tiny head that stands on his shoulders like a potato on a sack. I reckon he's only in his thirties but the years have been as unkind to his countenance as they have been to his hairline; to top it all, they have conspired to expose his piggy ears that stick out like two large sea anemones, feeding. I decline his offer by shaking my head and look around to see if I fancy anybody.

'Long queue, isn't it?' he says.

I make a sour face, for I hate queues like I hate wine recorkers.

'Such is life,' he says philosophically.

I shrug my shoulders, realising I haven't answered back. Rude, I know, but what the hell, I find him creepy.

'Been here before?' His English accent was very shire. I look ahead. One person on the line gets in, *one hundred thousand million to go!* Might as well be sociable; I'm stuck with this guy like others are born with unsavoury relatives.

'No, first time,' I reply. 'What's it like? I'm surprised such a place exists.'

'Yes, remarkable. It all started recently. I wouldn't exactly say the PAP has embraced homosexuality, but –'

*The PAP?*

'The People's Action Party. The ruling party since independence. We have one-party democracy in Singapore.'

He laughs.

'You live here then?' I ask.

'Oh, yes! Yes. The only way I'd leave is if they expelled me for corrupting the youth.'

Another person from the line gets in. At this rate we won't get in until Friday week.

'So, has the government changed their policy now?'

'It's been some time. In 2003 the then Prime Minister Goh Chok Tong told *Time* magazine how they would accept openly gay people in the civil service.'

*You don't say.*

'It was considered a blackmailable predicament.'

'But gay sex is still illegal?'

'It is. But it's a dead law. No one has been prosecuted for more than a decade.'

'Why the change of heart?'

The potatohead fixes me with his stare. 'You are a tourist. British aren't you? You don't understand.'

'Don't understand what?'

'How you create a nation where none exists.'

'Singapore is many nations,' I retort.

'It's early days yet.'

The queue is almost racing now. They're going in in threes and fours...

'How do you create a nation by being nice to homosexuals?' I ask.

He was waiting for that, if only to find my name.

'Singapore, my dear – what is it?'

'John,' I said.

'I'm Nick. Pleased to meet you,' he says and assumes a schoolmasterish tone. 'Singapore, dear John is surrounded by Indonesia and Malaysia, both Islamic countries. If you want to forge a distinct identity from your neighbours, you try to highlight your differences. And, if necessary, you create some.'

'You mean –'

'Nothing happens by chance in Singapore. Everything is the result of serious high-level debate. In the past they liked being the leader of the Asian tiger economies. In this post-9/11 world, they decided to differentiate. They want to attract creative people but creative people don't like living in straitjackets. They like living in a tolerant, gay-friendly, open environment.'

We're almost at the door.

I was expecting – well, I don't know what I was expecting, but whatever it was, it wasn't *this*.

Taboo is spread over two storeys. On the ground floor the DJ is spinning his funky techno, acoustically not a million miles from London's own DTPM. A long bar on one side is staffed by more peroxide orientals. One wall by the dance floor slopes down with makeshift wooden poles and seats. It is brimming with ladyboys: effeminate, ethereal and very, very young. Well-dressed, in designer gear and thankfully low on the oxygenated follicle front, they dance suggestively or sit cross-legged femme-fatalishly. As soon as I come within their line of sight, they all smile in unison as if I were snapping at them with an imaginary camera and their pimp closes in on me. I assume he is the pimp because he is dressed in a cheap Madonna T-shirt. All the firm's money must have gone to those embroidered D&G tops for his employees immediately behind.

'Alone, *lah*?' the pimp asks without wasting much time.

I smile, as I do when I don't want to talk back.

'You like boy?' he asks me straight away and points at his flock like a shepherd at his cattle.

'No, thanks,' I whisper and try to move – in vain, as I have reached the most crowded section.

'*No like boy?*' he exclaims in mock surprise.

I refuse the glass of beer he offers me. I like my drink but I also like my internal organs, thank you, and I don't want to wake up in a Kallang bathtub with one kidney missing – and when I say 'one' I am being optimistic.

'*No like drink?*' I hear him say but by then I have escaped to the centre of the dance floor.

Maybe it is the shock of dancing in a decent club in Singapore, maybe it is the pre-club drinks at Backstage, or maybe it is the overtures of the pimp, but I feel uneasy. Don't get me wrong: the music is good – better than good – but I think that everyone is watching this new face in hell with his lame left arm in his pocket. I last ten minutes before I decide to take a walk. The first floor is a chillout, abuzz with polite conversation, awash with boys looking longingly into each other's eyes, and almost aflame because the air con is busted. I attempt to open a window but they seem to have been welded shut to keep the noise in: don't offer the police a stick with which to beat you.

*This does not compute*, I keep thinking as I walk downstairs: nightlife, dance music, aggressive pimps – what next? Will someone offer me drugs? But no, the death penalty hanging over a pusher's neck like an open noose is deterrent enough for at least one decadent Western practice not to have found its way into this most upright of states.

When I buy my next drink at the long bar, I feel someone's gaze at my neck. Scientists who question paranormal experiences should explain how people can sense within *seconds* when someone in the same room is staring at them. I can describe the symptoms: a warm tickle starts on the neck below the hairline, the ears itch and the Adam's apple jumps inadvertently as a stare is transformed into an invisible caress. I wish Glaxo or Pfizer put some money into researching the subject, because then we might be able to solve the other conundrum: how to spot who it is, without looking around. In most cases we're disappointed, anyway – why, sometimes we can be positively insulted.

I certainly am not. My man is on the small side (well, if you want to pick up Vikings, go to Sweden) but sweet. Our eyes lock and he smiles first. I smile back and, losing no time, he walks towards me.

'Hello,' he says to me.

'Hi.'

'You sexy, sexy, SEXY man,' he says, and I knew then he was more drunk than me.

I weigh him with a glance. He is short, thirty-ish and slightly stocky with broad shoulders and a pale, round face. His eyes are small and drooping at the outer edges – just like, just like…

'Are you Japanese?' I ask.

Night falls quickly on his face as if someone had closed shut a skylight above his head. 'Japanese?' he repeats with his voice raised. Call the orientals impenetrable if you like, but you do know when they are upset, for they bark like pit-bulls.

I realise I have some explaining to do.

'Erm, I just said what came to my head,' I grovel. 'I am not a great observer of characteristics where Asians are concerned.'

'Nobody says this to me befo',' he shouts.

'I am sorry, I thought…'

'My grandmotha' Japanese. But I no Japanese! I, Chinese!'

'You do look Chinese,' I correct myself. 'It's me. To me everyone looks Japanese in Asia. What's your name?'

'My name is Dan,' he says.

'Hardly a Japanese name, is it?' I laugh nervously. 'It's very, ermm, *Chinese*. Like, like –' I stop. Dan Dare? Dan Brown? Dan Ackroyd?

'I'm John,' I belatedly introduce myself. 'Glad to meet you Dan.'

And I am. Sometimes you can't make out a genuine person in the hydra-headed pick-up falseness that permeates clubland from Soho to Singapore, but Dan's eyes still glow with that guileless innocence that comes from within rather than without. The gallivanting of the ladyboys further down only serve to emphasise Dan's affectionate stare as he leans at the bar; he gives my belly a warm feeling that, for now at least, only I matter in his world.

*This is someone I can wear my sling in front of and not feel awkward.*

'First time in Singapore?'

'I was here a long time ago. Long, long time.'

'You like Singapore?'

'I do,' I reply. 'There are some scenes that are difficult to forget.'

*Like the songbirds.*

I am the nightmare of maids everywhere and with good reason: it's only some really major catastrophe like global thermonuclear war or a Richter scale nine earthquake that can wake me up early on a weekday, let alone on a weekend, so my room is the last one to be made. I have found that different nationalities react differently to lie-ins. In South America the maid and her friends and her friends' friends start gossiping in a loud voice outside the door until you emerge beaten and hung over. In France and Italy they bang on the door – if you are lucky – or just barge in and feign surprise that you are still in bed and not up with the chickens to admire the Duomo/*Hôtel de Ville*/magnificent coastline. In Asia they leave you alone, but at a cost: they never replace items like soap or toilet paper ever again.

But that Sunday the maids were happy and pleasantly puzzled to see the hotel's sleep demon emerge from his room before they had even started to lay down the breakfast table. See, I have grown up with tales such as that of the Emperor and his Nightingale that personify the passion of the Far East for songbirds and the bird-singing competition at Tiong Bahru was unmissable. Malays also cherish their melodies, especially those of the *merbok*, a zebra-striped dove that is supposed to trill verses of the Qur'an if you but hear closely. The Chinese prefer the *mata puteh*, the white-eyed zosterops, a tiny olive-green songster with a powerful soundbox and a distinctive white circle around the eye; the *shama*, a beautiful and bossy member of the thrush family with a glossy ink-black head, back and wings contrasting with an orange chest; and the sparrow-sized red-whiskered bulbul, called *jambul*, whose voice is as close to human whistling as can be.

I knew that bird singing contests are common in South East Asia, but nothing had prepared me for the scale of the spectacle in the Bird Arena Café: a roof of railings with hooks on which dozens of identical 20-inch round bamboo cages were hanging, one bird per cage; competitors, almost exclusively male, sitting in a row of chairs parallel to the line of cages above, sipping a mug of coffee; waiters bringing drinks, collecting dishes and taking orders; judges walking around making notes; and spectators sitting at tables, eating – whenever Singaporeans sit down, they get pangs of hunger – or walking with necks stretched, because the cages are hung high to leave the birds undisturbed and minimise interference from man-made obstructions.

But my overwhelming memory is of the aural tapestry woven by the birds themselves – seemingly *shamas* on my Sunday – caressing my eardrums and imprinting their love songs into my unconscious. Yes, love songs they were, as only the male *shamas* sing, competing to find a mate who appreciates their musicality. And theirs was no twitter or squeak, no chirp nor chip: occasionally they sang as if with themselves as a duet, a strange a cappella tune arising from their lungs; sometimes the melodic air went on for minutes on end, its resonance lingering on for longer. I'd have liked to know what they were on about, but my even greater wish was to hear them in the wild where a mate could and would fly to them to make them content. How would a happy, satisfied *shama* sing as opposed to the ungratified avian choir above me laden with perpetual longing?

I am not sure if Dan has heard me recount all this, because, fortified by several beers, he has been leaning on me for the past quarter of an hour.

'Go to yo' place?' he finally proposes.

I think of the signs at reception: <u>*Absolutely*</u> *no guest in room after midnight.*

'I live in a hotel. They don't allow guests after midnight.'

Dan isn't so sure. 'Can, *lah*,' he says, which in Singlish means 'Of course they can and will.'

The lights come on and force a decision. I could at least try to sneak him in.

Well, the native Singaporean was right: he walked into the lift while I went straight to reception to ask for my key. But no, Mr Censor, you can pass this chapter with a PG certificate: as soon as Dan lay on my bed, clothes and all, he fell asleep. This is more than I can say about me, since he turned out to be a nightmare of a sleepmate. He tossed and turned every five minutes like a crackhead in rehab; he kneed my spleen with panache; and he spread himself upon the bed as if posing for the Crucifixion.

I jump. Now he is scratching himself all over.

I push him away and look carefully. There are no marks on him, no spots, no rashes.

*Except–*

On his back I can see a soft, mother-of-pearl scar where an incision appears to have been made. Now that I pay attention, his body has many such scars, as if he's suffered the death by a thousand cuts. I do not understand, and I'm uneasy with what I don't understand.

I wake Dan up. He sits up fuzzily.

'You were scratching – badly,' I say to him.

'No worry,' he says timidly.

'What's going on?'

He looks dejected.

'Before, when I was little, I had eczema,' he says, though the pronunciation of his affliction was such that he has to write it down ('exma') for me to understand. 'I am fine now but when I sleep, I scratch. No worries.'

'Only when you sleep?'

'Only,' he repeats.

'How odd,' I murmur.

'Odd,' he whispers – affirmation by repetition.

'I mean, you might bleed. Your scratching is so vigorous.'

He shows me his nails. Well trimmed.

'I take medicine to make my skin soft. But can no' stand in sun. Danger,' he replies.

I sigh. 'Can anyone sleep in the same bed as you?'

He nods.

'Can. My bo'friend. Only he can.'

'Your boyfriend? Where is he now?'

Dan rolls back into the sheets.

'No mo' boyfriend,' he says and almost immediately falls asleep. I don't. I can't – not a wink.

As soon as the sun comes up, I ask him politely to leave.

# CHAPTER FIVE

# THE DUTIFUL SON

Unlike his nickname, Wang 'Lucky' Xiang, was not fortunate; for a start, he lost his mother to illness at the tender age of five. His father, toiling in the fields from sunrise to sunset, could not bring up his son alone. So, six months after his dear wife had gone to meet the Jade Emperor in His Celestial Palace, he chose to marry beautiful but wicked Zhu. In the beginning all was well, and Zhu was kind to little Lucky Wang, for she was young and healthy and would have kids of her own. But a thousand days passed and then another thousand and, like a slowly uncoiling snake, the truth crept upon Zhu: she would never become pregnant. Her husband had a child, but she would have none to call her own.

Her heart poisoned with bitterness and envy, she turned against her stepson.

She punished him for the most trivial things. When he played with other children and returned home spattered with mud, she would not serve him his bowl of rice. When he had a nightmare and his screams woke her up, he got a beating. When one day he came back from the woods with hardly any mushrooms in his basket, she locked him outside in the howling wind. And every time she whispered calumnies in his father's ear: Wang gets into fights with other boys; Wang can't sleep at night because he's lazy and nods off during the day; Wang is disrespectful and doesn't do his share of household chores. Eventually, his father, too, turned against him and the poor boy was abused and beaten by both.

Yet Lucky Wang knew that the greatest virtue in this world is *xiao*, filial piety. How could he complain to his father who laboured and sweated everyday so that he, Wang, could have a roof over his head and a shirt – however worn out – over his shoulders? How could he bear a grudge against his stepmother who cooked him his meals – however meagre – and warmed his father's bed at night? So Wang kept his head down, and he patiently and uncomplainingly bore his cross.

One thousand more days passed and an unusually harsh winter set in. Deep snow covered the farm. The lakes were frozen and the small river that cut the forest in two became icily firm. It was as if life itself had gone into hibernation like the bears and the squirrels. Worse, Zhu fell ill with a fever, like Wang's mother. To lose one wife is a tragedy, to lose two is a catastrophe. Wang's father became a shadow of himself: he turned paler as Zhu turned more ashen in her bed and lost more and more weight as she became slowly emaciated. The family had slaughtered their last chicken weeks ago and had been on a diet of rice and water ever since. Nothing to hunt, nothing to rear, everything killed by the unrelenting frost.

# THE DUTIFUL SON

Zhu was drifting in and out of a coma, while Wang and his father stood praying by her side. One morning, she opened her eyes: 'Only eating fresh fish will cure me,' she whispered with difficulty. 'I saw it in my dreams.'

Her husband started weeping, for he knew then she was doomed. How could anyone go fishing in these inimical conditions? He cried so hard that he didn't notice Wang who got up, stuffed his clothes with paper and straw to keep the cold away, and walked out silently.

Wang marched to the Emerald Lake, where, only a few months ago, he'd caught the plump carp that swam in its waters. At first he tried to dig a hole in the ice with his hands, but didn't get far before his nails broke and his blood turned the snow red. He tried to beat through a hole with an oak branch, but the glacial hiss of the air numbed his fingers and his grip. Defeated, he lay prostrate weeping and tried to melt the ice with his body heat.

As his tears fell down his cheeks, he thought he heard a distant voice: 'Your stepmother beat you and turned your father against you and yet you are endangering your life on her behalf. Why?'

Through the mist of his tears, Wang tried to see who had been talking but in vain. 'Who's there?' he shouted.

Nothing. No one.

Ever obedient, he replied: 'Because she is a companion to my father. It is my duty to try and save her.'

He raised his chin and his eyes darted around trying to detect the slightest stir.

'Who's there?' he shouted again.

This time, the remote voice replied.

'Look down,' it said.

Wang lowered his eyes and they were immediately engulfed in vapour, for his tears had driven through the ice like molten lead. They created an inch-long opening that was steaming larger by the minute, as if a coal brazier had been suspended in the middle.

And lo and behold, two large golden carp flung themselves through the hole and landed next to him flapping their gills and gasping for air. An astonished Wang stunned them with the oak branch and carried them home running at full speed to take them to his stepmother.

We don't know what became of Zhu. The story doesn't tell us whether she survived the winter after eating the fresh carp or whether she appreciated her stepson's selflessness, felt ashamed and changed her ways.

That's not the point of the story, anyway.

- II -

The Orient might start east of Vienna and Asia east of Istanbul, but the real Far East starts in Singapore. Once upon a time, the Orient stood for sensual mystique and untamed wilderness: impenetrable mountains, subservient females and fearless warriors surfaced during your uncharted voyage. The Orient was for the adventurous, the defiant, the slightly insane. Its appeal was its cruel unpredictability: British emissaries could be thrown down a scorpion-infested cellar at the whim of a ruler; pirates could surface and 'rommage' your calicoes, your camphor or even your crew; sailors and ships might disappear in the eye of a typhoon and never be heard of ever after. Then again, guests would also be defended by a clan to the last teenage boy's breath; women respected and treated like precious jewels; and friendships forged would last a lifetime. Nowadays the Orient is mapped, its languages have been studied and its religious writings translated. It has become predictable as globalisation transports values to and fro and national values are forced to gauge their stock in the global mindplace of ideas. We now know what the Orient is about – and we should have noticed earlier, when we crossed the first bazaar.

It stands for retail culture.

Nowhere is this more true than in Singapore where consumerism is a marker of identity. Hong Kong may be the cultural hub of the Far East; Thailand its pleasure beach; Japan its locomotive; mother China the giant political spring – but Singapore is its marketplace. This lozenge-shaped island has been described as 'a shopping mall with UN representation' and sometimes the sarcasm almost rings true. As Prime Minister Goh admitted during his National Day rally speech in 1996, 'Life for Singaporeans is not complete without shopping'. What truly seems to unite the kaleidoscope of its communities is their love of the iPod and there's no better place to buy one than Orchard Road.

This stretch used to be an area with gambier and pepper plantations, Singapore's soil not being conducive for the cultivation of much else. When Raffles arrived, there were already such holdings on the island belonging to a Chinese family. It was their estate that Captain James Pearl bought in May 1822 – on today's Pearl's Hill – and started cultivating pepper; gambier vines lead a symbiotic existence with pepper trees entwining themselves around them and providing natural fertiliser. Gambier is not a shrub that gets a name-check in *Gardeners' World* but as a component of a well-known regional upper it is quite valuable; chewing a combination of betel seeds, gambier paste and tobacco wrapped in leaves soaked in lime brings a euphoric rush. There is a rather awkward side-effect: the betel nut turns the tongue and gums crimson red so an addict looks at best Ebola-diseased and at worst an extra out of a John Carpenter zombie spectacular as many a hapless rickshaw driver, who's driven his tourist clients away just by smiling, has found.

The desirability of gambier was high in the tanning industries – and no, I don't mean a beauty product to make you bronze under the sunbed: it was used to dye fabric what we now call the colour khaki. Singapore was the major world producer of gambier until its poor soil was depleted and the growers moved to Johore where by the 1890s there were reportedly 4,000 such plantations. Gambier continued to be one of Singapore's main exports until the explosion of the tin and rubber trade in the Malay peninsula took over and eclipsed everything else. The name of the street today originates after the move of the plantations out of Singapore and the emergence of fruit tree cultivation in the area.

As Orchard Road was close enough but out of town, it was an ideal place to bury the dead. Stephen King cognoscenti might relish the factoid that an old Chinese graveyard stood where the Mandarin Hotel is situated; that Indonesians from Bencoolen were buried in the premises of the Grand Central Hotel; or that a Jewish burial ground was demolished in the mid-1980s to make way for Dhoby Ghaut MRT station. The only reminder of the Orchard Road of old is the Thai Embassy at number 370, still housed in the premises acquired in the 1890s by His Majesty Rama V, King of Siam, immortalised in the musical *The King and I*. Hats off to their defiance, given that Thailand's balance of payments would skyrocket should they ever decide to let the developers get their hands on the 18,000-plus square metre estate. Because, as anyone who has been dwarfed among the back-to-back hotels and shopping centres can attest, there is nothing left on Orchard Road of fruit or gambier any more.

I walk around aimlessly, mentally groping the shadowy image of Singapore as I remember it, but it is not the opaqueness of my imperfect memories that frustrates me. It was not far from here, on Bencoolen Street, that I stayed in a cheap hostel seventeen years ago. Nothing remains of it or the Chinese family hotels around it. I splashed out for dinner at the Omar Khayyam on Hill Street, dubbed as 'the best Indian restaurant in the world' by more than one travel guide. I feel righteous indignation when I can't find any trace of it among the hotels and malls that have jumped up in its place.

The face of modern Singapore bears the stamp of a single man more than any other country in Asia outside Mao's China. It has been moulded in the image of Lee Kuan Yew – 'Harry' to his friends – one of *Time* magazine's 20 most important Asian leaders of the twentieth century. (Twenty? He easily slips into the top five). Singapore may owe its genesis to Raffles but its present character, appearance and constitution is the work of Lee Kuan Yew who led the city through decolonisation, union with Malaysia and, ultimately, independence to its current status as a global financial centre.

The verdict of the future historian will be tough, for Lee has been a ruthless, highly intelligent autocrat but one with the right ideas. Incorruptible, sharp-witted and abrasive, he is, like his city, a mass of contradictions. British-educated, his brand of *dirigiste* policies would not be out of place in centralised France. Hakka Chinese by descent, he abhorred the tribal politics of his neighbours. Democratic-minded, he didn't desist from making a deal with the communists in the early life of the PAP party he founded. He offered statutory seats to the opposition when there was a danger that his party would monopolise parliament using the first-past-the-post system, but he also sued persistent critics to bankruptcy and political oblivion. He created a powerful executive apparatus and imposed draconian laws – such as detention without trial – but he then used these powers judiciously and sparingly. He has created a state where capitalism reigns supreme, tempered with a programme of income redistribution unique in Asia. And in the true spirit of someone who does his job well, he has not made himself indispensable: in 1990 he stepped down to oversee his legacy as 'senior minister' under the prime-ministership of Goh Chok Tong.

If there's been a constant in Singapore's PAP governments, it is that nothing stands still and everything is mutable. A slip road is required for a new highway? The bulldozers come to flatten any houses standing in the way (Woodsville Road for the Pan Island Expressway). A new metro line is extended? Demolish hospitals and schools if need be (Youngberg Hospital and St Andrew's school for the North-East MRT Line). To us it may appear heavy-handed; to Asians, used to paternalistic rule, it comes as naturally as haggling. At least Singapore is keeping some nature reserves and colonial structures; if you want to witness some good old wholesale destruction of the past, let alone the environment, go to Hong Kong.

And so it is with Orchard Road: it has become a triumphal avenue to Mammon with monuments to the deity erected along its path; from the Forum to Plaza Singapura, I have never attempted to walk all the way in between in one go. Expats flock to the Tanglin Mall for the clothing and large sizes on offer, the bookworms to Borders in the seven-storey glass cone of Wheelock Place, the lower-income workers to the Lucky Plaza where they can bargain to their heart's desire, the music-lovers to the Heeren that boasts the largest HMV shop in Asia and the trendy to the designer boutiques of the Paragon: everybody has their own favourite mall on Orchard Road.

Maybe it's the name, maybe it's the convenient location next to the Dhoby Ghaut MRT station, maybe it's the fact that it was there that I bought my first-ever SLR and started a love affair that has lasted for two decades now, but for me, the greatest and the best shopping mall is Plaza Singapura. At least its gigantism has ensured it still exists after so many years. Once inside, you live in a parallel universe populated by the weird (Thai Bysr fashions), the mildly scary (Trumpet Praise Christian bookshop) and the sublime (Italian Gelare Café). From the digital world of Motorola gadgetry to New Age B-Hive honey, the Plaza exists in a warped space time continuum and even getting back to ground control – sorry, *level* – is laborious as the basements seem to grow as deeply as the upper floors.

By Bas Brasah Road, I notice the clocktower of an ivory-white, well-proportioned simple church with a tiled roof over a double-scalloped Roman moulding. It belongs to the Presbyterians and its history can be traced to 1829 when the Reverend Keasbury of the London Missionary Society arrived in Singapore. Originally built in 1878 but extended and remodelled half-a-dozen times, it is thankfully still coherent as an architectural whole despite the demolition of its manse in 1936. Unlike St Andrew's, the Anglican cathedral, or the Catholic Cathedral of the Good Shepherd, its simplicity is dwarfed by the developments around it and is almost blotted out by the loud, brassy colours of the adjoining YMCA building.

It's locked. *A church that's locked?*

My curiosity aroused, I walk across to the administration office expecting to meet a dour Scot and meet instead a dour

Chinese who barks at me 'Yes?' When I tell him I would like to see the inside of the church, he gives me a quizzical look, throws a bunch of keys to an attendant and growls: 'Show him in!'

I really don't know why I went to so much trouble, because I kind of knew what to expect. This is a part of Singapore that will be forever Scotland: pews, pews and more pews, not even made comfortable by the presence of a cushion. They're all facing a giant organ which dominates the interior like a giant squid in an aquarium. There is nothing of artistic merit inside which is how Presbyterians want it, I suppose.

I notice another locked glass door at the back. I walk straight there and stand in front. The attendant follows me grumbling and opens it. It appears to be shielding a few marble plaques on the wall.

'In Memory of Major Ivan Lyon DSO MBE Temporary Lieutenant Colonel, The Gordon Highlanders, killed whilst leading a raid against Japanese shipping in Singapore Harbour October 1944, aged 29 years.' And then in smaller letters: 'This tablet is erected by his sorrowing wife and family.'

Oh, yes, the third definer of this city: Raffles, Lee Kuan Yew and World War Two.

Back in Plaza Singapura, I find Coffeemania quite easily and very nice it looks too except for a gang of teenage schoolgirls whose gaze is immediately fixated on my sling. I walk to the old lady at the counter to make an order like one would do in Starbucks.

'I'll have a large cappuccino,' I say, ever conservative in the face of too much choice.

The old lady smiles. 'Please take seat,' she says.

'Don't I order now?'

The Chinese hate saying yes or no; they pummel you into submission through repetition.

'Please take seat and waiter will come for order,' she smiles again.

Under the questioning glances of the girls, I walk to a single table in a corner. A waitress appears out of nowhere and writes down my order in a pad. Then she gives it back to me.

'What do I do with this?' I ask.

She points at the old lady at the counter where I've just been. The girls around me hide their faces in their palms.

'But I've just been there and she sat me down,' I complain. 'Can't you give her the order yourself?'

The waitress looks back at me, not without some fright – complaining is *so* unConfucian – walks to speak to the old lady and returns.

'You must go there,' she repeats anxiously and points at the order which says 'SELF ORDER'.

I am mildly annoyed but fascinated enough to see the choreography to the end. I go to the counter in the midst of what I perceive to be choked giggling by the teenagers and give the order sheet to the old lady who is to finally brew my coffee. Or so I hope.

'Must have table number,' she says, after having a good look at it.

If it wasn't for Chang, I would have left Coffeemania there and then...

Chang is the barman's friend who had flirted with me at Backstage a few nights back. He also has a European name, but somehow he looks more of a Chang than a Reggie which brings back images of East End heavies fighting over a spilled pint. Mind you, as I said back then, Chang's appearance is atypically Chinese: he is tall, broad-shouldered, with more than a hint of that sensuous Malay mouth where his lower lip protrudes as if he's forever waiting for the host from a padre. He has that signature divine smile; I haven't found any people in the world whose faces sparkle more cheerfully than the inhabitants of the Malay peninsula. This is our first date on his time off, and we are treading the first discreet steps in a well-rehearsed opening. If conversations were dances, then ours would be entering the slow adagio in a careful pas de deux. It is clear he has noticed my sling, but he probably thinks it improper to comment at such a delicate stage of our lock step.

Chang is a student and is working as a waiter to supplement his income.

'Student of what?'

'Marketing,' he replies with a complete lack of Singlish. 'I wanted to study film and drama but my parents were dead against it. You Cow-casians,' – I cringe – 'are more tolerant than the Chinese.'

'In what way?'

'For example, allowing your kids to study what they want.'

'Well, it is the Brits who gave you those anti-gay laws,' I counter.

'But you moved on. Here we are rooted in the past. I must marry. I must have a son. I must not bring shame to my parents. I keep hearing "Your father's getting sixty when are

you going to bring him grandchildren?" Here, you must
marry by thirty. And you never divorce.'

'Are you going to marry then?'

Chang shakes his head.

'It's my life. Why should I do what anybody else wants?'

'But you did study what your father wanted.'

For the first time I notice a whiff of helplessness about
him.

'What was the alternative? Can't get through my studies
on my own. With marketing I can go into advertising which
is more creative. I could maybe direct an ad. Or I may get a
chance to go abroad – to study further.'

He takes a short breath.

'But I did tell my girlfriend. I broke up with her last
year.'

I am impressed. 'That must have been very brave. How
did she take it?'

'She loves me, she said so. I do, too, in a way. But why
should I marry a woman and make her unhappy?'

'That is a very Western thing to say.'

'I don't understand.'

I have to think a bit before I can formulate my ideas
coherently. 'Singapore made its fortune from globalisation.
But that doesn't just mean that I can come here and sell you
things or that you can come to the UK to study or buy bonds
in the Japanese stock exchange. It also means exposure to
other cultures and ideas.'

Chang's intelligent face looks puzzled.

'What you just said – "Why should I do what my father
wants?" – is against the Confucian ethos. What happened to
filial piety and all that? The first and most important tenet
is to marry and have offspring.'

'I love and respect my parents, but it's my life in the end,' he says.

Ah, individualism. There goes Singapore's *esprit d'état*: when a patriarchal, authoritarian society is sacrificed in the shrine of capitalism then all kinds of doors are open for uninvited guests to come and settle themselves on the sofa. Family ties and connections become less important as the relentless pursuit of personal profit fetishises the quest for individual happiness, come hell and high water.

I like Chang. I want to latch on to someone for reassurance in this city that keeps challenging my convictions. And I need somebody to cheer me up, because – well, let's say I haven't been too candid about this damned sling.

I touch his knee under the table, and he gives me one of those smiles.

- 12 -

A combination of chronic over-reliance on word-of-mouth for news from mainland China, a determined distrust of administrations elected, unelected or colonial and a flair for the bizarre have turned South East Asia, and Singapore in particular, into an urban legend jungle. They range from the barely believable: babies born on a flight will get free air-travel for the rest of their lives (what? even on Virgin?); to the utterly fnarr-fnarr: the worst job in the world belongs to a guy masturbating animals in the Singapore Zoo; or the downright distasteful: don't eat shellfish after the tsunami because they feasted on the drowned human bodies and can pass on the 'Zulican' virus. (You can laugh now, but in Chinatown the price of lobster plummeted in the immediate aftermath of the tsunami tragedy). For the record, expectant mothers: no such IATA regulation exists; bestiality practitioners: solitary animals in the Singapore Zoo need no help with self abuse; and, hey, hypochondriacs: what was the name of that virus again?

In this vein, you'd have thought that only those alien abductees in America's Midwest rectangular states would actually believe that *The X Files* was a documentary, but, no, you'd be wrong: in Singapore you can join SPI, the Society of Paranormal Investigators. Its members visit abandoned old forts that are said to be haunted (verdict: no ghosts); they check out famous apparitions (verdict: they don't exist) and they examine the rumours that Haw-Par Villa's extraordinarily vivacious statues used real body parts. Maybe it is them and not Glaxo who should research how people can sense when someone is staring at them from behind.

The taxi driver stops. 'Haw-Par Villa,' he announces.

We can't see it, because there are street scaffolding diversions. There is a sign with the now expected singular, 'Pedestrian This Way'; except that it has one arrow pointing to the right and another pointing to the left. To be doubly Zen, there is also one arrow pointing at both directions, maybe to paraphrase the Buddhist maxim 'There are many ways to the villa, all equally valid, and it's up to you to find your own.'

Upon first glimpse of those Haw-Par Villa statues, one is forgiven for supposing that the grotesque was an invention of the Chinese imagination. I had to keep reminding myself that no, it was Prince Eugene of Savoy, homosexual aesthete, military genius and scourge of the Ottoman Turks, whose own grotto in Vienna's Belvedere Palace was decorated with such, well, *style,* that he ended up coining the term, denoting an over-the-top caricature. It took two hundred years for Gaudí and his creations to top grotesque with 'gaudy', but only two decades for the Haw-Par Villa to surpass both – I mean, there's kitsch and there's *Chinese* kitsch. Singapore's authorities are so embarrassed to share the same soil with one of the prime examples of true bad taste that the site is downplayed in official brochures. As a result, the existence of this pinch-yourself monument to tackiness has remained a cult secret, and its style does not yet have a name. I suggest Haw-Haw.

The founders of the Haw-Par Villa were two brothers, Aw Boon Haw and Aw Boon Par born in Rangoon in the late 1800s. Their father was a Hakka herbalist, Aw Chu Kin, who sold a snake-oil ointment which his sons perfected and marketed aggressively in South East Asia as a cure for body aches and pains under the name Tiger Balm. (As someone who has bought and used a jar out of curiosity, I can reveal that it smells strongly of camphor and feels like a milder version of Vicks.) In the 1920s the brothers moved to Singapore; it was the decade when fortunes were being made, and they expanded into publishing, joking that ads for their product cost so much, it was cheaper to open a few newspapers to push it.

Boon Haw built the villa, a six-domed folly with a panoramic view of the sea and the islands beyond, for his beloved brother Boon Par in the 1930s. The furniture was imported from Europe, the inner domes were lined with gold and the terraced gardens covered with sculptures representing Chinese myths. The villa contained an additional extravagance for the thirsty city: a swimming pool. Despite the brand new Pulai Reservoir built in Johore in 1929, the island's perennial freshwater supply problem soon turned the pool into a pond. Swallowing his pride, Boon Haw had its sides ornamented with mermaids, crabs with human heads and giant fishes that could have swallowed Jonah and the whole of Judaea several times over. In accordance with their personal motto – *that which is derived from society should be returned to society* – the brothers opened up the gardens to the public so that their compatriots would be reminded of the traditional Chinese beliefs, for there they were, sculpted in all their gory glory. This is Singapore's oldest standing attraction, entertaining – I am careful choosing that word – visitors since 1937. The outbreak of the war made the brothers flee: Boon Haw to Hong Kong and Boon Par to Rangoon where he died in 1944. When Boon Haw returned the villa was decrepid, so he had it demolished and turned into a theme park, restoring many of the statues and building even more.

We pass through the gate under an inscription trying to explain what the villa is: 'It is a park. It is a big moral lesson. It is for everyone.' Well, it's not for everyone and many a Western – sorry, *Caucasian* – visitor remains perplexed among the morals to be gained from the parables depicted. For a start, irony, tragedy and subtlety are absent from Chinese mythology. Flawed heroes are a product of Western tradition: Hamlet, Faust or Madame Bovary are as alien to the Chinese as elliptic their own tales appear to us – and nowhere is that more blatant than in the Tableaux of Vices and Virtues.

So let's play guess-the-moral: Qing Chen is gambling all day while his wife is running her grocery business. There he is at bottom right, absorbed in his card passion. We see Mrs Chen sending her son down a slope to fetch his father from the gambling den, because her business is booming, and she needs help. But the son pays no attention to the traffic and a car – a plain blue Volkswagen Beetle – runs him over; his dead body, bleeding from the head, is the centrepiece of the composition. And the moral of the story? Is it, 'Look left, right and left again when crossing the road'? Is it, 'Keep to the speed limit in built-up areas'? Nah, it's 'Gambling can cost you everything' – silly me.

How about this scene? In the first panel, two friends have gone to camp in the woods. A bear appears while friend B is asleep. So what does friend A say? 'A bear! I must escape at once! No time to warn my friend! My safety comes first! I will climb this tree!' In panel two we see him being devoured by the bear: 'Friend! Friend! The bear has got me. It saw me hiding on the tree. Help me, please.' And what does friend B think, who is still seemingly asleep during this time? 'I am so afraid. Maybe if I lie down on the ground and act dead the bear will go away.' Now guess the moral. Is it, 'If you see a bear pretend to be dead?' Is it, 'Bears climb trees too, stupid!' No, it is, of course, 'Be a loyal friend'. Where is Aesop when you need him?

This one is a little easier, although its elaborate finale still eludes me. Wang Qing once saw a large sea turtle being carried to the market to be sold for soup. He bought it, and rather than cook it, he set it free back into the sea. So far so good, nice touch mate, I know people who are horrified to pick a live lobster from a restaurant aquarium, too. Years later, Wang was travelling in a boat that sank in a typhoon. As Wang was about to drown, the grateful turtle appeared and saved him. Moral of the story: 'Be kind to animals'. Right, a bit stretched, but a point I can at least get. But there is more. The turtle presented him to the Dragon King in his undersea palace who showered Wang with presents. Fine, the turtle owed him one and now they were even, so what's the point of the extra presents? In my books he now owes back to the turtle! And there is more: the turtle then took him to his destination where a rich heiress fell in love with Wang and married him. Hold on, this is not a moral tale, it's an advertisement for the World Wildlife Fund!

While I am pondering all this, a sudden shower makes us seek refuge in Hell. Well, it is the only covered space in the villa and better in Hell than wet.

'So you Chinese believe in hell?' I ask Chang. 'I thought everyone east of Karachi believed in reincarnation.'

'This is *before* reincarnation,' says Chang. 'When you pass the nine courts of hell where you are punished, you end up in the tenth court. There, the presiding judge determines your future fate, an old lady, Meng Po, hands out the tea of forgetfulness and your past life is wiped from your memory.'

'You know the story well.'

'My parents used to bring me here,' Chang admits with a blush.

Well mine didn't, and I can't get enough of these slasher dioramas that depict punishments on human statues with extraordinary ferocity. In the first court of the cavern that is Hell, the newly-arrived souls look at themselves in the Mirror of Retribution where all their past sins are revealed to them so that their torture could begin. And so it goes that in the second court prostitutes drown in a pool of their own blood and gossipers have their tongue pierced. In the third court we observe in lurid detail how 'social agitators' are tied to a red-hot copper pillar and grilled alive. On the other hand, officials who were convicted of graft have their hearts removed, their knees crushed, and their faces scraped like an onion. At that point it hits me: it is impossible to penetrate the Confucian mind unless one appreciates that crimes against the order of society are as important as those against an individual; no wonder the PAP insists on exemplary punishment for any officials found guilty of corruption. In the fourth court not only those who stole or refused to pay rent to their landlords, but also those who evaded taxes are ground by a stone mallet.

In the fifth court of hell, moneylenders who extracted exorbitant interest rates are rolled down a hill strewn with sharp blades. As for the sixth court – woe betide those who were caught with pornographic material or those who committed blasphemy: some kneel on iron nails, some are sawn in two and others are gnawed at by rats. Drug dealers and rapists are boiled alive in the seventh court whereas in the eighth, those who violated the code of filial piety have their intestines torn out alive. In the ninth court, smugglers and arsonists are being bitten by snakes and stung by bees. As for the tenth court, the Hall of Oblivion, Chang was dead right about Meng Po and her potion. But even in reincarnation our free will is being exercised: it's up to us to cross one of six bridges and 18,000 ways leading to a particular form of future life.

I check. The torrential rain has subsided. We can safely leave Hell now.

'Do you believe in all this?' I ask Chang as we move out.

'I believe in the ethics,' he replies.

'And in filial piety, too?' I tease him, as the statue of Wang 'Lucky' Xiang awaits us just by the exit from Hell. There he is with two carp fish next to him, flung from a hole carved on the ice by his boiling hot tears.

Chang looks away. 'I am a good son,' he protests. 'Anyway, I have a brother. He will pass the family name on.'

Right next to Wang is a tableau David Walliams would appreciate. *Bitty* I think, as a certain *Little Britain* sketch comes to mind. Madam Zhang Sun, emaciated and hungry, is being breast-fed by her stepdaughter in order to survive a famine – at least grandma has no teeth. I find such affection both touching and nauseating. It has kept a whole culture subservient and conservative, but at the same time, it provided a safety net for older people – provided they had offspring. What can such a society make out of Western concepts of individual 'inalienable rights' and 'the pursuit of happiness'?

We walk towards the battle between the rabbits and the rats. This is a huge and violent composition with larger-than-life rats and hideous, sharp-toothed rabbits attacking and devouring each other with gusto. A sign explains the background of the story. A couple of white rabbits were happily married, but a black rat moved into their hole, seduced the wife and ran away with her. The other rabbits became angry, attacked the rats and a fierce battle ensued. In a touch of that wonderful oriental logic we are told that the orange guinea pigs were unsure which side to cheer for and as a result they were attacked by both sides. I know it doesn't read as odd as it looks but it's in the details that the weirdness manifests itself: two rats with red armbands use a stretcher to carry away a casualty whose four paws have been bitten off and reduced to bloody stumps; a guinea pig spears a giant rat with a lance; a rabbit steadies himself up to fight with a guinea pig in a boxing ring.

I despair: 'What is it all about?'

Chang points at the sign that provides the moral: 'When outsiders interfere, trouble can result'.

'And you understand that?'

Chang, like the educated Singaporean he is, knows how to argue his corner. 'Of course. Look at what happened in Iraq.'

I take a long breath. 'No, no, but this is... a private matter. Single male rat seduces married female rabbit. It's their problem. Why do all individual sins have to be acted out and punished collectively?'

'Private matters start a train of events that lead to a war,' he replies. 'Like Helen of Troy.'

*Smartarse*, I think. Chang stands next to me arms folded, a huge smile in his face, his intelligent eyes sparkling mischievously. I want to leave the Haw-Par Villa immediately and take him straight to my hotel before that midnight curfew.

'The *Iliad* was an epic poem,' I start but I know I am on a losing downward spiral, 'and it didn't have a black and white moral like this, and anyway, if you want an alternative interpretation, this rats and rabbits business can be interpreted as a parable against interracial sex!'

Like a good Singaporean, Chang avoids any more confrontation and walks on. We follow the story of the Eight Immortals Crossing the Sea; we stop by the Three Gods of Prosperity: Fu – the deity of Luck, Lu the deity of Wealth and Shu the deity of Longevity and pause to ask for all three; we check out the panels of the Journey to the West depicting the adventures of Xuán Zàng, Monkey, Friar Sand and Pigsie; and we marvel – if marvel be the word – at Boon Haw's cars. If you thought that there must be limits to pretentious exhibitionism, think again: his first car was a 1927 German NSU with a metal tiger's head and a horn that reproduced the animal's roar. The second was a 1932 Humber with gold stripes on the body and a much bigger tiger's head – complete with fangs – welded to the radiator.

We come to a stop in front of one of Singapore's most photographed statues: the Maitreya or Laughing Buddha. You all know the one: he's bald, ludicrously pig-eared and dressed in an orange robe that exposes a long necklace gracing a round belly, one that you rub for luck while having your photo taken. As the inscriptions inform us, the Maitreya was not a full Buddha, but a bodhisattva, an enlightened being who kept postponing his entry into nirvana in order to help the human race. His last documented incarnation was as the monk Chi Tze who lived an itinerant life in the ninth century AD teaching the principles of Buddha.

'I quite like Buddhism,' I say to Chang. 'I like the way it isn't prescriptive. Buddha's teaching points to the moon; it isn't the moon itself. There are many ways to the top of the mountain, and each one of us can follow a different one, our own private *tao*. It doesn't matter if you follow Christianity, if you follow Islam or whatever, as long as you reach the top.'

'Yes,' Chang says. 'That's what my parents taught me. There are many ways to the top of the mountain.' He suddenly grins. 'And mine is through gay sex!'

*If this is how you will 'know thyself'...*

'Dutiful son,' I tease him.

'Dutiful son,' he repeats, and his eyes shine.

# CHAPTER SIX

# WHAT THE EYES DON'T SEE

King Hui of Liang was sitting smugly on his throne on the great wooden dais made out of Chen-hai hardwood timber whose underside was ornately carved with birds, dragons, flowers and human figurines. He was looking over the winding, sloping road to the shrine of Guan Yin the Goddess of Mercy, who saves us from the Three Calamities and the Eight Disasters.

King Hui closed his eyes for he felt ethereal, drifting, up on his balcony. The autumnal day was bright, but not too warm, and the few clouds in the sky appeared more as a decoration for the distant mountains than as a threat of rain and thunder. And there was he, a ruler – a just ruler everyone claimed – of a vast and prosperous land, in peace with itself and its neighbours. The world was a benign place and nowhere more so than today, here, and now.

In order to put a brake on his daydreams, he cast his eyes on the street below where a man had appeared, leading a black hulk of a bull from a rope attached on a nose ring.

The King was perplexed by the spectacle and asked: 'Where are you taking this beast? This is the way to the shrine of Guan Yin.'

The man immediately fell on his knees and replied, 'My Lord, I was going to consecrate a bell with its blood.'

The King looked at the bull and amazingly the bull looked back with a piercing, mournful glance as if it could comprehend what had been decided and what was to follow. More remarkably, the bull's gaze was not furious or frenzied, but calm, stoic, unruffled.

The King was moved. 'I cannot bear its demeanour,' he said. 'It appears to me as if it is an innocent person going to a place of execution. Let it be.'

The man, still kneeling, asked deferentially. 'Shall I then dispense with the consecration of the bell, my Lord?'

The King deliberated for an instant and replied: 'An unconsecrated bell will not be heard by Guan Yin in the realm of *sagga*. Perform your sacrifice, but swap the bull for a sheep.'

As the man obediently made his way back, King Hui rose from his throne and left the balcony. He wanted to make sure that he wouldn't be there to witness the scene when the man, this time pulling a sheep behind him, made his way to the shrine – for what we don't see, we don't know and what we don't know, doesn't hurt.

- 13 -

With over 9,200 birds and 610 species in 20 hectares of lush and misty jungle greenery, even the raging avian flu could not keep an inveterate twitcher like me from Jurong Bird Park. I admit, there is some Cringe Factor Seven involved: a birds-of-prey show, a 'Breakfast with the Birds', a 'Be a Falconer' experience, a children's 'Parrot Panto' and worst of all, an hourly chit-chat with pelicans, hornbills and starlings. (Did I get this right? What do you do there? Exchange gossip about the flamingos?) Yet despite such family-style tweeness, this is also a site of serious research. Amongst other firsts, the zoo harbours the world's largest breeding colony of Humboldt penguins outside Patagonia and has pioneered a successful conservation programme of the highly endangered golden conure whose sweet amiability turned it into one of the most sought-after aviary birds. You are excused if you've never seen any, because they normally live in Brazil and they are on the verge of extinction; but if you *do* know what they look like, then you must own one, so shame on you.

Still, don't underestimate the ability of the bird park to switch suddenly from the scholarly to the seriously syrupy: immediately past the entrance I am confronted with the spectacle of half-a-dozen grinning kids posing for photos with parrots perched on their shoulders. Kids also love miniature railways which is why the elevated 'panorail' – an automatic motorised train that allows you to observe the park from above – is so popular I have to queue to board it. Once on the move I look down, and sometimes sideways, at golden-backed and fulvous-breasted woodpeckers, roseate spoonbills, snowy egrets and scarlet ibises until we reach the first stop at the Lory Loft, a large lory aviary. There, forty feet above ground level, I wander on an elevated boardwalk where tittering lories feed literally from my fingertips. They are of unimaginable variegated brilliance: rainbow, dusky, blue-streaked or yellow-bibbed, they come and perch fearlessly on my shoulders as I place the odd mango peel by the central feeding tower. Now let me put on my professor's hat for a second and make the distinction: *lories* – to be found in Australia, Indonesia and Papua New Guinea – should not be confused with *louries* that live in Africa (nor, of course, with *lorries* which are a different proposition altogether). As if to emphasise the lories' native habitat, there is an Australian Bushman's hut by the aviary exit. I order a cappuccino and thankfully I pay and get served without those complicated Coffeemania quadrilles.

The waiter proudly proclaims his provenance with the thickest Aussie accent this side of Porpoise Spit.

'Do you like the coffee, mate?' he asks me.

It's not often you get that sort of question, but maybe he wants a chat with a fellow Caucasian. I had to admit the aroma was exquisite.

'Now you mention it, yes, it's excellent. The best coffee I've tasted in Singapore.'

'I grow it myself.'

'Sorry, you mean *grow* it or *grind* it?'

The waiter grins in the mocking way Australians do when they know something you don't.

'I have a business here in Singapore. I grow beans – in a large garden or a small plantation, I don't know myself.'

'Good life?' I ask.

'Great life, mate,' he replies. 'Singapore is a place where you can make a lot of money very quickly. They micromanage your life, but they don't regulate your business'.

Rather abruptly, he points at my sling.

'What happened to your arm?'

*Time to go.*

'Swimmer's arm,' I reply. 'You know, like tennis elbow.'

I get up as the panorail arrives.

The next stop is Waterfall Station and I disembark to marvel at its special attraction. At one hundred feet, Jurong Falls is the world's highest man-made waterfall – this being Singapore, the water is recirculated – and provides the setting for a humid tropical aviary. Hoopoes, crested louries (note the 'u'), bee-eaters, weavers and starlings nonchalantly cross my path as I walk there and back. But the real special attraction awaits me as I return: two white parakeets are perched right above the station seats copulating with loud gurgles. All children look up – many giggling, most befuddled, some expressionless – whereas every parent pretends not to hear the orgiastic noises and checks the clock in the hope that the next panorail would show up *now*! Not even its eventual arrival makes the parrots flinch, for they are well into their mating with ardour that puts any semi-respectable rodent to shame.

I've heard that Jurong had a fantastic 'World of Darkness' but I'm still surprised at its prodigious size. The extensive owl section feels almost complete – what with barn owls, spotted-wood owls, those huge eagle owls, arctic snowy owls, Malay fish owls and the great Ural owls (what, no ear-tufts?) Despite all this and more, everyone queues up to see the 'mad woman bird' (bush-stone curlew to the rest of you) which is a short, gangly, grey-streaked Australian bird with large plaintive eyes and an eerie call that's been compared to the howl of a mad woman – sound engineers who are working on *Jane Eyre* adaptations, take note. Poor bird, it has probably lost its voice with all these kids tapping on the glass to make it shriek. I catch the eye of their unresponsive parents and tut-tut. To my horror they mistake my disapproval for impatience and start tapping on the window themselves.

Back outside, I stroll past the African hornbills and South American toucans but make a stop by the Window on Paradise. Much that I consider myself well-travelled, I have not seen any paradise birds before. Observing the intricate plumage displays of the twelve-wired bird of paradise – so named for the dozen fragile feathers that delicately sprout from its tail – I can understand why those first Portuguese sailors chose to conclude that such beauty belonged to angels and named the birds accordingly. *All this adornment and for whom?* I wonder, as I spot the drab, reclusive female, that keeps her beak open like a dog and looks more like a moorhen than the mate of those dazzling males. What do they see in her?

I've left for last the jewel in the crown of Jurong: its Penguin House. Here, the temperature is a constant 16°C and penguins, unseen outside Antarctica, waddle around a pool set in a landscape of cliffs, nesting alcoves and burrows. There are emperor penguins, fairy penguins, macaroni penguins (so called because their stringy crests look as if they've been attacked with a plate of spaghetti) and that colony of Humboldt penguins. The success of their breeding program is due to a unique lighting system that recreates the passing of the seasons and allows the birds to maintain their annual biorhythm. But forget the science and watch them dive, for Jurong Park treats the visitor to a specially constructed viewing gallery with a ninety-foot wide window that allows us to witness the antics of these fascinating birds underwater; they swim swiftly like torpedoes and playfully like dolphins, their movements as graceful as they are dynamic.

I hear the thunder and decide to leave. It is not easy to get to Jurong Bird Park by public transport – you have to take the MRT to Jurong East and then you hop on a bus – and it is not easy to leave either. Just take care that it doesn't start to rain while you're waiting because the bus stop has no shelter. There is no downpour like a South Seas downpour and after one minute's non-stop drenching, I might as well have taken a dive with the penguins in their pen.

- I4 -

What caused this jumble of people to storm into the train compartment? Is there a special event, a football match or whatever? There is one British whimsicality that has not rubbed off on the ex-colony: the scrum to get in is as vigorous as the struggle to get out. As usual, my sling acts as a pot of honey to a grizzly with everyone pinning it on me with as much strength as they can muster. But hey, I make it to Farrer Park above ground, and my immediate impression is that I've landed on planet Bangladesh.

The recent rainstorm has just flooded the empty area in front of the exit and through the clean, crisp air I can glimpse something novel: rotting rubbish, unmaintained high rises and moulding fruit being pecked off by mynah birds and magpies. For the first time in Singapore I see swallows flying. They probably shoot them in the CBD – if the streetcleaners can't stand gum, they must go ape with birdshit – but here any droppings would make absolutely no difference, lost as they would be among the, well, *dirt*. Yes, real dirt – I nearly cry for joy. What's more, the food shops do not offer *char kway teow* or prawn *mee* but good, fine English fare like chicken Madras or sheek kebab. They don't call this district Little India for nothing; what, with the lack of hygiene and all, I feel like I'm in London.

Yet this India is more like that of old: both Muslim and Hindu. At Farrer Park, the temples are mosques like the tired Masjid Angullia in the corner – looking more like a villa in Marbella than the Taj – and as for the names, well, there is only one plastered all over Serangoon Plaza. Here is Mustafa Jewellery, there is Mustafa Foreign Exchange, an Al Mustafa restaurant and a Mohammed & Mustafa general store. That's discounting the Mustafa Centre, a sixties glass-and-frame box where bhangra muzak hums shrilly in the background. Like the other shoppers, I am prepared to surrender my bags in the entrance, but they wave me on. Why this racial profiling? Don't they think I can shoplift like the best of them? Mind you, there is nothing to tempt me. The Mustafa Centre may only be a few metro stops up from Orchard Road, but the product choice, budget manufacture and stacking (one shelf full of detergent, the opposite full of light bulbs and Mickey Mouse pencils) is unequivocally subcontinental.

What is this on Jalan Besar? Is it a bazaar or the most tired and limp car-boot sale, I have witnessed? The sellers are all gloomy, tetchy and uninterested; maybe the sheer god-awfulness of the second-hand crud has got to them: old typewriters from the age of Noel Coward, black-and-white dusty television sets, mountains of mobile chargers (as if the average user doesn't already own a dozen), well-worn trousers, boxing gloves (not exactly superwaxed), useless currency notes hardly in mint condition, pens that do not write, clocks that do not tick, penknives that do not cut, muddy boots, mouldy video tapes, soiled tennis balls. I stop, stunned. Who will buy this guy's faded family pictures? That fax machine, will it turn on? As for that Coca-Cola can, easily the most functional commodity on sale: it is past its sell-by date. I look around for the holy cows but thankfully they're missing. Lee Kuan Yew's autobiography is titled *From the Third World to the First*. Looking around, this designation is sorely tested.

I shake my head as I head up Race Course Road, a street that used to lead to an equestrian arena that opened as early as 1843. On non-racing days, sheep – kept in sheds nearby by the Muslim population – were left to graze on its grounds, eventually to become rogan josh on the feast of Eid. The road kept its name in defiance of efforts to rationalise it, because the racecourse moved to new grounds in Bukit Timah in 1935 (and more recently to Kranji) so the name was judged 'deceptive'. I'd like to see those bureaucrats come to London and walk down Poultry: they'll have a fit if they intend to buy chicken livers.

It is the Temple of 1,000 Lights I've come to visit, but the Leong San opposite steals my attention. It is constructed like a traditional Chinese Palace with black ornate timber beams welded together nail-free like an Ikea cabinet. I discover that it is relatively recent, built in 1917 by Venerable Zhuan Wu. He came to Singapore with a statue of the Guan Yin, the Goddess of Mercy who, upon entering Heaven, was so moved by the cries of unsaved souls that she decided to stay back and help mankind. Protector of children, she is often seen with a baby in her arms, her iconography similar to the Christian Madonna. Revered as a kind of Asian earth mother, her blessing is an unconditional requirement for the new harvest to flourish. She is worshipped wherever rice is the staple crop, as far as Korea and Japan, where she is called Canon. Yes, like the cameras and printers: the giant corporation is named after her and its original 1934 logo was an image of the deity herself.

Originally Guan Yin's statue presided over a simple lodge on Race Course Road. which was expanded by a rich local merchant in the mid-1920s, as this was the age of fortune and philanthropy. It has been constantly maintained and restored and, now a temple, it contains a main hall, corridors, guest rooms, monk's chambers, a kitchen, an ancestral worship yard and several rooms for meditation. My eyes focus on the wavy, tiled central roof. Its ridge contains a blazing pearl flanked by two protecting dragons whereas its gables depict dramatic warrior scenes. As I enter the narrow courtyard, a stone bell stands on the left; I am told that its sound fends off Bai Hu, the man-eating White Tiger, Guardian of the West. *What does it all mean?*

The instantly recognisable statue of the Laughing Buddha greets me warmly at the entrance to bring luck, happiness and a good, all-round vibe, but this is where any familiarity with images or symbols ends. Directly behind the Laughing Buddha and facing the main idol in the holy of holies, towers Wei Tuo, the guardian of faith, poised serious, demonic, macabre. He was a general devoted to one of the incarnations of Guan Yin as Miao Shan, the Princess who remained a virgin, spurning her father's orders to marry. Wei Tuo, in return, remained faithful in his unrequited, platonic love and helped her escape from the clutches of her father, the king. Although his dedication was his undoing – he was captured and executed – Buddhist folk memory has elevated him into a *deva*, a human being of great moral authority, forever called upon to guard the main deity of a temple. In our case, this is his old flame, Guan Yin, looking imperious like Turandot frozen in time in the middle of '*In questa reggia*'.

An elderly monk emerges out of the temple depths maybe attracted by my camera flash. I guess he is the Resident Monk. He's followed by a round-faced boy. I point at my camera with a questioning look.

'*Can*,' the Monk says, which I take to mean 'yes'.

He sits by a statue of Confucius on the right watching every move I make, while the boy directs me silently to the left and gives me a leaflet explaining that I should walk in a clockwise direction: it is good feng shui (does this change in the southern hemisphere?) Anyway, I like the idea, because it means that Europe got it wrong and Britain got it right: driving on the left brings good luck which is easily confirmed when you check the accident rates on French roundabouts. Then again, it could also be that the boy has sent me to the donation box where two statues are coiled together in permanent struggle; donations help them uncurl from each other and at the same time let us resolve any quarrels with our own loved ones. I hesitantly put some money in.

The boy looks happy and points at a bell and drum hanging high above my head. Tradition dictates that the bell be rung 108 times and the drum beaten 3,000 times every morning whereas the order is reversed at dusk. I look at the boy's arms – he was sixteen, maybe seventeen but his arms were surprisingly muscular: even if as rapid as one second per beating, 3,000 seconds corresponds to a 50-minute battery twice a day.

My examining look was reciprocated.

'Your arm?' asks the Monk.

*That question.*

'A fall,' I say. 'Down some stairs.'

He disappears behind a screen.

The boy stretches his arms and opens his palms pointing at the Qi Xing Deng, the Lamp of Seven Lights. This is the lamp lit for prayer on the first and fifteenth of each lunar month; it remains open on those days during which the appeals to the gods are more propitious. It is placed opposite the miraculous statue of Guan Yin and a white marble statue of the historical Buddha-Sakyamuni; both are encased behind glass.

He wants me to pay reverence. I don't do prayers.

*Maybe I should.*

Under the boy's gaze, I close my eyes and stand there for a few minutes pretending to meditate. I have no idea what to do. I should ask that my arm be healed. *Aum*, I cogitate. *Au-au-au-aum*. It has to originate from the navel, does it not? I concentrate and contract my abdominals, but they are of no use: I haven't been to a gym in weeks.

I open my eyes. The boy is smiling. I am glad and relieved he likes it, and I become more pleased when he leads me to a door next to the main altar and through that to a yard in the innards of the temple. In the middle stands a four-faced status of Brahma to ward off evil from all directions. On the western side are 18 *arhats*, the first disciples of the Buddha who, being devoted Brahmins, attained nirvana. On the eastern side there are individual boxes and vases with various calligraphic ideograms arranged in five altars. This is the ancestral worship hall where prayers are being said on various days for the souls of those who passed away. They are never far from us, ever watchful, ever caring and ever critical if their descendants stray from the Way.

I think of Chang.

*To come out as gay in a culture like this...*

- 15 -

'I thought of you today,' I say to Chang who picks me up from my hotel.

'You did?'

'I was over at a Buddhist Temple in Little India in a kind of memorial hall for ancestors.'

Chang doesn't like to talk about this again so I change the subject.

'And you?'

'I was at home watching DVDs.'

'Like what?'

'You'll laugh. *Sound of Music.*'

'How very gay.'

Chang looks at me bewildered. 'Is it?' he asks.

It's my turn to be taken aback. 'But of course. It's part of the gay stereotype.'

Chang looks seriously surprised. 'Really? I'm shocked.'

'You thought you were unique?'

'Not unique but –'

'C'mon. You're kidding me. Do you also like Barbra Streisand?'

This time Chang's jaw drops.

'YES!' he cries. 'How did you know?'

'It's another gay thing.'

'NO! I can't believe it.'

'And I can't believe you didn't know about it.'

'I thought... just in Singapore... or just me and my friends...'

'You are shocked for liking something gay you didn't know you *ought* to, is that it?'

Chang is speechless.

'Don't believe in this homosexual lifestyle crap,' I tell him. 'We are genetically predisposed to Barbra.'

Chang puts an end to the conversation by stopping in front of a door. 'Happy,' he says. It is a Sunday night and we are at the only late night club in town.

I walk in and am impressed: this is not a seedy here-today gone-tomorrow dingy hole. From the soft sofa furnishing to the mood lighting and the international DJs to the quality of the hi-fi speakers, the ambience screams 'I am a no-expense-spared superclub' – no wonder Happy has been dubbed 'Singapore's hottest nightspot' by *Wallpaper*★ magazine. The pervading thick smell of expensive eau de cologne works like a strong room deodoriser, and the sartorial creations worn by the city's ultra-thin metrosexuals give the place the atmosphere of a Dolce and Gabbana show during Milan fashion week. Not for the first time in Singapore, I feel an outsider: sharp, short, sideways glances scrutinise me and my sling, which I'm now oblivious to, and instantly put me in my place in the pecking order of sexual attraction which is down, down, *down*.

It is with a sense of relief that I lock eyes with the creepy potato-head from Taboo standing at the bar. Well, at least I am not at the bottom of the food chain.

'Hello John,' he says immediately, checks out Chang and winks at me with studied clumsiness so that everyone – especially Chang – might think that we were old buddies parading our conquests for the benefit of the other. It is for this reason that I pointedly ask him for his name.

'Hello errm,' I say 'sorry, I didn't catch your name.'

I hope that Chang heard me there.

'I'm Nick,' says the guy 'don't you remember? We met before you broke your arm. In Taboo.'

He is beginning to irritate me. 'Not really,' I say, 'it is not broken. I came to Singapore with my arm in a sling –'

'Ha-ha,' Nick interrupts 'in Singapore with a sling. As if you couldn't buy enough of those at Raffles.'

'… but I wasn't wearing it in Taboo,' I add. 'Excuse us.'

I chase the barman down the bar to avoid Nick but to no avail: he follows us. I notice that Chang feels excluded, so I am forced to introduce him.

'Marketing, eh? I have some contacts in advertising,' says Nick poignantly. I can sense that the plan to get Chang's phone number has commenced. Feeling another alpha male's competitive chat-up breathing down my neck, I ask Chang what he wants to drink. Right, an orange juice. I don't look at Nick, and I don't offer.

When I return, they are deep in conversation.

'… explain that to me,' Nick was saying.

'Explain what?' I ask.

'David Beckham. Why do you all go crazy about David Beckham in the Far East?'

'It's a matter of success,' Chang replies with his usual intelligence. 'He's photogenic and the message he conveys is success and money.'

'Is that why you have Caucasian faces in ads? Why you don't have any Asians?' Nick continues.

Chang shrugs his shoulders. 'We've been a colony for so long,' he says. 'We still look up to Britain. We go there to study. And America now is a superpower. Caucasian faces are synonymous with success.'

'And beauty,' says Nick. 'You get Hollywood movies with an implied ideal of beauty and you fall for it.'

I don't like the direction the conversation is taking so I steer it back to safe ground.

'What about China? She's also successful.' I say, clearing my throat.

'China is on the up, yes. It evokes positive images for consumers regarding family, children, homeland.'

'And Japan?' I ask mischievously.

'Never really took off. The Japanese are not so popular in Singapore,' Chang replies matter-of-factly which for him is as curt as he can be.

'You should know that,' says Nick. 'You slept with Dan.'

I wish the earth could open up and swallow me. *How did Nick know that?*

I put two and two together. 'You knew him already –'

'… and I pointed you out,' says Nick. 'He asked about you and I said I knew you.'

'Someone I met in Taboo,' I explain to Chang whose face betrays no emotion. 'I didn't sleep with him.' I stumble. 'I mean, yes, I did but that's the only thing I did. I took him back to the hotel, but we were too tired and we fell asleep. Or rather he did and I didn't.'

*Hell, I'm off to Sydney in two days.*

'Dan kept him awake,' says Nick lowering my discomfort level to Torture Level Nine.

I do not comment and neither does Chang who senses my annoyance. If we only kept quiet for longer Nick might just go away. But then, the bastard tells me this.

'Poor guy,' says Nick. 'He's been very ill, you know.'

I look at him, the obvious question forming in my eyes.

'No, not *that*. Cancer.'

*But can no' stand in sun. Danger.*

I shiver underneath the air con. Some dissidents in Singapore have complained of police abuse claiming that they've been forced to sit underneath the full blast of the air con. So that's normal treatment, then.

'So far he's in remission,' says Nick. 'But –'

We lean at the bar, sipping our drinks. I feel guilty for Dan; I really liked the guy and I don't even have his phone number. Happy is proving very sad, indeed. Maybe it is the company, or maybe it was the knowledge I have acquired. Ignorance is bliss while it remains ignorance.

'What happened to you anyway,' asks Nick eventually, pointing at my arm. 'Car accident?'

I shake my head. 'No.'

'Fell down the stairs?'

I take a deep breath. What did I know of Dan? What did I know about Singapore? Or, for that matter, what did they know of me?

'If you want to know, it was self-inflicted,' I say. 'The most stupid thing I've ever done.'

Stupid or not it has diminished in importance which makes it tolerable.

'Well, it had been painful already and I thought it was, well, muscle tension, so I exercised it by swimming. But it was still painful, so I went to a sport injuries masseur. No improvement. Then I went to this club. I was – you know how it is – I was dancing and shaking my arms around. And after that I went to another club. I was so out-of-my-face, I didn't feel anything. I remember feeling some stiffness, going back home and using half a tube of Deep Heat on my shoulder.'

I can tell Nick is enjoying this.

'When I woke up, I couldn't lift it.'

By now, I am cycling downhill with no brakes.

'I had an MR scan. Two rotator tendons had snapped. It was tendonitis I suffered from, not muscle spasm. Tendonitis requires cold compresses, I was putting on Deep Heat. It requires immobility,' – I point at the sling – 'and I was going swimming. Movement repetition makes it worse. And I went clubbing.'

'So?'

'I'm taking some non-steroidal anti-inflammatory pills. They are so strong, I have to take more pills to protect my stomach or else I'll end up with an ulcer.'

'You're still taking them?'

'Yes. And putting on cold compresses. For another two weeks.'

'And you're drinking?'

'I can drink moderate amounts of alcohol. It's not as if I do so every night.'

Nick sniggers, but Chang looks concerned. 'So what happens now?' he asks.

'If it doesn't heal within a month, I will need surgery.'

'Will it be OK, then?'

*This is the moment of truth.*

'It might leave me crippled.'

The three of us stop for minute, overwhelmed by the weight of so many revelations.

'What are your chances?' whispers Chang.

'The doctor said fifty–fifty.'

Chang squeezes my hand.

'Bloody stupid,' interjects Nick.

'I know.'

I feel my sling. I put my other hand in my pocket, partly out of habit and partly to hide my discomfiture. There is a piece of paper inside. I take it out. It is yellow and thin.

*Oh that.*

I had walked out of the Leong San – as Chinese as dim sum and as traditional as chopsticks – to confront the sight of the Burmese-Thai Temple of 1,000 Lights, as low-key and unobtrusive as Siamese Buddhism itself. It looked rough-hewn compared with the exuberance of the Leong San, and inside the austere decoration won no prizes: a 50-foot high, 300-ton statue of Buddha dominated the chamber, its garish colours emphasising its artificial look. I should have guessed: having been born in Rangoon, the Haw-Par brothers were prime donors, so any statues would have been built to their taste.

A sign above the entrance proclaimed confusingly that the temple was built in the Chinese year 2470, but it made more sense in the Thai calendar that translates as 1927 CE. Light bulbs were arranged in a circle around the Buddha but, although I didn't count them, I estimated that '1,000' must be a relative superlative rather than a numerical exactitude. Somehow it didn't feel like a temple: the prevailing silence was more akin to the impatience of a bank queue rather than the meditative calm of the Leong San. There was no one praying, there were no monks, and the few faithful were involved in commercial transactions in this world and the other: a couple were burning paper money in the kiln outside; custom has it that mock paper money burnt as offering becomes real money in the domain of the souls. The practice is Chinese, not Thai, but no belief can remain pure in this syncretic mixture that is Singapore, as a statue of Ganesh, the Hindu elephant-headed God, demonstrated further in.

Ganesh faced a basement chapel where I entered, curious to witness the sacred relic: Buddha's own footprint. I expected some vague indentation set on clay like those dinosaur tracks in Utah, but I should have known better. At the end of the statue of a reclining Buddha dressed in an orange robe, the print was an abstract foot carved out in ebony with inlaid mother-of-pearl. If it matched the Buddha's, then the Enlightened One wore sandals size 30 which may explain why He preferred to walk barefoot.

There were similarities with Leong San: Guan Yin sitting on a lotus, the *arhats* praying around the Buddha, the four-faced statue of Brahma, the stone tiger of the west. But there were some extra touches: a diorama depicting the life of Prince Siddharta, and a Wheel of Fortune shaped like a windmill and divided into 12 sectors, each one with a loose flap that was caught by a nail sticking out as it rotated, so that it eventually stopped.

I approached the caretaker who was manning the contraption and paid him 50 cents. He asked me to give the wheel a roll – clockwise, because I was male. When it stopped, he took the sector number down and asked my date of birth. He then checked today's date and, after some calculations, he opened a shelf and chose a yellow divination sheet.

'Very good,' he said in English and, pointing at my sling, he repeated: 'Very good'.

Back in Happy, I read the prediction aloud.

*'The Wheel of Fortune says your fate is bright as a starlit night. You will be free from care, money you will have and if you seek a suitor you are sure to win her or him soon. The object you lost will be found. Lawsuit you have no reason to fear, all will come right in the end. In illness you will recover. Your family will enjoy happiness. In all you do, you will not be without luck all your life.'*

'This looks optimistic,' says Nick.

'I don't believe in Wheels of Fortune,' I say.

'Why did you try then?'

'For fun. Something to do.'

'Would you rather it said you'll be extremely unlucky all your life?'

'No, but –'

'There you are then.'

'You'll be fine,' says Chang reassuringly.

*I don't know…*

'So what if the wheel proves correct?' asks Nick.

Chang straightens his back and thinks for a few minutes.

'If your arm heals properly, you must return,' he says.

I am typing on a keyboard on a free Internet link at Changi, trying to kill time before my flight to Australia, but I might as well be in Plaza Singapura again. The shiny, glitzy airport is as huge, as busy and as dirt-free as any mall on Orchard Road – rendering every public space into a retail cash machine is this city's unique touch. I am supposed to be here for only 15 minutes, but I have surreptitiously logged half an hour, because surfing helps me overcome my boredom. Robert Louis Stevenson famously said that one should travel for travel's sake and that the point is to move, but he had no experience of waiting at airports, one of those Sisyphean punishments of modern life like peak-time commuting or Saturday afternoon queuing at a Tesco checkout.

It's when I log on guiltily for a third time that it hits me: why have I been looking back rather than forward? I've spent all my time visiting Singapore websites. Shouldn't I google something about Sydney, my next destination? Yet curiosity gets the better of me and I return to Singapore's cyberspace even as I am about to leave it in real life. For I have found so much to savour: apart from the ever-entertaining Singapore Paranormal Investigators' pages – which alone can keep me wired in a permanent cyberpunk state like one of Bruce Sterling's characters – I have been sniggering at sammyboy. com, a sex-advice website for South Asian males in need of female company. At the other end of the spectrum, there is fridae.com, an all-Asian equivalent to UK's gaydar, where male posters from Japan to Jakarta communicate in broken English and, oh how sweet, send hearts to each other. Incredibly, both sites are hosted in Singapore. Since the Internet is the bread and butter of the global city, the ever-pragmatic authorities must have decided that, if you can't beat them, get their tax money at least.

I have also discovered Yawning Bread, a Singaporean blogger and relentless opponent of censorship, religious dogma or bureaucratic pettiness. His witty and incisive criticism of the city's high and mighty turns him into an instant hero to my eyes. I skim over his topics and nearly fall off my seat. there are some truly courageous men in Singapore, indeed.

You see what I mean about looking back, not forward? I kind of know what awaits me in Sydney, whereas unearthing Singapore's uncensored forums is a revelation.

The computer clock flashes – I have three minutes left. I send the web links to my e-mail account and log out.

*If your arm heals properly, you must return.*

Maybe I should. I'm leaving with so many open questions about this city, after all.

Like, how did Raffles' exotic siren turn into the hospital matron everyone keeps dissing?

# PART TWO:
# ... AND WITHOUT

# CHAPTER SEVEN

# GHOST FOR SALE

Ding Bo led a dangerous existence.

No, he wasn't a pearl diver in the seas of Nanyang, nor a bandit in the mountains of Hunan, but still his wife kept nagging him to be more circumspect. He simply wouldn't observe the taboos of the seventh month when all the Hungry Ghosts, the *yau gui*, are released from heaven and from hell. What concerned her the most is that he wouldn't change his routine during that dreaded month. He wouldn't retire home before nightfall but insisted on walking all alone from the tavern to their house through the winding narrow alleys. Unsurprisingly, the more she harried and harassed Ding Bo, the more he seemed to ignore her and want to straddle the village at closing time which sometimes – *Guan Yin give me strength* – was well after midnight.

No wonder then he eventually bumped into a ghost.

'Oi!' said the ghost. 'Who are you and what are you doing out on such a night?'

Ding Bo had had a few drinks and returned the question with Dutch courage. 'And I don't recognise *you*. Who *are* you?'

'I,' said the ghost, 'am a ghost. G-H-O-S-T. No wonder you don't recognise me; I have been dead for seventy-nine years. Even if you knew me, my hair has been in such a mess for the last decade that my mother, bless her, sometimes has problems identifying me in the netherworld. But then again she always *was* short-sighted. But even if she weren't short-sighted –' the ghost stopped as if remembering something. 'Anyway, who are *you*?'

Ding Bo had sobered up quickly and tried to appear unperturbed. 'I am Ding Bo. I only died last week so I'm a bit new to this.'

'A virgin!' cried the ghost excitedly. 'Let me come to your aid; I have always wanted to meet someone right after they snuffed it! Oops, sorry, I hope that wasn't too crude for you. Remember I've been dead for seventy-nine years and I'm quite blasé about it.'

'No problem,' said Ding Bo.

'There are of course those who have been dead much longer than me, but they are of no use. They get confused with modern life. Whereas I died at sixteen and I'm still interested in all the latest inventions. Seventy-nine years is short enough for me not to lose the plot but long enough to know the ropes. You are so lucky to have met me! Where are you heading to?'

'To the capital,' Ding Bo said with only a split-second pause. He needed to get away from this built-up area in case someone turned up.

'So am I,' said the ghost and followed him into the forest. 'There is always someone new there to spook out of their skull. Watch me and you will learn a lot.'

He suddenly turned into a nine-feet tall monster with sharp claws and pointed teeth. He roared and spat fire for several seconds like a dragon before he became himself again.

'Well? What did you think?' he asked his arms akimbo.

'Excellent! Bravo!' Ding Bo replied.

'You can do that with practice. Unless a human spits on you, of course.'

'Why, what happens then?'

'*Wa lao*, you know nothing,' the ghost said. 'We lose all our power with man's spittle. We can't change our shape any more and remain with the last form we have assumed. Yeuch! Horrible!'

'Will you teach me how to change shape?' asked Ding Bo.

'Sure. Where shall we start? How about... a tiger? Yes! Yes! A tiger!'

The ghost was ready to metamorphose, but Ding Bo held it by the sleeve.

'Let's go easy first. How about a little lamb for starters?'

The ghost's eyes rolled upwards and forced a yawn out of his jaws. 'A little lamb? Dull City, mister. What were you when you were alive? A mandarin?'

'C'mon, I'm a complete beginner. You have to take me gently through my paces.'

'Oh, alright. But I don't like that "little lamb" bit. I will become a proper, adult-sized sheep. Anyway, there's nothing to it, you'll see. You just have to think hard "I am now a sheep" and, hey presto, you *are* it.'

At once the ghost shrunk to a sheep in front of Ding Bo's eyes. Without hesitation he spat on it and picked it up by one of its hind legs, while the animal baa-baa-ed helplessly. He waited for a while to see if the ghost would change back, but no, it was well and truly stuck to its form.

Ding Bo threw the ghost over his shoulder and retraced his steps to his home. His wife was awake and in a heated mood. 'DING BO! What are you doing staying out so late at night during the seventh month? And what is this? A sheep? Did you steal it?'

'I won it in a game of mah-jong. I'm going to the capital to sell it tomorrow.'

Ding Bo's wife temper mellowed. 'Alright. You go tomorrow. But come back before sunset, *ah*?' She said this on auto pilot not expecting an answer from her husband.

So it was to her amazement and delight that she heard Ding Bo agree: 'No more staying after dark. I promise.'

## - 16 -

I use my chopsticks to pick up the finely cut cabbage from the common platter. It is translucent and crisp, like sauerkraut that has been pickled to perfection.

'This is delicious,' I tell Uranium.

'Yes,' he agrees. 'I like jellyfish, too.'

*Jellyfish?*

Despite my unease I go through with the chewing. 'I thought it was cabbage.' I say.

Uranium chuckles. 'First time you try jellyfish, is it?'

'It is,' I concede.

'And?'

I give up. 'I have to admit it is delicious.'

'Yes. Food for wedding feast, like shark fin soup,' he adds.

My fellow diners agree. On my left is Uranium, a big, solid, twenty-something bloke with a baby face and a number two haircut. In front of me sits the only female, Sunkist, a shy, diminutive, dainty figure with beautiful black eyes that stare intelligently behind a pair of modish spectacles. MJ, a good two decades older than his friends and very recognisably the leader of the group, is speaking slowly, confidently and clearly on my right. Guess what? I dared contact them, so I'm having dinner with some of the elite of the Singapore Paranormal Investigators: office workers by day, ghostbusters with peculiar *noms de guerre* by night.

I am a little tetchy but not because of them; I have refused their offer to take me to Swensen's, a restaurant with Western cuisine, so we're having supper at Mouth, Singapore's oldest teahouse. Now, I like Chinese food, but when I read the house signature dishes (pig's knuckle in black vinegar, goat stomach with dried vegetable and sea cucumber with mushroom and abalone) I became a little jumpy.

'So, your society is like an after hours social club?' I ask.

They shake their heads in disagreement. 'Not at all. SPI was created to conduct investigations into the paranormal. We use sophisticated instrumentation and perform scientific experiments to understand supernatural phenomena. We also help free of charge those who have witnessed something that can't be explained.'

'How big is SPI?'

'There are about a dozen elite members, about one-hundred ordinary members and about 16,000 participants in our online forum.' says Uranium.

'We've grown a lot in five years,' adds Sunkist. 'We are now a registered, non-profit organisation. We have to keep books and all that.'

All three are at pains to stress that they do not perform exorcisms or encourage superstition; look, they are well-educated and abhor fuzzy thought and woolly science: Uranium is in IT support, Sunkist does research for a manufacturing company and MJ is a marine quality assurance engineer. Still, Sunkist would make an excellent Scully although, as I look around, the place of Mulder remains vacant.

'Were you inspired by *The X Files*?'

Uranium sighs. 'Well, yes, we do like *The X Files*, or some of us do, but our organisation has nothing to do with the programme. We're only interested in scientific explanations.'

He puts some *ling* fish on my plate. A huge platter has arrived and the fish head puts me off. The Chinese love serving everything complete with heads, beaks and claws, whereas squeamish me prefers the decapitation of all comestibles; it makes them look more like food that way.

'Define "scientific".'

MJ picks up the topic. 'Suppose someone calls us with an unexplained sighting. Or thinks he has captured something on film. First we'll go to the scene and have a visual check. Last time this guy walking around in the bush spotted something that went whoosh and passed by. It was some kind of plastic. If we can't explain it, we investigate with our equipment.'

'What do you do?'

'We may set up an infrared camera with sensors and leave it on over a period; we will then capture and analyse the images.'

I am reminded of those *Most Haunted* programmes on Living TV. Derek Acorah eat your heart out.

'And what's the percentage of the cases you have investigated that can't be explained?'

Uranium pauses. 'About twenty per cent,' he says; the others nod in agreement.

I am unconvinced.

'Let me tell you one story,' says Uranium. 'This is an investigation we undertook recently. A Malay guy wrote to us saying that he had a recurring dream of a woman asking for help. She was leading him to a burial place opposite his house which is in a forested area called Telok Blangah. Even after he left the house and moved away, he kept getting those dreams. So, he contacted us. We went to his old house and searched the forest, and we actually found a grave. The tombstone was quite old and from what was written on the stone it was a woman's.'

'He could have discovered it himself.'

'When we searched the area he didn't direct us to it. He just told us it was opposite his house. It could be that he had been there, but the tomb is not easy to get to; it is well-hidden and even we came across it by accident. After determining the grave's position we found that the tombstone was far away *but directly opposite the house*. He couldn't possibly know that, you couldn't figure the position from the vegetation. It is too much of a coincidence.'

I want to try one giant mushroom, but it has the texture of raw liver and is slippery. I try to spear it with my chopstick, but it slides off and lands just by MJ's bowl. I try to pick it up with the Chinese spoon but it's still difficult as its catchment area is way too small for the slithery cap. In the end I just nudge it to a fine balance and bring it to my mouth with the nervousness of an unseasoned acrobat.

'Plus he was Malay and the grave inscription was Chinese. He can't read Chinese so he couldn't know it was a woman buried there. *Spoo-ky*. Do you want more soup?'

Hm, it's called 'old cucumber soup' but I can see large pieces of unidentified meat floating in it. I'll just have the broth, thank you.

'I read that you did an investigation in the Haw-Par Villa. Someone contacted you and said that the statues were made out of real human parts. *Pur-lease!*'

Uranium doesn't laugh. 'Yes, we were there two years ago. Someone told us of the existence of a graveyard where they dumped body parts; we had to investigate. Of course, we found nothing *lai dat*. There was a sort of "graveyard", a locked room really, where they dumped statues – defective ones. But if they dumped them in the open, people might steal them and sell them as antiques. That's why they had to keep them under lock and key.'

A tale is debunked – pity. The idea that the Haw-Par Villa's tableaux were constructed with human corpses was far too satisfactory – maybe because it reinforced stereotypes about the Chinese believing in urban legends.

'Are most of your members Chinese?'

All three look at each other uncomfortably. Talking about race, even innocently, is a no-no in Singapore.

'Our organisation is non-profit, non-political, non-religious and non-racial,' explains Uranium. 'If it is mostly Chinese, it's because Singapore is mostly Chinese.'

'Don't get me wrong,' I say. 'I mentioned the Chinese because they are very superstitious. I would expect a society of paranormal investigators to be composed mostly of Chinese and of men. Am I right?'

We look at Sunkist.

'You are right about the men bit,' she says. 'It's eighty per cent men. I don't know why.'

'Well, I do,' I say. 'Mucking about in the dark with high-tech equipment, playing Mulder and Scully – surely it attracts the male of the species. Like it should attract the more superstitious of the races.'

In the ensuing long pause, I pick up a piece of barbecued duck and decline more soup. It definitely smells of something funny – a later google reveals it was chicken feet. As the other main ingredient is overripe cucumber, whoever thought of the combination can have a job at the Fat Duck in Berkshire preparing egg and bacon ice cream.

Uranium breaks the silence. 'In one respect, yes, you are right. We Chinese have the Hungry Ghost Festival and its taboos.'

Please elaborate.

'It is believed that all the dead spirits in the netherworld are released for one month's holiday during the seventh lunar month. They come up to our world floating around. As a form of respect and for them not to bother us, we offer them food and drink. It's like Halloween, but that's only one day.'

Actually it's more than Halloween. It is a touching remembrance of those souls who have otherwise been forgotten: the ghosts of the unwed, of the childless, of those to whom no offerings were made through the year – and no offerings means they are hungry.

Sunkist joins in. 'The Japanese have the same custom except that it lasts one week. For us, it lasts one month.'

I contemplate the havoc 'trick or treat' might cause for 30 days.

'There are lots of taboos that our parents passed on to us about this seventh month,' says Uranium. 'Not to go swimming, not to get married, not to move house, not to stay out at night. Of course that is *exactly* what we do in SPI. This is our busiest month!'

'The main taboo that still gets observed is not to get married,' says Sunkist and looks at Uranium with an unmistakeable stare.

But he's in full flood and doesn't notice. 'The reason why the Chinese believe it is not good to get married during the seventh month is because when we are talking about a wedding, we are talking about a feast. Even if you're not superstitious, you don't want your guests to freak out at the idea that during the dinner ghosts will also be sitting around the table. And, of course, the food will not taste any good.'

'Why won't it?'

'It is believed that when Chinese make offerings, the food will lose its original taste and smell because the ghosts eat it. We did a scientific test *lai dat.*'

I notice that they are discreetly leaving the rest of the jellyfish for me. I oblige.

'Like what?'

'A blind tasting. We asked people to try the food before and after it was offered to the ghosts. Then we asked them to distinguish between the food that had been offered and that which had not.'

'And?'

'About fifty per cent could tell that the food had lost its taste after the offering,' Sunkist says coolly.

Could it be chance? I am trying to calculate the odds, but my probability theory is hidden in the cobwebbed attic of my cortex. Whatever – it sounded like good fun.

'You can join in the fun,' says MJ. 'We have an outing in two weeks' time. Will you still be around? Do you want to join us?'

I jump at the invite. 'It's a date,' I say.

They pay for my dinner.

- 17 -

I pass through Chinatown on my way back to my hotel. It's only been a few years since I arrived in Singapore beslinged, dispirited by my debility and with a fifty–fifty prospect of a potentially crippling operation. To my own surprise and delight, the medication and the rest during long intercontinental flights healed my arm enough for me to climb glaciers in New Zealand – that is, completely. True to my promise, I have returned the same – if not a little healthier – but Singapore has changed. Even six months is a long time for this bite-size state, as they told me in Tiong Bahru.

Yes, one of the first things I did is return to the Bird Arena early on my first Sunday morning, before the nightlife devoured me, as is its wont. This time, I knew something about the suburb itself: it was the first public housing project in Singapore, the brainchild of the Singapore Improvement Trust which operated until 1960 when the Housing Development Board, the HDB, took over. Despite the lack of maintenance, there is something earthy and liveable in those three- and four-storey houses that still stand – most noticeably in Seng Poh Road and Eng Hoon Street – compared with the later Gotham City tower blocks of the HDB. The pavements may be cracking and the smell of mould spores might permeate the air, but the curves, the lines and the dimensions are more agreeable and convivial.

*Huh?*

I stop and look at my map. Was it here? Yes it was, but –

The old café is no more. A high fence informs us of 'Danger/ Keep out/*Bahaya Jangan Dekat*' and in a few more alphabets I can't interpret. The block of flats next to it has been covered with green netting as if ready-wrapped for a takeaway. I know where to look: up, where a wiry old signboard is only just discernible: 'Tiong Bahru Bird Arena – Mata Puteh'. I shake my head. It can't be! Tourist leaflets are still advertising the song contests! They just can't *demolish* it!

Well they can. I approach the fence and read the poster with trepidation: 'Proposed conservation... Addition... Alteration' – I am too upset to read the lot – 'Change of use... Hotel development with provision of restaurant at roof and erection of bridge link...'

Yep. Just what Singapore needs: another hotel.

Mutely, I move to a café nearby and fight the inclination to have a stiff drink, opting for a strong cup of coffee instead. I notice another backpacker couple with a map walking around, lost. And another. And another. If you didn't know where to look you'd have missed this minor catastrophe.

When the waitress brings me the coffee, I quiz her about the Bird Arena. How long has it been closed?

'Six month,' she says with a jaded expression. Obviously I'm not the first person to have asked her that.

'When I was last here, there were birds,' I say, 'there was singing...'

She is busy and doesn't want a heart-to-heart. 'Six month long for Singapore,' she says curtly and walks away.

And it is over two years since I've been here.

On the grander stage the PAP is still in power. Goh Chok Tong's interregnum had just come to an end by the time of my last visit, and Lee Hsien Loong, Lee Kuan Yew's son, is now in charge. But, as has become tradition in Singapore, none of his predecessors has left Cabinet. Lee Kuan Yew, now in his eighties, has been retained with the title Minister Mentor and Goh Chok Tong as Senior Minister. I've heard of guarantees regarding smooth transition of power, but this verges on the extreme.

The monsoon has not yet finished, and it is raining relentlessly. Over the Johore Straits, there are permanent floods and two people have died from leptospirosis, a disease transmitted via rat's piss. Even parts of Singapore flooded temporarily ('an unlucky combination with high tide', taxi drivers keep telling me in order not to lose face). At least the constant downpour keeps the bloody mynahs out of sight.

Along with the monsoon, a ban on smoking indoors has descended upon the city that seems congenitally attracted to prohibitions. Inside the Pearl Centre, a public notice is barking threats: the National Environment Agency has apprehended several people smoking within the complex and is proceeding with summary action against the mall management; the management in return threatens to forward the particulars of any smokers to the agency and hold them liable for all costs incurred. All in all, a rather neat angle on the subject: we save you from death but sue you to death, instead.

Chinatown is wearing red, the auspicious colour of celebration, for it's the time before Chinese New Year. Despite the incessant rain, awnings and marquees have been erected and the passing hordes of shoppers are asphyxiating: if a house is full during this period, it will be full throughout the year, for Happiness equals Abundance equals Wealth. Stocking up the larder is a must: cured meats, candied delicacies, glutinous rice puddings, fruit with special connotations. You can buy melon seeds and pomegranates signifying many children; pomelos whose name 'yo' also means 'to have'; kumquats that symbolise prosperity since the first character is also that of gold itself; pineapples whose name is homonymous with 'good luck has arrived'. And everywhere you turn there are red papercuts, red lanterns, red candles and red calligraphic epigrams in golden font.

I sort of give up on central Chinatown for the duration except for the Samsui women's restaurant on Smith Street;

during my compulsory visit there, I am unnerved to see a male chef's head peeking from behind the kitchen door. I know that sounds stupid but I had bought the medicinal lore hook, line and sinker: the least I expected was to see a centenarian sorceress slowly steaming that ginger chicken to perfection. To top it all, a blasphemous newcomer proclaimed brashly its existence outside: 'Erich's Wuerstelstand: the Last Sausage Kiosk Before the Equator'. I sigh; is nowhere safe from the Bratwurst?

Yes, I am back at the Chinatown Hotel. I admit it's a little frayed around the edges and I note that it now charges $40 for every guest who stays in the room after midnight but I'm used to this place. I did try staying at one of a bunch of new 'boutique' hotels nearby, but in an Asian context you should think of them as 'bijou'. The shower head was over the toilet, the fridge was only large enough for a single can to fit snugly inside and there was no cupboard: instead, a long horizontal pole with three hangers emerged from the wall at eyebrow level. I didn't last a full day, especially since, after I lay on my bed, my trousers hung on top of me menacingly like the legs of hungry ghosts. I escaped to the Chinatown Hotel where my double bed is almost as big as the room in that 'boutique' hotel and the fridge is the size of a minibar – after my purchases in a day or so, it would look like one, too.

The Kreta Ayer HDB flats are being 'upgraded'. This is the carrot the government has been offering to the voters: PAP wards get their tired-looking skyrise honeycombs to look like Docklands maisonettes. Mind you, the government doesn't need to promise anything here, since they'd even vote for a Haw-Par statue if it ran under the PAP banner: this is now the Tanjong Pagar multi-MP constituency, where Lee Kuan

Yew himself gets re-elected year after year. Disturbingly, for the first time in Singapore I notice homeless people. Maybe it is the monsoon that's made them seek shelter inside the Kreta Ayer estate but there they all are: old, flimsily thin and wearing only a vest and pantaloons, they sleep on the concrete floors, their head resting on their sandals. The bunch of keys that lets you march into the First World Club seems to lock more doors behind you than it opens up in front.

I walk to the end of Keong Saik Road and I hardly recognise it. Last time I was here I counted 15 brothels. I can now spot only eight, but I'm reliably informed there are ten. Hotel Pacific has disappeared and those above mentioned 'boutique' hotels have opened plus a dozen or so eateries. At Number 20, I locate one of the successes of gentrification: *Whatever*, a New Age shop and vegetarian café, whose walls are lined with books on everything kooky and holistic – from Alpha-alignment to Yoga and Beyond. Its coffee is the biggest attraction, although the leaflets advertising 'Egyptian Shenu Attunements' and 'Past Life Workshops' make compulsive reading. The Indian corner shop is still there but, along with my Pokka aloe vera juice with pulp bits, I can also buy time at one of their four Internet machines. The seafood restaurant still serves king prawns the size of lobsters but it must have changed chef, because they serve them with enough monosodium glutamate to turn you allergic even if you are immune. On my first day there, I left looking like Madam Mim in Disney's *The Sword in the Stone* after she has caught the virus with which Merlin the Wizard finally defeats her.

Backstage is still defiantly flying the rainbow flag over the New Year's revellers in Central Chinatown. On my first night there, I met a Malaysian visitor who urged me to fly to KL on the next plane. *The Etiquette Guide to Singapore* explicitly suggests avoiding the topic of politics during small talk, but there was no stopping this guy dissing all things Singaporean and painting an idyllic paradise to be found on the other side of the Straits of Johore. When I steered the conversation to the delicate subject of leptospirosis, he got agitated as if it was my piss that spread the pathogenic serovars.

*Manazine*, the only attempt at a gay magazine in Singapore, has gone out of business. Ten thousand free copies were distributed in selected outlets but, come the third instalment, 'concerned parents' complained about the 'easy accessibility of the magazine's homosexual content'. Immediately, the MDA cautioned *Manazine* to restrict its availability and sounded its death knell: it was the last issue that I read at Backstage last time I visited. Happy has also closed and Nation, the international gay party, after running for four successful years, was discontinued despite the Singapore Tourist Board advertising it abroad; the government decided that it was not prepared to allow any more public gay festivities. It seems that the new PAP brooms under Lee Junior are more prudish than the old mops.

This time around, it is Tantric I frequent the most, with its candle-lit tables and muted *Little Britain* videos. There's a good balance of smoking in the yard in front, drinking in the middle and dancing at the back. It is there I meet Jacky. She is sipping a Martini and, as I look anxiously over the bar, she tries to put me at ease.

'Something's bothering you. What are you looking for?' she asks me.

'I am looking for Little Boy Lost,' I say.

'Aren't we all?' she counters.

I explain to her that I had an Internet date but the picture was fuzzy. What I know is that the guy works here and his online handle: littleboylost.

'Leave it to me,' she says and before I can stop her, she leans forward and whispers to one of the barmen. By the time I pay for my drink she's back with the information.

'It's Richard,' she says and points at a cute guy at the other end who waves at me.

I'm embarrassed but pleased. 'Can I buy you a drink?' I ask her.

She looks at her half-empty glass.

'Oh, yeah, stack them, why not? A lychee Martini, please.'

I give the order and try to catch Richard's eye, but he's working non-stop like a steam locomotive on speed.

'He doesn't like me in real life,' I tell Jacky.

'Patience! It is Friday night,' she scolds me. 'Wait a little bit.'

I examine her closely for the first time. She is a petite thirty-something, carrying a stylish Prada bag as large as herself. She is also very pretty, her delicate features more Eurasian than oriental.

'What do you do?'

'I'm a fashionista,' she replies mysteriously.

I don't probe further. 'And what are you doing here?'

She narrows her eyes. 'I'm here every Friday, my sweet. And afterwards I cross the road to Taboo. I'm going back to my roots.'

That she has to explain.

'I'm clubbing with my gay friends again,' she tells me with a hint of drama. 'I've been married for fifteen years and I recently separated from my husband.'

'I'm sorry.'

'I'm not. There's no better place to be single than the gay scene. I'm rediscovering my past.'

'You mean you are fag-hagging your way around Chinatown,' I tease her.

Jacky laughs heartily. I like her because I like people who open up to strangers in dimly-lit bars.

'What about the straight scene?'

She looks up, over-elevating her eyebrows like a diva. 'Pur-lease! I don't need any of *that*.' And after a pause. 'Are you coming to Taboo with us?'

I forgot to mention that Jacky comes with an entourage.

'I don't know,' I say, pointing at Richard with my chin.

'Well, he's not going away.'

'He doesn't like me. He doesn't want to speak to me.'

'Doesn't he?' she asks and looks on as Richard hurriedly comes over and greets me.

'I'm sorry,' he says. 'We're so busy on Friday nights. It's John, isn't it?'

'It is – and you are Richard?'

'Yes.' He hands me a piece of paper. 'And this is my cell.'

'I'll text you tomorrow,' I promise, as he dashes off.

Jacky is purring like a Siamese cat, her expression one of feline satisfaction.

'*He doesn't like me*,' she says mocking my accent. 'HE DOESN'T LIKE ME!'

I can do nothing except pout contentedly.

'So are you coming now with us?'

*She likes me, too.*

Like Singapore itself, Taboo has spent a lot of money desleazing and refurbishing, since I've last been here. The sound system is better, Hoegarden is on tap and the sofas upstairs have been newly upholstered. Caucasians abound as everyone straight, gay and all the shades in-between mix with each other. The most noticeable – and unmourned – difference is the disappearance of the ladyboys. ('Who cares? They were Indonesian, anyway.') Their corner has been transformed to a drinking area with benches and stools. Young sophisticates, amongst whom the design and fashion industry is over-represented, are sipping cocktails at the same spot where pole-dancers used to tease the well-heeled sugar daddies. Exhibitionism has gone upmarket: male punters, who spend their lives in the stale humidity of gyms, dance shirtless on the bar instead. Waiters, wearing a red top with the club's logo, mix with the clients, offering to fetch drinks from the bar.

One of them is coming towards me.

'Can I have that?' I ask and point at his vest.

He looks at me. 'Wait until I finish,' he replies.

I sober up. 'I mean the *vest*.'

'Oh,' he says and his face turns to stone. 'We only have small and medium. You are, what? Large?'

I await the bad news, for this is not a size they are used to in Singapore. When orientals are big, they are not just large – they are massive enough to create their own gravitational field. Chubby chasers are thwarted in a part of the world where waist size 30 is considered XXL, but when they eventually meet Mr Sumo Wrestler – which they do, they do – they are more than compensated.

The waiter sizes me up. 'Let me check,' he says, leaving never to return. There are predictably no sizes between medium and baby elephant.

I buy myself another drink and wonder if I will meet Nick; not sure I want to. I know I won't meet Chang again. I kept in

SINGAPORE SWING

touch with him while he was in Singapore. Then he came to
London and I lost him, or rather he lost me. Last time I tried
to contact him on MSN, he didn't remember who I was.

I shrug my shoulders and check that I still have Richard's
number safely tucked in my wallet. I take out two pieces of
paper. *Two?* Oh yes, I got Jacky's number also.

'Let me know how you get on with Richard,' she'd said.

# CHAPTER EIGHT

# ON MERITOCRACY

Here is a well-known Malay myth to keep the book's race quotas above board.

'Twas in the reign of the Paduka Sri Maharaja, one of the kings of ancient Singapura, that a unique plague befell his kingdom. When the Maharaja himself heard about it, he could hardly believe his ears. Short-tempered and mercurial, as he was famed to be, the semi-naked *orang laut* who brought him the news was fearing for his life.

'You said *fish*?' asked the Maharaja.

'Swordfish, my Lord.'

The Maharaja tapped his fingers nervously on the throne.

'Let me get this straight,' he said. 'A school of flying, ahem, *swordfish* is terrorising our southern shores?'

'Yes, my Lord.'

'And they're spearing the fishermen with their, ahem, *snouts*, I suppose?'

'Yes, my Lord.'

The temperamental ruler exploded.

'Listen here! I would understand it if the swordfish speared our people in the sea. I would understand it if they speared them in their boats. But, in the name of Allah, *on the beach*? They are fish! Out of water!'

'They fly back into the sea, my Lord.'

The Maharaja lost his patience and threw his embroidered slipper at the messenger.

'Put this man in jail!' he bellowed. 'I'm going to the beach to see for myself whether this is true. And your swordfish had better be flying like djinns in an oil lamp shop or else you'll see what a real sword feels like.' He clapped his hands: 'Eunuchs! Prepare the howdah!'

And so it came to pass that the Maharaja marched to the beach on top of his favourite elephant, accompanied by the Bendahara, his prime minister, who was riding a black stallion by his side. He was preceded by 50 men from his Royal Guard, specially selected for their loyalty, and a dozen trumpeters who declared to his subjects that their Supreme Ruler was approaching. Behind him rode in formation his ministers, his mullahs, his eunuchs, his wives...

A swordfish suddenly flew from the sea and speared one of the men of his Royal Guard through the chest.

After a moment's silent disbelief all hell was loose. The Royal Guardsmen lanced the swordfish before it had time to fly away. The mullahs started praying. The women started ululating. The elephant raised his front legs and blew his trunk with a trumpeting sound as if to compensate for all the stunned court musicians.

Another swordfish flew by. This one was aiming at the Maharaja. Miraculously, it only ripped the long sleeve hanging by the sides of his silken shirt. The resulting uproar, as the shocked ruler gave the order to retreat, was heard as far as the island of Bintan.

Once back at his palace on top of Forbidden Hill, the Maharaja collapsed into a sulk, while his government met in a closed session for three days and three nights. But, despite such brainstorming, the problem appeared insoluble.

On the fourth day, a boy of 12 was brought to the Maharaja with a petition. Choleric as usual, he asked the boy what he wanted while glancing sharply at the courtier who let him in.

'I beg you to let my father out of jail, my Lord.' said the child whose voice had not yet broken. 'I have no other family.'

The Maharajah turned to the Bendahara. 'What is this boy talking about?' he asked.

'His father is the messenger who brought you the bad news about the swordfish, Your Majesty.'

The Maharaja jumped; he had forgotten all about him. Nervously he made a gesture to his retinue to let the man free. Then he regally dismissed the boy with the back of his hand. But the boy wouldn't go.

'You, my child?' he asked impatiently.

'My Lord, I think I know how to get rid of the swordfish,' the boy replied.

The Maharaja's irritation was so great he didn't even flinch. Things were getting more ludicrous by the minute. There he was, humouring a lowly-born boy who purported to have solved the biggest problem facing his government.

'Yes?' he said, whilst innerly debating whether the boy's father should not be now boiled alive for bringing up such a brat.

'Sharpen up tall bamboo stakes and place them tightly on the beach next to each other, like a wall. The swordfish will impale their snouts there, as they fly to the beach.'

There was a long silence while everyone's brain in the room started processing the boy's words, a silence only broken when a jubilant Maharaja rose and clapped his hands.

'Do it!' he shouted. 'You heard the boy, do it!'

The scheme worked as predicted and the people of Singapura were freed from the worst nightmare that had befallen the Kingdom since, well, the last one.

The story should end here, but – that's the point – it doesn't.

About a week after that crucial audience the Maharaja called the Bendahara for a meeting in his private chambers.

'Do you remember that boy whose plan rid us of those marine pests?' asked the Maharaja.

'I do, Your Majesty. How could I forget him?'

'Do you know where he lives?'

'Indeed, Your Majesty. Only yesterday I took the liberty of sending him a few presents on your behalf to thank him. Nothing expensive, of course. He and his father were easily satisfied. The poor normally are.'

'That's it,' the Maharaja said. '*The poor*. It was not me or you or any members of our exalted court that thought of the solution, but a *poor boy*.'

'A boy with a bright future, Your Majesty.'

The Maharaja stopped him.

'A boy with *no* future. I want you to send two of my most trusted guards to kill him and his father tonight.'

The Bendahara choked on his saliva. 'I don't understand...'

'Make it look like a robbery. Good timing with those presents. Say it must have been some jealous neighbour.'

'But –'

'But what?'

'The boy did us all a great favour.'

'No. The boy spoke and thought above his station and caused a rift in the natural order of things. I rule by divine right. You preside over day-to-day matters because I have delegated you that right. If we let excellence decide promotion and start judging people by worth and not by birth, then society will collapse throughout Malaya and I can not allow that.'

That same night, the bright boy and his father were strangled by strangers. None of the Maharaja's presents were found.

Two neighbours were arrested and were never seen again.

- 18 -

So how come Singapore is a city-state?

The story may be lengthy, but boring it isn't. Biographies sometimes read like fiction – the more so if you don't know anything about the subject. A country's history can equally be as fantastic, especially if you approach it with a clean slate. And so it is with Singapore.

Let's start in 1945: Year Zero. Colonialism is dead in South East Asia. Chairman Mao's long march to power is galvanising both the intelligentsia and the proletariat of the South Seas. The Dutch returned expecting to plunder according to the status quo ante and are being chucked out unceremoniously. The French pretended there is no distinction between 1950 and 1850: they are about to get the biggest slap of all in Dien Bien Phu. The British are withdrawing willingly and gradually, but not before they try to raise a bulwark in Malaya which is in the throes of a communist resurrection. Little credit and fewer congratulations still have been offered to the British forces and political operatives who succeeded in putting down such an insurgency in a region where even the Americans would flounder two decades later.

London convened its own colonies, the various sultanates, and the independent Malay states to create a centralised and strong Malayan Union. Although colonial policy had been to favour the Malays as the native ruling class, the Union was to give everyone the vote, thereby enfranchising the Chinese immigrants and lessening Mao's penumbra that fell upon the peninsula. But when the numbers were added, the results were shocking. Chinese immigration under the Empire had been relatively unchecked; the inclusion of the Straits Settlements of Malacca, Penang and Singapore would make the Malays a minority in their ancestral land. There was only one answer: Singapore, with its massive Chinese population was not to be included. This left a more acceptable 55:45 Malay/Chinese ratio in the Malayan Union founded with pomp and circumstance on 1 April 1946.

The omens for a state inaugurated on April Fool's Day are not good: the Union disintegrated as soon as it was formed, with the Malays – let alone the sultans – outraged at the loss of their privileges. A federation was formed and a new constitution gave the 'sons of the soil', the *bumiputra*, political supremacy: Malays born in the federation were citizens; non-Malays were subject to restrictions; a Malay was the supreme head of state; Malay would later become the official language and Islam the state religion. Politics turned sectarian: there was an assertive Malay Party, the United Malays' National Association (UMNO), a pliant Malay Chinese Party representing the Chinese community and a small Congress Party for the Indians. Sensibly, they fought and won the first Malayan elections together as an alliance where the UMNO was predominant.

And Singapore?

Singapore was to remain a British colony like Gibraltar, Hong Kong or Cyprus. However, the armed struggle in the jungles of Malaya – fought almost entirely by Chinese Communists – had fomented enough unrest in the island-city for some form of autonomy to be put in place in 1954. Not long after, Singapore was granted a constitution and attained self-government with an election in May 1959. This was the beginning of Singapore's modern age, the first time when the bulk of the Chinese residents – soon to be citizens – were able to vote.

The 1959 election was contested and won by a left-wing party called the People's Action Party; its strangely totalitarian insignia – red lightning in a blue circle – would not look out of place in Gerald Scarfe's drawings for Pink Floyd's *The Wall*. It was headed by Lee Kuan Yew who became Singapore's prime minister at the age of 35. Lee's great achievement was the creation of this political body claiming to represent every race, religion and community – just imagine whether this could ever have happened in Northern Ireland. But ours is a Hegelian tale: three steps forward, two steps back – what was young and radical yesterday, becomes tomorrow's conservative establishment.

The PAP's broad anti-colonial front also involved collaboration with the outlawed Communists in order to bridge the gap with the proletariat it was supposed to represent in the first place. Once in government the PAP set off on a course with three objectives: to unite all communities together; to isolate itself from the communist support that had brought it into power in the first place; and finally to achieve complete independence from the British via a merger with the Federation of Malaya (adding a 'Si' for Singapore to build the new country of Malay-Si-a). It was this policy that resulted in a split with the PAP's left wing that defected to form the Barisan Sosialis, a party Communist in all but name and implacably opposed to the union: had not the peninsular Malays been their mortal enemies during the insurrection? The defection forced the PAP to run a minority administration, but it achieved its aim in distancing itself from the far left and redefining its character. Its main thrust was now union with Malaya and to this effect it started talks with the UMNO and the rest of the Alliance parties.

By now you would have thought that a Malay-dominated, Islamic and staunchly conservative government would have little in common with a non-communal-but-Chinese-controlled, moderately left-wing, secular party.

And you'd be right.

- 19 -

There is no mistaking Kampong Glam: the landmark golden dome of the Sultan Mosque is perched dead on North Bridge Road. This is the area Raffles conceded to Sultan Hussein Shah and his descendants under the 1819 agreement. It is here, from Arab Street to Changi Road, that the heart of Malay and Muslim Singapore has been beating for nearly two centuries. The *kampong* has a rather unfortunate-sounding name – with its connotations of that seventies musical trend whose prime exponents were Bolan and Bowie, clad in velvet and chiffon – but it derives from the *gelam* tree that used to thrive in the area. The only samplings left today are planted inside the Malay Heritage Centre at Sultan Gate for the benefit of tourists.

The first mosque, built by Sultan Hussein between 1824 and 1828, was bankrolled by the East India Company who wanted to keep their ruler sweet. Faded photos show a brick Indonesian-looking building with a tiered pyramidal roof like a squashed pagoda. It served the community for a century before being replaced by the current two-storey Saracen-style mosque – designed, incidentally, by the British firm of Swan and McLaren. It is being administered by a board of trustees that represents the meshed Muslim make-up of Singapore: Arab, Malay, Bugis, Javanese, North Indian and South Indian. The Saudis have paid for several major repairs and renovations for the last forty years and their most visible contribution is the vast carpet that covers the prayer hall. It is on this carpet that I must not walk, I'm told, as I leave my shoes at the steps of the mosque entrance.

The time is outside prayers so the mosque is not busy, but there are still a good fifty people inside meditating (or sleeping, it is difficult to tell). There is no furniture except for some glorious chandeliers, a dozen pedestal fans facing the congregation and several sets of wooden bookshelves set against the pillars, containing what I presume to be copies of the Qur'an. I take great interest in the chandeliers because they are of similar design to those hanging in the Grand Mosque in Mecca itself and, since my chances of visiting the latter are nil, this is as close as I can get to the holy of holies of a great religion. That Saudi carpet with its pattern of white convex arches set against a wine-red background is, indeed, a marvel. It covers like wallpaper the whole 3,000-square-metre floor, snugly girdling every pillar base. How did they lay it? I try to distinguish the seams, but in vain.

The street that leads to the Mosque entrance, Bussorah (Basra) Street, is exceedingly picturesque but pedestrianisation has rendered it lifeless. The shophouses are freshly painted, the pavement is tastefully patterned and tall palms have been planted at regular intervals, but it's the state that owns the shophouses flanking the street: no one *lives* here. Handicrafts are geared for the tourist: rattan, bamboo and willow baskets, scarves, shawls and brooches, prayer mats, carpets and sarongs plus batiks, batiks, batiks. So much on sale, so photogenic, and yet so soulless. Maybe that's why it is here I see my first and only example of graffiti in Singapore. Someone has defiantly changed a 'No Dumping' sign to 'No Humping'.

This never fails to raise a chuckle but it is no laughing matter: vandalism is one of the forty-plus offences for which caning is a mandatory punishment in Singapore. Some are serious like rape, others less so, like overstaying your visa. The beatings are administered by specially trained prison guards using a wet rattan whip – as long as a broom handle and as thick as a finger – on the naked buttocks of the prisoner who is strapped face down on a wooden trestle. Being under 16 or over 50 might exempt you from the cane, but being a foreigner doesn't, as the widely publicised case of Michael Fay demonstrates.

During the latter part of 1993, cars in the Tanglin area of Singapore were being spray-painted at night. The police laid an ambush and arrested a 16-year-old student from Hong Kong, Shiu Chi Ho, and the son of a Thai diplomat who was released having diplomatic immunity. After a seven-hour interrogation, Shiu named several students attending the American School for expat kids. One of them was Fay, a photogenic, 18-year-old American. His parents had been divorced and he lived in upmarket Regency Park with his mother and stepfather. In his room the police found stolen Singapore flags, 'Not for hire' taxi signs and 'No Smoking' notices. He was arrested, spent nine days in custody and finally pleaded guilty to two charges of mischief, two of vandalism and one of possessing stolen property. On 3 March 1994 he was sentenced to four months in jail, a $3,500 fine and six strokes of the cane. Apart from Shiu who was arrested red-handed, he was the only one to be sentenced to a beating: other boys were too young (under 16), jumped bail and fled Singapore, or pleaded not guilty and were acquitted.

The case put the spotlight on Singapore's caning laws and caused an international debate on the difference between those famous 'Asian' and 'Western' values. 'Unlike some other societies which may tolerate acts of vandalism, Singapore has its own standards of social order as reflected in our laws. It is because of our tough laws against anti-social crimes that we are able to keep Singapore orderly and relatively crime-free,' said the Singapore government. The US administration disagreed: there was a large discrepancy between the offence and the punishment. As the buttocks bleed and are permanently scarred, isn't caning torture? Were such 'Asian' values exclusive to Malaysia, Singapore and Brunei that still administered what was in reality an old colonial punishment? Why did Hong Kong abolish it in 1990?

Fay's mother tried to mobilise US and world opinion but was surprised at the strength of the 'flog 'em and hang 'em' lobby, as the Singapore Embassy in Washington was deluged with messages of support. Even in Fay's hometown of Dayton, Ohio, a radio call-in proved strongly pro-caning. Bill Clinton asked Singapore's President to waive the punishment. As a gesture of goodwill the strokes were reduced to four, but the caning went ahead having united the country's citizens against the interference of the world's only superpower. It was also a reminder of the vast grassroots support for PAP's disciplinarian legislators.

Some Malays have been openly complaining about the 'Hollywoodisation' of their culture in letters to *The Straits Times* and I can see why when I reach Istana Kampong Glam.

This was the residence of Sultan Hussein himself, who originally lived in a timber-and-atap bungalow surrounded by high walls *'exhibiting effects of age and climate'*, as one contemporary traveller observed. He goes on to give us a rare description of the Sultan himself: well in his forties when he made the deal with Raffles, his teeth were blackened from chewing the betel nut, and his neck, suspected rather than conspicuous, supported a large shaven head with a handkerchief tied around it that left the top exposed in the old Malay fashion. He was no more than five foot tall, pot-bellied and with small, deformed legs that made him look like a waddling duck as he moved about. Since he had the attention span of a five-year-old and fell asleep whenever he sat down, it comes as no surprise that, when his brother usurped the throne, there were few mutterings.

It was Hussein's son, Ali Iskander Shah, who commissioned a new, two-storey building designed by Singapore's top architect, George Coleman. It stands in front of me, at Sultan Gate: semi-Palladian in style with tiled roofing, it features a protruding middle section with three round archways that lead into a long veranda. Unfortunately the construction took a hit on Ali's finances and, as his debts increased, his star waned until he was forced to pledge his British annuity to an Indian moneylender.

In 1855 the British came to his aid and brokered a deal with his supposed vassal, the Temenggong's son Ibrahim. The Temenggong's family had been much luckier. The British had granted them land in Telok Blangah which shot up in value as plans for the new deep port, Keppel Harbour, started being drawn. The deal offered Sultan Ali a large cash payment in return for his birthright and his land – only his title would remain. (Ali's descendants still receive a stipend by the Singapore government of $250,000 a year, although this is being spread thinner and thinner as the recipients multiply.) Despite all this the indomitable Ali managed to die heavily in debt and in 1886 his son Allum Shah finally ceded the title of Sultan of Johore to the Temenggong's grandson, Abu Bakr, whose lineage continues to this day.

When Allum Shah died without direct heirs, the British authorities claimed ownership of the *Istana*. His half-brother, Mahmud, who claimed the inheritance for himself by right, obeyed the colonial rulers but lived in protest in the Gedong Kuning, the Yellow Mansion, to the left of the *Istana* itself. It is now a top-class restaurant – closed for a wedding when I try to have a peek. The only sign of its past is the canary yellow it is painted in, the colour of Malay royalty.

I turn into the *Istana* compound, advertised as a Malay Heritage Centre, but there is no one at the gate when I slip into the garden. I seem to be the only living thing around, bar the starlings and the mynahs. Maybe they are all taking a siesta; maybe it is prayer time; or maybe they don't care anymore. Restored and beautified Kampong Glam looks better than ever, but it stands inanimate, like a fragment of Bollywood scenery expecting a crowd of extras. The anonymous planners have forgotten that you don't admire a graceful old lady when she is all tarted up like a teenager with lipstick and hair extensions. It is the dignified way she carries those wrinkles and double-chins she has collected over the years that you notice and respect – and more importantly, you want to keep her alive rather than embalm and perfume her corpse.

I look at my watch. I had better be going back. I have a date with Richard in a few hours.

- 20 -

Numbers, numbers: in order to solve the thorny problem and keep the Malays in the majority in the new Malay-Si-a, three British Borneo territories comprising Sabah, Sarawak and Brunei were added to the Federation along with Singapore. (Brunei pulled out early on providing us with a blueprint of how some Malay sultanates might have looked, had there been no union: a peppering of absolute rulers like the Sultan of Brunei collecting Rolls Royces, breeding prize-winning racehorses and buying hotels in Mayfair). The final population totals added up as follows: 3.7 million Chinese versus 4 million 'sons of the soil'. Never mind that the Indonesians who ruled South Borneo and were claiming the rest of the island, started a slow-burning conflict, the Konfrontasi, that exploded in Singapore itself with terrorist bombings; never mind that the Malays were not strictly speaking the absolute majority in the new Malaysia since the indigenous people from Borneo like the Iban were, well, *indigenous*; the Chinese were in the minority and that was that.

It is hard to think of a people that comprise a quarter of the planet's inhabitants as discriminated against, but it is even harder to settle upon a better word to describe the Malay attitude towards their Chinese neighbours. The sentiments were not a million miles away from the feelings that eastern and central European peasants harboured against the industrious Jewish and Armenian communities in their own midst. So, it was yes to Singapore, to its wealth and its location, but no to the Singaporeans who bent over backwards to accommodate the Malays. The seats they accepted in the new, combined assembly were way below what their population warranted, whereas those of the counter-balancing Borneo territories were bumped up artificially. Separate citizenship continued to exist; Singapore nationals could only vote and stand for election in the city itself but not in Malaya. When the chips were down, outnumbering of the Chinese was what mattered, and this is what the border-shifting was all about. The political dominance of the Malays would not be challenged.

It was at that point that the PAP leadership showed the political nous that has characterised it for half a century. It called a snap election in September 1963 just around the time when the euphoria regarding the union was at its highest. The result was a glimpse of the future déjà vu: the electorate gave the PAP a resounding 37 out of 51 seats and confirmed the PAP's crossover appeal; the Singapore Alliance, the coalition supported by the governing parties in peninsular Malaya, won no representation. This was truly not just another Chinese community party: the Malays in Singapore – and other minorities – voted for the PAP in droves; it even came first in the overwhelmingly Malay ward of Geylang Serai. So, not only was the PAP going into the new Malaysia stronger than ever, but could also claim to represent every community on the island. This was a real threat to the parties in Malaya with their sectarian politics. When the PAP decided to sit in the cross-benches rather than blindly support the Alliance government, relations between Malaysian Prime Minister Tunku Abdul Rahman and Lee Kuan Yew became frosty. When, in April 1964, the PAP decided to contest the federal elections in the peninsula, the kris were out.

The spectre of a Chinese prime minister loomed large: here was a social-democratic Chinese-dominated party whose leadership was British-educated, competent and with a reputation of efficiency, challenging a right-wing Malay government on its own soil. It was also a party that claimed to represent all communities: 'It took us some time to convince the 200,000 Malays in Singapore of the PAP's sincerity,' Lee Kuan Yew commented during the election campaign. 'I do not think it will be all that difficult to convince the three million Malays in Malaya.' The Alliance challenged the PAP's decision to field candidates in the courts, but lost; although

Singaporeans couldn't vote in Malaya, there was nothing in the new constitution to stop the party expanding its local rank-and-file. Had the Malayan parties not contested elections in Singapore via their own offshoots? And, ominously, *had they not lost to the PAP*?

The Alliance need not have worried. It was impossible to set up an effective party organisation so quickly. The PAP fielded only 17 candidates for the 104 Parliament and 282 State assembly seats contested and most of them lost their deposits. Only one candidate won, and he was Malay. When threatened by an external menace – in this case, Indonesia's Konfrontasi – voters rush to the government of the day. As for the Chinese: why vote for the opposition outsider and reduce the strength and subsequent division of spoils of their own Chinese party in Malaysia? The PAP had grossly misread the mood of the electorate and had rushed head-on to an electoral disaster.

It was to prove a bigger catastrophe than anyone could have suspected.

It's past ten o'clock at night when I step into Outram Park station. This time I'm not going to be snookered in front of vending machines with single tickets that have to be returned at once at the end of every trip: I have bought myself an ez-link card that can be topped up electronically and offers discounted travel, not unlike Ken Livingston's Oystercard. Who copied whom, I wonder.

The MRT has not changed – well, a new line is being built – but a slight climate of alarm permeates Singapore's underground system, most conspicuously at Clarke Quay where a sign proudly proclaims: *'For your safety 40 CCTV cameras are monitoring this station'*. The Madrid, London and Bombay bombings have been gravely noted, and a film keeps looping in the flat screens in every carriage. A vigilant lady challenges a youth with a baseball cap who leaves his luggage behind: 'You left your bag!' she says; he claims it isn't his and runs away; she pulls the emergency cord and stops an impatient guy who is about to touch it. The fears are not misplaced. In Malaysia, an Islamist party is contesting the elections. In Singapore itself, three dozen local members of the Jemaah Islamiyah terrorist group that carried out the Bali bombings have been arrested, after video material was found in Afghanistan.

I stop. Everyone is looking at me. I just had a gulp from a water bottle. Shit! I forgot. *'No Eating and Drinking: Fine $500'*. Thank my lucky stars that we're arriving at Farrer Park, my stop.

Ah, it's different. The unsightly high rises have been demolished and cranes – mechanical ones – occupy the spaces where swallows used to nest. A government official must have visited the place, glimpsed the dirt and disapproved.

The Mustafa Centre still dominates the Serangoon Plaza, and they still let me walk in with my backpack. Inside, the place is as chaotic as I remember it. Imagine a shop where wares of every colour and size are right in front of you, rather than in the storeroom, out of sight. I slip quickly through the watch stalls where the whole stock is mangled like snakes in a pit. Special offers abound: *Buy Two Citizen For $90* – hey, what are they, melons? It's at the luggage section that I begin to warm up to this leviathan of department stores. Wow, I can replace my ageing bags for a tenner! As for the digital camera section – it's enormous, and I spend a good half hour browsing the brands. They are cheap, oh so cheap, and suddenly I realise that I've become a dedicated Mustafa shopper – especially since it's just before midnight; the place is open 24-hours.

Guidebooks revel in remarking that Singapore ain't no Bangkok. It's an unfair comparison, like saying, 'Goa is not quite Gomorrah'. But where else can I go shopping for camera equipment or change pounds at the foreign exchange centre – maybe deal in gold – after midnight? If I'm peckish, I can have a curry, a Hainanese chicken rice or sit out and enjoy a coffee at any hour of the day. And when I do, and I sit at one of these plastic chairs, I am not alone for long. Soon a young Indian ensconces himself next to me although there are empty seats as far as the eye can see. I check him out with the corner of my eye. He's well-groomed, unmistakably excited and steals glances at me.

Whatever I said about Gomorrah, I take it back.

- 21 -

Attack is the best form of defence and if you want to bully someone, follow them home and make sure they notice you. After the poor showing by the PAP in the peninsular elections, the Malay right-wing press took advantage of the party's post-election blues and started a hysterical denunciation of the Singapore government with imagined wrongs where none were intended or, indeed, had transpired. Editorials wondered why there were more unemployed Malays than Chinese in the city, although the Chinese formed the majority of the population. Columnists raged that the PAP had forcibly moved the Malays out of their *kampongs* to house them into flats. Accusations of gerrymandering by splitting the Malay vote through displacement were being bandied around. A phrase started appearing menacingly in the commentaries: *'Do not treat the sons of the soil as stepchildren!'*

Lee Kuan Yew was disturbed at the course these attacks were taking, so he called a conference with Malay groups on 19 July to discuss any grievances including any perceived slights from the government's slum clearance and tower block building operations – to be fair, this was a policy common in the sixties worldwide. A fiery demagogue and UMNO member, Syed Jaafar called his own conference a week earlier than Lee's. On 12 July he delivered an acerbic speech at the New Star cinema in Pasir Panjang in front of huge crowds that included representatives and observers from Malay bodies, and fifteen Alliance members from Kuala Lumpur. Syed Jaafar started by claming that Malays had been oppressed subtly or blatantly in Singapore and, like Mark Antony at Caesar's funeral, he spread doubt by refutation: *'I do not want to accuse Lee Kuan Yew of being a communist, but I feel suspicious.'* By the time he'd finished, cries to kill Lee were being heard.

It is hard to think of Lee Kuan Yew as a model of restraint given his latter-day defamation writs against dissenting voices, but during that period he was as patient and composed as a Vestal Virgin. This, in spite of headlines in the Malay press that ranged from overt threats *'If some undesirable incidents should happen… Lee Kuan Yew should not blame the Malays, but he himself should take full responsibility,'* to Mohammed-cartoons-style agitation: *'Teacher forced student to smell pork!'* Despite all this the government-sponsored conference went well with most of the invited organisations attending. Lee himself was subjected to a grilling which he handled skilfully and everything appeared to be on track again.

Two days later, on 21 July, a celebration of the birthday of the Prophet Mohammed was due to be held at the Padang. It was to prove the match that was thrown into the tinderbox.

The Nadezhda Russian Restaurant is the only incongruity on Arab Street where the live-above-the shop terraced houses are distinguished only by the dividers between their sloping roofs and their deep mauve, pink and peach colours: there is Makkah Trading, Aladdin's World of Silk, Haj Textiles and Batik Exchange (Authorised Money Changer). This is one of the oldest neighbourhoods in Singapore, demarcated to a community of Bugis that had already established themselves by the Kallang river and later settled by Arab merchants. The Bugis were seafaring folk from Sulawesi who regularly traded in the Indonesian archipelago. The cry 'The Bugis are coming!' created a frenzy of anticipatory mayhem in the Singapore docks among peddlers, provisioners and prostitutes. But in other places of the archipelago the reputation of the Bugis was one of bloodthirsty cut-throat pirates: the sight of their slender, pointed praus on the horizon was enough to lead a whole *kampong* into flight. I like the plausible but unproven theory that their name has been forever immortalised in the expression '*the boogie man is coming*'.

Today's eponymous MRT station at Victoria Road is where the fearsome-looking Bugis used to make merry until the early hours of the morning. It has replaced what some have called '*the best-known tourist attraction in Singapore until the late 1970s*': a grid of narrow streets full of food and drink stalls through which transvestites and transsexuals openly paraded their wares. It is not widely known that in the 1970s and 1980s Singapore was a centre of excellence for gender reassignment surgery. Professor Shan Ratnam, Head of Obstetrics and Gynaecology in the National University Hospital of Singapore, pioneered the first Asian sex change back in July 1971 and, until his retirement 25 years later, he performed something like 500 such operations. In 1973 – astonishingly for such a homophobic society – the Singapore government allowed transgendered individuals to marry with their new identities and the change of sex to be denoted in their ID cards, a normalisation that would wait for another thirty years to be effected in the UK.

With such, let's say, *infrastructure* behind it, Bugis Street and its *mak nyah* became the porn centre of the town for decades. It is *Saint Jack* territory, a novel where the 'Sin' in Singapore is vividly described by Paul Theroux. A viewer of the 1978 Peter Bogdanovich film, based on the book and shot on location for six months, can catch a glimpse of a seedy underside – less Padang and more Pat Pong – that has ceased to exist. The film was made under false pretences and when it came out *The Straits Times* reported that the authorities *'were aghast at its portrayal of Singapore as a fleshpot of a country, rife with gangsters, pimps and prostitutes'*. Needless to say, the resulting movie has been banned since.

I don't know whether it was the book or the film or the feeling that they'd been had that led the government to sanitise the area, but they have succeeded. The bulldozers and cranes arrived in October 1985 and produced a pedestrianised, covered bazaar with narrow lanes and an endless two-way flow of people where it is difficult to walk with a daypack, let alone sashay in high heels, hair extensions and a 36D bra. Two-dollar cheap watches killed the transgender trade.

Or rather, pushed it elsewhere.

The origin of the July riots of 1964 was much debated at the time, but now that the non-partisan diaries of the western high commissioners in Singapore have been published, a general consensus has emerged. On 21 July 1964, 20,000 Muslims gathered at the Padang for the Mohammed Day celebrations. Inflammatory leaflets were distributed ('*Before the blood of Malays flows on Singapore soil, it would be better to see the blood of the Chinese flooding the country.*') and provocative speeches were made by UMNO officials conflating ethnicity and religion: '*It is clear that Allah does not stop Muslims to be friendly with non-Muslims as long as they do not drive them out of their homes and disturb their religion.*'

At 4 p.m. a parade started with the Malaysian head of state and other personages leading the way to Lorong 12 in Geylang. As the marchers moved on, they became rowdier and rowdier. Shops started closing their shutters in advance of the procession. Just before 5 p.m., a Chinese federal constable saw two Malay youths throw an ice cream at a Chinese cyclist but did not interfere; he kept an eye on them, instead. Soon after, half a dozen of their friends broke off from the march. He told them to join up. One of them refused and pushed him away. Twenty-odd Malays ran over and surrounded the constable shouting 'Allahu Akbar'. A second, Chinese, policeman rushed to his colleague's aid.

The group of protesters swelled to fifty. A third constable, a Malay, tried to calm down the demonstrators but failed. At 5.15 he ran into a coffee-shop to call for reinforcements.

It was then that the two Chinese policemen were set upon. The first one was jostled and kicked until he disappeared under the legs of the crowd. The second one, bleeding from a gash in his head, ran into a bicycle shop on Kallang Road. Before the – Chinese – proprietor could close the door, the mob had smashed their way in and started beating him up, too. He eventually broke free and escaped through a door at the back.

By 5.30 p.m. there were scuffles all along Geylang Road. Police cordons formed and the crowd broke through. By 7.30 p.m. clashes were occurring on Queen Street, Victoria Road, North Bridge Road, Jalan Besar and Palmer Road. Military assistance was sought: the British put the Gurkhas on alert, but wisely stayed out of the melee. At 8.15 p.m. an American diplomatic car had its windscreen smashed by a hail of stones. At 9.30 p.m. a curfew was imposed. By then 178 persons had been injured and four had been killed. At 10.45 p.m. Lee Kuan Yew spoke on the radio in Malay, Mandarin and English and appealed for calm.

The lifting of the curfew at 6 a.m. next morning was like a green light to a wave of new inter-ethnic clashes. Federal ministers flew in for a show of solidarity but turned down the offer of a joint broadcast with Lee. The curfew was re-imposed at 11.30 a.m. but widely ignored. The Chinese were hitting back: Geylang was ablaze. The police went on a pre-emptive strike and started arresting Triad members, suspected of being behind the retaliatory attacks. The second day of rioting was worse than the first: 179 injured, 11 killed.

On the third day there were reports that 4,000 Chinese were being organised for battle at Kampong Chai Chee. A call for jihad was made by an imam to avenge the alleged massacre of a certain Sheikh Osman and his family. The sheikh – shaken – appeared on television to dispel the rumours. Moderate community leaders scoured the streets to calm down their brethren. They slowly succeeded: clashes were down but continued sporadically, fed by the rumour mill, until 7 August. The final toll was 23 dead, 454 wounded and 2,568 arrested. More was to come: at 8.50 p.m. on 2 September, a Chinese was hit by a stone thrown by two Malays while travelling on his scooter at Kampong Amber and sparked off the September Riots. Eleven days later, 13 more people were dead, 106 injured and 1,439 arrested.

The political fallout was volcanic. The PAP wanted an enquiry, certain of the UMNO's guilt in precipitating the riots by exporting their racial politics to Singapore. The Alliance, on the other hand, mocked the PAP's non-sectarian claims: it was on *its* turf that the riots had started. Relations between Abdul Rahman and Lee Kuan Yew turned from frosty to downright polar.

- 22 -

Those who think Singapore is not Asia but a precocious corner of the First World, should come to Geylang on a Saturday night. Here, at last, you can find the hustle and bustle of the Far East and catch a glimpse of a non-air-conditioned Singapore. Amusingly, it doesn't feel hot any more; a welcome breeze cools me down. Maybe it is the multitude of fans or maybe the stifling heat elsewhere is actually *generated* from the scores of air conditioners. After all, what do they do but take the heat from the inside and pile it on the outside? With all its air conditioners at full blast, the carbon footprint of tiny Singapore must look like Australia.

In Geylang people travel pillion on scooters Bangkok-style in the main drag – which, unlike Chinatown or the CBD, is choc-a-bloc at midnight – or lean timidly on railings next to the numerous karaoke hostess clubs. Over at the New Shanghai, a girl sits bored on a stool by the door. The prices outside prepare you for what to expect: Martell VSOP $148, vodka $98, Black Label $128. At every corner a big TV is blasting the Kop's noise with snippets of 'You'll Never Walk Alone'. Men – almost invariably men – are watching a Liverpool–Chelsea game with half-litre Carlsberg bottles at a hand's reach. There are people everywhere: squatting, sitting on steps, talking on their mobiles, drinking beer, hustling. I see one Chinese guy with a pigtail and my shock is such – pigtails having gone out of fashion ever since the Manchu dynasty went to pot – that I stare at him so intensely, he feels my gaze on his neck and turns around. He is a mean motherfucker with a devil's tattoo on his shoulder, so I split.

For the first time I see dogs in the streets. They are lying down, plainly unafraid of the dogcatcher. I wonder if they have been licensed after careful vetting of their pedigree. I take a look at them: nah – they wouldn't even be allowed in the toilets at Crufts. They are – goodness me *strays*! How come the first three days of each month have not yet been set aside for their extirpation?

It's on the sidestreets, the *lorongs*, that it gets *really* exciting. In front of Hotel Fragrance Emerald on Lorong 6, the girls are at the lobby with their hot pants, high heels and handbags, the standard uniform of the prostitute from Southampton to Shanghai. Hotel 6 opposite advertises its rates: $12 transit, $40 overnight. The girls there are bold enough to parade outside – or perhaps the air con is full blast and they are certainly not dressed for arctic conditions. Over at the New Darlene Hotel at Lorong 8 they are undercutting the prices: $10 transit and $37 overnight. I'm surprised that this *lorong* faces a mosque; the locals must not give a damn. Look, a family of three is heading for Hotel Fragrance Emerald. The mother covers her little girl's face with her palm when they reach the parading female flesh by the elevator. The prostitutes, unruffled, separate to let them pass.

On Lorong 10 by Hotel Fragrance Sapphire – there is a Hotel Fragrance Pearl further on, in what seems like Starbucks-style saturation market coverage – someone talks to me: 'Hello John,' he says. He can't know my name; does he understand the connotations of the epithet? A man opposite winks at me. Is he a pimp or rent? I decide he is a pimp; not long after, I see him being followed by a Western gentleman of some age to the elevator of Hotel Fragrance Sapphire where the girls are waiting.

There is a whiff of danger in the air. As I try to cut through the *lorongs* by the back alleys, a Chinese guy with a fully-tattooed torso stops me with a hand signal. There is a makeshift pile of tyres and large green bin containers placed on the street to form something looking remarkably like a barricade. I try to look through by squinting. The alley is seeped in total darkness, but it attracts far too big a crowd for my liking. I walk back up to Geylang Road and look up to the first floor of a shophouse. The light is on and the windows are wide open, their frames set against a rickety building that wears its mould like a badge of courage. I can make out three sets of twin bunk beds. Washing lines hang inside the room; a drying pair of trousers dangles deeper inside. Topless, sweaty males look down onto the street. I stumble against a beer bottle.

On Lorong 22, the streetwalkers are distinctly more corpulent and less fragrant than the sweet, soft souls I saw earlier. I wonder whether the further out you go, the older and uglier the prostitutes become. I look at my map: Geylang Road reaches all the way to Lorong 44; there must lie the sight of Medusa. Although extremely curious, I decide not to tempt fate and risk turning into stone. I turn back instead and browse the window of an adult shop which takes the usual pains to state that no porn is available. What is in stock instead are various dildos, creams, natural aphrodisiacs and female hygiene products, though I doubt whether the claims of one particular feminine cream (lightens vaginal pigmentation using French nano-technology) would pass EU advertising standards.

For the first time in my life I feel invisible. Although I am the only Westerner, people are not interested in me. It is Saturday night, they have worked goddess knows how many hours, and they are here to eat, drink and socialise. Everyone is either sitting watching the football or staggers by me looking down, as if ashamed of the state of their neighbourhood. *You oughtn't be*, I think. *At least you're real.* Look, a car is parked against a sign showing a car being towed away for those who can't read English: 'No Parking at All Time'. Someone smokes underneath a 'No Smoking' sign. The people seem to be giving two fingers at the rules and regulations that mire this city. I bet some are even chewing gum.

There, at last, dirt, glorious dirt. Rush to Geylang Lorong 14 to see it before it is pedestrianised over: a muddy field with puddles of water and unkempt trees with rubbish strewn against them.

Trust me to find the dirt in Singapore once more.

The cab driver who takes me home is as garrulous as his colleagues the world over.

'There is no special red-light district before,' he tells me in his beautiful, glorious Singlish. 'Five year ago, there is bro-tel,' – rhymes with hotel – 'all over town. In Chinatown where you live, there is bro-tel. Worehouser we call 'em. But government not renew the license, *lor*. Except in Geylang. So red-light district move to Geylang. But now too much. You have streetwalker walking *lai dat*. You are talking girl come from all over the world, Thailand, Malaysia, Indonesia, Vietnam. China girl there is a lot, *lah* – even Russia. There is girl from Russia in Geylang! They come as tourist, government can' do anything, *ah*?'

I tell him that the locals seem to accept it: 'I saw a family walk into one of those hotels with the girls standing outside'.

He is not surprised. 'I carry a family from Malaysia. I ask 'em why you stay in red-light district? They tell me agent book for them, they don' know. Those who been to Singapore they know hotels operate short term only. We call them fuckshop.'

'I bet there are many backpackers who wouldn't mind if they were only paying $40 a night.'

The taxi driver doesn't answer, not versed in backpacker psychology.

'I was also surprised about the life in the streets,' I continue. 'It's buzzing.'

'On main road many many different kind of food. Young people go there.'

'But there are a lot of rundown areas. How come they have escaped the clutches of the government?'

'They all private-own,' so government can' do anything. Up to individual owner, but who upgrade? No value. Red-light district wan' to buy? Bank don' lend money. No value.'

The explosive lifting of the lid of Pandora's race box scared everyone in equal proportion and some kind of truce was established: inflammatory pronouncements, especially on the position of the Chinese in Malaysia and the Malays in Singapore were voluntarily restrained. But when the time came for the first all-Malaysian budget, all hell broke loose once again. Malaysian Finance Minister, Tan Siew Sin, was a member of the Malay Chinese Party who stood to lose most if the PAP made inroads in Malaysia. So when he needed to raise extra taxes for the defence expenditure – these were the days of the Konfrontasi – he imposed a payroll and turnover tax that hit Singapore's commerce hard; it was estimated that the island would shoulder forty per cent of the extra financial burden. When Lee complained, Tan retorted that the PAP was a party with a strategy to share the wealth of the haves with the have-nots. He mocked Singapore's willingness to be a fully-fledged member of Malaysia. Who should the government tax? Rich Singapore merchants or poor Malay tin miners?

This, of course, is the crucial question that defines the cohesion of a country. Taxation is only acceptable when its distribution is acknowledged as just. Notions of justice are normally confined to a particular group, be it a gang patch ('hey, only *our* drug dealers are allowed in this club'), a village ('those city folk are buying holiday homes and pushing up the prices') or, more broadly, a nation: when the SNP in Scotland campaigns for independence, references to 'their' North Sea oil abound. Under different circumstances, Singaporeans might have accepted the tax burden to raise the standard of the Malay miners, but in riot-fogged times mob passion is never clear-sighted or visionary. When, during his speech at the opening of Parliament, the Malaysian Head of State made a pointed reference to 'threats from within', both parties knew it was time for divorce.

For such a momentous decision it was a surprisingly cloak-and-dagger occasion. It was kept secret until the very end in order not to upset the British who first and foremost wanted a strong Malaysia protecting their naval base in Singapore. Nor did anyone want to give a propaganda boost to Indonesia who kept claiming that Malaysia was not a country, but a geographical construct to serve British interests. Abdul Rahman was convalescing in France after an attack of shingles, so it was Tun Razak, his second in command who conducted the negotiations. Lee summoned his senior ministers to Kuala Lumpur on 7 August 1965 and, at half past noon, they all covertly signed a separation document.

The British High Commissioner was not told until 36 hours later and was as astonished as Harold Wilson who kicked up a fuss. He sent a personal message to the Malaysian PM, but it was too late to reverse the process; the gulf between the two parties was as deep as the straits physically separating them. On 9 August the Alliance members of the Malaysian Parliament were told the news. At 10:00am the

Singapore Independence Bill was given its first, second and third readings at once and passed with 126 votes in favour, none against and one abstention. At the same time Lee Kuan Yew briefed the British, Indian, Australian and New Zealand High Commissions in the City Hall. There, at noon, he gave a tearful press conference: '*For me it is a moment of anguish because all my life, all my adult life, I have believed in a merger and the unity of these two territories,*' he said. '*It broke everything we stood for.*'

Oblique references to the origins of that 'si' in Malaysia cause blood to boil, still today. When Lee Kuan Yew was asked in June 1996 whether he could envisage an eventual reunion, he replied in the affirmative, '*provided Malaysia adopted a meritocratic system like Singapore's*'. The Malaysian Prime Minister Mahathir Mohamad was quick to reply with the profoundly paradoxical '*We do practice meritocracy, but one based on race.*'

# CHAPTER NINE

# THE RABBIT'S SACRIFICE

Once upon a time, the animals of the forest heard from the ravens – flying like shoddy paper planes, crazy as they were with enthusiasm – that the Buddha himself was going to pass through their valley and that the Enlightened One would spend the night under the old *pulai* tree by the Spring of Pure Happiness.

'The Buddha is coming! We must prepare a feast of celebration that will eclipse the memory of the most sumptuous banquet ever offered!' cried the animals excitedly and spread this way and that collecting fruit, herbs and grains. Come the afternoon, makeshift ovens were glowing and large cooking pots were steaming on top of blazing fires.

By the time the Buddha appeared in his guise as a wandering beggar, the banquet was ready.

First the Bear came forward who had brought pure honey and royal jelly, collected by tricking the fierce bees on top of Fire Mountain that normally protect their treasured produce to death.

The Buddha saw, and He was pleased.

Then came the Tiger who had brought the plumpest and juiciest of durian fruit, having swam all the way to Turtle Island, where the tallest and oldest trees were to be found.

The Buddha saw, and He was pleased.

The Rabbit was somewhere in the middle of the procession and realised that his offerings were below par. He was holding just a bowl of tonic made of fresh lime and galangal, whereas in front of him other animals were depositing hot herb soups, spicy curries and gold-leafed, luscious cakes. When his turn came to appear in front of the Buddha, he faltered for he knew not how to demonstrate that his heart was full of spiritual fervour.

Except –

Without thinking any further, the Rabbit jumped into an open fire, for the best sacrifice he could think of was himself.

And the Buddha saw, and He cried.

## - 23 -

I suppose, it's only when faced with a durian ice cream that you realise what your background really is. I was in Little India waiting for a tour of World War Two locations when I decided on the spur of the moment to ease myself into tasting that damn fruit by trying an ice cream. It, of course, stank. My insides protested violently and a foul burp came up after a few licks, as if something has crawled and died inside me and I was exhaling its decomposing gases. And, yes, I must mention the wind I passed soon after, because it lingered low and poisonously over the minibus. Pythagoras believed that when you fart part of your soul escapes; this one was Lucifer personified. It belonged to a separate fartan universe where time bends and smell is four-dimensional. Soon, every window was open, as we all craved for a hit of some good, old-fashioned carbon monoxide expelled by a passing juggernaut. You have been warned. You try that fruit at your peril.

Anyway, I am on the minibus – luckily old-fashioned with windows that can open – and if the other tour members have perceived my faux pas, they hide it with chivalry. The tour is composed in equal parts of Americans, Australians and Brits, all World War Two buffs who test to the limits our guide's expertise. But Razeen holds his own – of small and scrawny build, he is an informed, eloquent and witty live wire.

He must first dispel some misconceptions.

'Ladies and gentlemen – they said Singapore fell because "the guns faced the wrong way". Yes, the Japanese invaded Singapore from the north-west,' he says, 'and yes the town's guns – twenty-nine of them – were pointing south-east. But Lieutenant General Arthur Percival, the commander-in-chief and Major General Gordon Bennett, the head of the Australian Imperial Forces, were not as clueless as popular history makes them out to be. They were prepared for invasion from the north. British High Command had even predicted the exact location of the Japanese landings in Malaysia.'

Razeen was right. A plan had been devised, called Operation Matador, to capture the narrow Thailand isthmus at Singora and throttle any invasion from the north-east. But Britain was fighting for its existence back in Europe and North Africa and had no manpower to spare, so the avoidance of a third front was of paramount importance. When the reports came in that a Japanese fleet was sailing for Malaya, the pre-emptive strike was held up in case this was an elaborate manoeuvre to coax the Brits to capture Singora and force the Thai government to call for Japan to liberate its territory. Of course, the Japanese move was no hoax, and Operation Matador was held up for so long it never even started.

'Nor did the Japanese invade on bicycles. They used bicycles, for sure, but they also used tanks. The British and Australians did not have any tanks. Nor much airpower. Nor ships, really. The Royal Navy could not spare any big ships. The ones they could afford were a modern battle cruiser, the *Prince of Wales*, fresh out of sinking the *Bismarck* and an older, patched up World War One battle cruiser, the *Repulse*. They were both sunk on 10 December, three days after war broke out. They were sailing towards Kota Bahru when a false alarm made them turn back towards Kuantan, a strategic coastal airfield in the middle of the Malayan peninsula. But when they arrived, they only saw some dead water buffaloes on the beach. The troops in Kuantan had fought a battle with an imaginary foe all night. But by then the ships had been spotted.'

What happened next is one of the most painful episodes of the Royal Navy's history. Admiral Tom Phillips – nicknamed 'Thumb' because of his small height – commanded the fleet. He was a traditionalist with blind faith in sea- rather than air-power, and an unshaken belief that a battleship could not be sunk from the air. It led to arguments with Air Marshall 'Bomber' Harris who jokingly prophesied: *'One day, Tom, you'll be standing on a box on your bridge and your ship will be smashed to pieces by bombers and torpedo aircraft. As she sinks, your last words will be, "That was a fucking great mine!"'*

This, sadly, is exactly what happened. The Japanese sent squadron after squadron of aircraft against the two enemy ships outside Kuantan, while Phillips obstinately kept radio silence and refused to request the RAF's assistance. When the captain of the *Repulse* found this out, he disobeyed orders and telegraphed HQ, but, by the time the fighter planes arrived, it was too late. The two ships along with 840 men had been lost in their first two hours of battle – including Phillips who, with stubborn but misplaced heroism, went down with the *Prince of Wales*. Churchill's reaction when he heard the news was typical of the impact it had worldwide: '*In all the war I never received a more direct shock,*' he wrote in his memoirs.

We have reached Mount Faber. It is a typical Singapore day, hot and humid with a grey, pewter-coloured sunless sky and misty visibility. Butterflies fly all around us and the shrill sound of cicadas is the soundtrack to our meandering. Amongst the pine trees and rhododendrons, white and mauve cat's whiskers are flowering in landscaped patches. Encircling the vista point are 15 wood carvings that tell the history of Singapore from its legendary naming to today's multicultural society. At the top itself, a tree is wired through with a lightning conductor, a reminder of the ferocity of the sky-splitting South Seas thunderstorms that have to be heard to be believed; even operating mobiles during this period is risky as the occasional electrocuted user can attest.

Razeen gives us a small talk. 'Here is where Faber Five command was based, ladies and gentlemen. It was the main control centre for the coastal guns at Fort Siloso on Sentosa Island over there and the Labrador battery you can see opposite. For ten years Fortress Singapore had been reinforced and its naval base was built to accommodate twenty ships. This was to be the headquarters of the Far Eastern Fleet to protect India, Burmah, Hong Kong plus Australia and New Zealand that were still relying on Britain to protect them. But come the beginning of the hostilities and there were only two big ships available. Figure that.'

He points towards Sentosa Island in the south.

'The main Singapore defense was the guns that could hit a ship in twenty miles. And no, the guns were not useless as has been suggested. The fact that the Japanese did not attempt a landing by the obvious route, the south, was evidence of their deterrent value. And they weren't silent, nor were they "pointing at the wrong direction". They *did* fire north; they could turn on their axes except one that couldn't and one that didn't have a turning cable.'

'They were ineffective,' says an American who clearly knows his stuff.

'Yes, they were. Naval bombs are supposed to pierce armour first and explode later so they are not that useful against ground troops. Unless you were unlucky enough and your head took a direct hit, the bomb just made a crater. The Japanese fell on the ground, got up, had a good look at it, decided it was a naval explosive device and then calmly spread for cover. But don't underestimate the effect on the Allied soldiers – hearing those big guns blasting was great for morale.'

Razeen points towards the south-east; our hazy view is full of the red, brown, white and blue containers that put the 'pot' into the entrepôt. 'That's Keppel Harbour and Tanjong Pagar. It means Cape of Stakes. Legend has it that Singapore was once attacked by a shoal of swordfish. A little boy suggested that they put up a wall of bamboo stakes to trap them. More likely there were fishing snares. You know what happened to the boy? They killed him because he was too smart! The boy was murdered and his blood painted the earth read on what we now called Redhill. There is an MRT station there.' He points west.

'You see those HDB flats?' he continues, this time pointing directly north. 'Everyone in Singapore lives in those flats. Chinatown, Kampong Glam: very few live there any more. Little India? That was named in the eighties with the building of the MRT station. The Indians originally lived by the river. By Dhoby Ghaut. Where are the old temples? In Chinatown next to the Chinese ones.'

He stops for us to ponder over this.

'Everyone in Singapore speaks two languages. At school we are taught English and one of the other official languages: Mandarin, Tamil or Malay. But we are not allowed to choose. We have to learn the language of our ethnic group.'

'And if it's a mixed marriage?' asks the American.

Razeen laughs. 'Your lineage is determined by your father. Which, in my case, was useless. I am a Peranakan Chinese. We are so integrated with the Malays, we have forgotten our Chinese. But I had to learn Mandarin although in my house I spoke Malay. That's written with the Latin alphabet. You write it down as you speak it. But Mandarin! It's impossible! I flunked it year after year.'

And with that he gives us a sign to get on the bus again. The driver has thankfully – or perhaps intentionally – left all doors and windows open, so my little adventure with the durian has been consigned to oblivion.

- 24 -

After a short drive, we get out at Labrador Park, where the chirrup of birds replaces the rattle and hiss of the cicadas. The erstwhile fort that used to be full of observation posts, gun turrets and ammunition stores has been turned into a park that is surprisingly serene for Singapore. Tall *ketapang* – sea-almond trees – stand defiantly on the rocks, right by the sea. They are semi-deciduous and some of their large, leathery leaves have turned red already providing a strange New England colour to the tropical landscape. Taller still, the *tulang daing* – purple millettias – give shelter to hanging lianas. Wild cinnamon and sea-grape bushes occasionally peep at us through the forested path, as we trundle along until we reach the fort's original casemates hidden under a wall of creeping ivy.

'The first fortification in Singapore was Fort Canning defending the old river port but when the new deep-sea harbour opened it was necessary to defend that. This is the entrance to what was Fort Pasir Panjang. Just before World War Two, it was reinforced and renamed the Labrador Battery, under Faber Command.'

He points at a bunker door. 'Until recently we knew of three bunkers, but if you look at this map, which we copied from the Public Records Office in London, you'll see a fourth one. I was a member of the archaeological team that tried to open it from there. The Parks Board refused, so we had to break through from the inside. What we found was that the ceiling had collapsed. We knew that some guns here had taken direct hits from airplanes – with the loss of three Indian gunmen – but the collapse of the walls showed that it had been blown up just before Percival surrendered.'

We walk on past a large *beringin* tree, the weeping fig. Malay lore has it that once the moon had fallen on the earth and animals and humans were wiped out except two males and one female who propped it back up in the sky using the trunk of a *beringin* tree. That's why its handsome bleached-grey bark looks like the face of our silvery satellite.

'I wonder if he would have given up so easily if he knew what would happen next: imprisonment, maltreatment, the

Death Railway. Percival had it easy; he ended up in a jail in Manchuria. When the Japanese themselves surrendered on the USS Missouri in Tokyo Bay, he was sitting right behind General MacArthur who gave Percival one of the pens he used for signing the surrender documents – nice gesture. Here in Singapore the situation was different, ladies and gentlemen: the Japanese were advertising an Asian co-prosperity sphere, but they lost the "co" on the way. One in five of the military would die in prison, but the figure for civilians was one in four.'

Soon after surrender, the Japanese rounded up the Chinese and butchered those they suspected might rise against them. Like Herod slaughtering the new-born infants, the biblical horror of this act lies in that conditional 'might'. The main aim of General Yamashita, the army commander, was to eliminate the surviving members of Dalforce, the volunteer regiment that fought bravely in the battle of Singapore and *might* become the focus of organised resistance to the occupation. On 21 February 1942, all Chinese males were ordered to gather at five assembly points where they were interrogated by the Kempeitai, the Japanese secret police (headquartered in the YMCA building on Orchard Road). Men were singled out for execution for reasons such as that they had tattoos (members of secret societies), could sign their names in English (pro-British) and being a schoolteacher (they are always dangerous). Lee Kuan Yew was also rounded up, but, showing the sharpness of thought that would characterise him later, he surreptitiously jumped off the lorry before it left. He did well: the men who were selected were taken to the beaches of Punggol, Changi, Tanah Merah, the island of Sentosa and the docks of Tanjong Pagar to be machine-gunned to death. A few survived the massacre, pretending to be dead and lived to tell us about the atrocities. The total number of Chinese executed in Singapore may never be known. In 1945, the Japanese War Office claimed 5,000, but a figure of 50,000 was put forward in the 1947 War Crime trials and is being considered as reasonable by modern historians.

We leave the tranquillity of Labrador Park for the traffic-choked streets of Alexandra, driving by some of the most expensive real estate in Singapore. This was a military residential area; the old barracks have been renovated and turned into flats. Everything here is a reminder of the melting pot of the old Empire: next to street names like Bury, Canterbury and Berkshire, a sign shows the way to Hyderabad Road. In this web of streets, perched on top of landscaped lawns and half-hidden by palm trees, are Edith's Black and White houses. They were built in the 1920s by merchants and administrators who transported the traditional half-timbered cottage design to the lush greenery of Singapore. Some of them are two-storey, the upper floor balancing itself on the base via wooden beams like a Tudor mansion on stilts. The beams make space for verandas that open on all sides providing air and light to the ground floor living rooms. Only company CEOs can afford them now.

'Only once did I enter one of those and saw how the other half lived,' comments Razeen wryly, as we drive away. 'Then I realised I was born in the wrong half.'

Just before Alexandra Hospital, he passes around a picture taken in 1938 when the building opened as the principal military hospital for British forces in the Far

East: a handsome, Mediterranean three-storey structure of austere elegance, looking more like a hotel than its function calls for.

'It's exactly the same as it was then,' I say.

Razeen jumps. 'Exactly! Ladies and gentlemen, look: the hospital has remained as it was in the war. Inside it has been modernised, but the exteriors are the same. And it is surrounded by tunnels and secret chambers. Now the government wants to close it and demolish it.'

*No!*

'The services will be transported to a new hospital that will be built in the north. Historians, of course complained, but the government has already decided its fate. Civil servants are not keen on preserving history. They even tore down Changi prison in 2005 to build a new maximum security prison. Only an original wall remains.'

He shakes his head.

'And now they are knocking down this hospital, despite what happened here on the fourteenth and fifteenth of February 1942.'

The Alexandra Hospital massacre started on the 14 February around 1 p.m. Japanese troops – having suffered many casualties in the battle of Opium Hill further up – stormed down in a rage and claimed they were being fired on from the hospital roof. Captain J. F. Bartlett came out, with red crosses sown on him and his hands held high, to make sure the soldiers respected the hospital. They fired at him at point-blank range. They then burst into the operating theatre, stabbed the medical officers who were performing an operation and bayoneted the patient who was under anaesthetic. We know this because Captain Smiley, the surgeon, survived despite suffering multiple stab wounds. The soldiers then rounded some 200 staff and walking wounded, tied them up together and squeezed them into three small huts where they left them overnight, having barricaded the doors and nailed the windows. Some of them collapsed and suffocated. The rest were marched off next day in twos and threes and bayoneted to death. The massacre sickened everyone including the Japanese, so much so that the division's commander, General Mutaguchi, conducted an enquiry and those responsible for the killings were executed.

'And now,' Razeen says, 'to Kranji.'

- 25 -

There are many soldiers in front of the Kranji cemetery steps. In full combat gear. With guns.

Razeen either ignores them or hasn't seen them yet as we park the minibus – their camouflage must have worked.

'Although Changi was a bigger camp and its graveyard greater, it was Kranji that was developed into a permanent war cemetery by the Commonwealth Graves Commission,' says Razeen, 'because the cemetery at Changi could not remain undisturbed. So the bodies were exhumed from all other places around the island and reburied here. Bodies also arrived from the cemetery in Saigon. Altogether about 4,500 people are buried here.'

Only now Razeen notices the soldiers. 'Let's join them,' he says. 'They are here for their graduation ceremony. You are lucky; this doesn't happen all the time.'

'Is there conscription in Singapore?' asks the curious American.

Indeed there is. Like in Switzerland, every male goes through basic training and is then called up once a year for training exercises until the age of 50. The north-western tip of the island, beyond Sungei Buloh belongs to the military and is permanently out of bounds, its features appearing on no map. Given Singapore's history of conflict and its geographical position – being squeezed between two larger neighbours – this is understandable. Would Kuwait have been so easily invaded, if it could call up every man under arms?

The soldiers congregate around the memorial while we walk between the well-tended grid of landscaped graves. Every headstone bears a name, regimental arms and an inscription with some 850 bodies still unidentified. I look down. 'Private J. C. Auton, 2/19 Infantry Battalion, 20th January 1942. Age 27'. Next to him lies 'Private R. Currey 2/20 Infantry Battalion, 10th February 1942. Age 22'. Like many others, his inscription simply says: 'His Duty Fearlessly And Nobly Done, Ever Remembered'. They were both Australian, from New South Wales. Among the crosses, there is the occasional Star of David: 'Private H. Sanders, 2/20 Infantry Battalion, 30th December 1942. Age 37'. No crescents, though; the Muslim soldiers are buried on the other side of the hill, forever facing Mecca. Most graves are of men, but there are also women: here is nurse Ruby Margaret Brooks, from Cambridge and next to her Diana Mary Cooper from Hitchin, both 23, both volunteers of the British Red Cross Society.

Razeen gathers us around a particular grave. It is that of Lieutenant Colonel Ivan Lyon who died on 16 October 1944, aged 29.

*Ivan Lyon?*

'Is there a commemorative plaque for him in the Presbyterian church on Orchard Road?' I ask.

'You've noticed it?'

*In what now seems another lifetime.*

'There are many heroes buried here and their story deserves to be told,' says Razeen. 'Major Ivan Lyon was a Scotsman who was attached to Z Unit – special operations – and who commandeered one of the most successful acts of sabotage during the war, Operation Jaywick, yes, named after the toilet cleaner. A group of eleven British and Australian commandos sailed from Australia in fishing boats and on 26 September 1943 they sneaked into Singapore harbour, paddling in small canoes. They attached magnetic limpet mines on several vessels that were moored there and sank seven Japanese transport ships. All returned successfully back to Australia.'

Razeen pauses. 'So why is his grave here?'

At the main memorial on top of the hill, the soldiers gather to hear a pep-up speech by what looks like a very young major. I hear him use the common adage that those who do not learn from history are doomed to repeat it.

'One year after operation Jaywick, Lyon volunteered for a repeat performance: Operation Rimau, which is Malay for tiger – after one of Lyon's tattoos. But this time the Japanese had learned their lesson and his team was spotted. They escaped on Merapas Island where two of them, Sub Lieutenant Gregor Riggs, another Scot, and Sergeant Colin Cameron, an Australian, stayed back to engage the enemy while the others tried to escape. They both died heroically on the island, but in vain. The Japanese ran in hot pursuit and eventually ten of the group were captured and the rest killed, including Ivan Lyon. Just one month before the final Japanese surrender those ten were executed as spies.'

The last post sounds from the soldiers' ceremony further up.

Razeen points at two tombstones. 'Look: here are those two who sacrificed themselves: Gregor Riggs and Colin Cameron. Their remains were found in 1994 on Merapas

Island. They were the last two military burials here at Kranji War Cemetery, on 27 August 1994.'

I check. They were both 21 when they died.

'And here, ladies and gentlemen, lies Rodney Breavington,' Razeen says. 'He was a true blue ANZAC: born in New Zealand, settled in Melbourne. He, and three others, another Australian and two British, escaped from their POW camp but were caught by the Japanese 200 miles out on a small boat.'

I know the story. Because of them, the whole of their division was asked to sign an oath that they would not try to escape. They refused. So the camp commander dragged the four escapees to Selerang Beach to make an example out of them. Before they were killed, Breavington stepped forward and asked the firing squad to kill him but save his mates. It was him, he said who was the mastermind of the escape; they were only executing his orders. The incident was captured in a poem, *The Corporal and His Pal,* part of Australian military folklore. The firing squad was symbolically made up of four nervous Sikhs who had defected to the Japanese. After they fired, one of the condemned stood up and pleaded: *'You have shot me through the arm. Please shoot me through the heart.'* The second volley hit him on the leg. He cried *'For God's sake, shoot through the HEART!'*

When the war was over and the war crime trials began, the Japanese commander who ordered their execution was shot on the same spot on Selerang Beach. Razeen shows us a picture: a corpulent, middle-aged man is tied to a pole, his trousers inside his well-polished high boots, stooped forwards, a hood over his head. The caption identifies him as Major General Shinpei Fukuye.

The soldiers are dispersing, as we approach the Singapore Memorial. A large semi-circular stone inscription explains:

On the walls of this memorial are recorded the names of twenty-four thousand soldiers and airmen of many races united in service to the British Crown who gave their lives in Malaya and neighbouring lands and seas and in the air over southern and eastern Asia and the Pacific but to whom the fortune of war denied the customary rites accorded to their comrades in death.

'Here,' says Razeen, 'are the names of the bodies that were never found.'

'Perished at sea?' asks the curious American.

'Many of them. But there are some that stand out.'

He goes and points to a name: 'Captain Patrick Heenan, the Singapore traitor.'

Let me take over once again. The fact that the Singapore Memorial wall bears the name of a court-martialled traitor is worth exploring if only for the Anglo-Saxon notions of innocence and guilt.

Captain Patrick Heenan was the illegitimate son of a Eurasian mining engineer and a girl from New Zealand where he was born in 1910. He grew up in Burma and, when his father died, his mother moved to London where she remarried. His stepfather was well-off and forked out the fees for Cheltenham College where Heenan joined the cadets. He became an officer in the Indian army's 2/16 Punjab Regiment and was posted in Malaya. His mixed parentage and dark skin colour appears to have been the target of overt racism in the British mess, so, disgruntled, he bought the Japanese pan-Asian propaganda directed against the British Empire; he seems to have turned into a double agent during a long holiday in Japan just before the war. Further unauthorised trips across the Thai border made his commanding officer suspicious, and he sought Heenan's removal from the

Punjabi Regiment. So where was this suspected spy moved to? But of course, to intelligence – Air Liaison to be exact, where he was promoted to second in command in a border post. No one seriously believes that the initial Japanese successes in the air were simply the result of information by Heenan, for there must have been other spies, too, but the fact remains that he was caught hiding a wireless transmitter in a Catholic padre's communion set. More incriminating maps and reports were found when his locker was searched. He was jailed in Changi prison; two days before Singapore fell, he was secretly court-martialled, taken out to the docks and shot in the head. His body has never been found.

Which is why his name is now on the memorial wall: there is no body and there exist no documents that prove his guilt; the fog of war has seen to that. The Singaporeans and their historians have no doubt, like Razeen, and there have been many attempts to wipe his name from the memorial. But as there was no confession, the Commonwealth Graves Commission in charge of the memorial wants irrevocable proof. I can't see why a conviction by a court-martial at the time isn't good enough.

The soldiers are preparing for the final ceremony. Rifles are being unloaded from a lorry and arranged on a table in a row. I approach and caress one rifle-butt as I would a lion. The Commander sees me and comes over. He is young, early thirties, and Razeen confirms my reading of the epaulets: this is *Major* Marcus Tan who greets me.

'A wonderful place to bring your soldiers, Sir,' I say half-respectfully, half-fearfully for I have been a bit too close to those weapons. But the major, assertive, self-confident and very congenial does not notice – or does not show it. He points at the conscripts standing saucer-eyed at ease, for whom the sense of occasion appears overwhelming.

'They're getting their rifles for the first time,' he says to me. 'I believe that this place enhances the significance of the ceremony. There are many brave men and women buried here.'

'I couldn't agree more, Sir,' I say, as martially as I can muster, and shake his hand firmly.

Jacky is waiting for me at Tantric. She buys me a pint.

'Heavy day,' I say. 'World War Two. Kranji.'

She's not interested.

'Did you meet Richard?' she asks instead.

'Yes.'

'And?'

I smile mischievously. 'It was good,' I reply.

'I'm glad you two got on so well together.'

I am not so sure. Richard has been cool since that first date and is always busy whenever I come into the bar – or rather busier than usual.

'Meet Tim,' says Jacky introducing a long-haired, bespectacled Caucasian who is standing next to her.

'Hi, I'm a geek,' he says to me and, as if in a rush to prove it, he tells me a joke. 'You look as if you are going to get this. No one else understands it.'

'Go on,' I tell him.

'Kurt Gödel, Werner Heisenberg and Noam Chomsky walk into a bar –'

'Hold on,' I stop him. 'Noam Chomsky I know. He defined formal grammars, cognitive psychology and that. Heisenberg is he of the Uncertainty Principle. But Gödel?'

217

SINGAPORE SWING

'He was a pioneer of mathematical logic,' Tim replies grinning. 'No one knows him, hehe.'

I have a bad feeling about the joke.

'Anyway,' he continues chirpily, 'Heisenberg looks around him, and says "What unusual company. And we're in a bar. I am certain that this is a joke, but I have no idea whether it's funny or not". Gödel considers the proposition for a minute, and replies "It could be. But in order to tell whether it really is, we'd have to know whether it was funny to someone outside the story, and as we're inside the story we'll never be able to know." At which point Chomsky interrupts "Of course it's a joke, you're just telling it wrong!"'

Jacky and I glance at each other as Tim pisses himself laughing.

'I like him,' I whisper. 'He's weird.'

'Me too,' she replies and squeezes my hand.

I take a good look at Tim who has gone to the bar.

'He's straight, isn't he?'

'Yep. But he's really cool.'

I tend to agree with her. 'Do you like him?'

She nods.

'A lot?'

She wriggles away.

'As a friend,' she whines. 'As a *friend*'.

I put a mental bookmark to follow this up while Tim returns with a bottle of champagne and a carafe.

'What's this?' I ask.

'A French 75,' he replies, and he clearly doesn't mean a vintage. 'Try it.'

'What's in it?' I ask.

'In the bottle? Gin, lemon juice and sugar.'

He half fills my flute glass with the lichen-coloured mix and tops it up with champagne. I taste it. A champagne sour if ever there was one, and very nice it is, too.

It doesn't take long to get me drunk on an empty stomach. So I don't know whether it is the effects of the French 75 or whether I really do see Dan walking through the door.

If it is him, he looks the perfect picture of health.

# CHAPTER TEN

# THE WISE OLD MAN

The Wise Old Man had lived at the edge of the village for what seemed like centuries. Even the wrinkliest inhabitants remembered how, as children, they used to pass by his hut part afraid, part curious, but always – always – respectful. Such deference arose not simply because the Wise Old Man was, well, *old*, but because he managed to live without possessions and without needs, surviving only by the charity of strangers. This was not any Wise Old Man: this was the wraith of an *arhat*; the exhalation of a true bodhisattva.

The Thief wasn't local; he had come from afar. He didn't know of the Old Man, of his station in this life and the next, of his suspected and expected holiness. What the Thief knew was that this hut, casting a ghostly silhouette under the bold full moon was situated away from the village. Even if its occupants were not asleep, they could summon little help by shouting.

The Thief kicked the door in. It fell on the floor, broken, unused to sudden lurches. The Thief entered and checked his surroundings.

There was nothing inside.

No, not nothing worth stealing; *nothing*. No bed, no sheets, no table, no clothes, not even an empty rice bowl.

*Does anyone live here?* wondered the Thief. *Someone must, because it's clean. And the door was closed properly.*

Behind him, he heard steps.

He turned around abruptly only to confront a wizened old face with a long white beard and a bald head that reflected the moonlight like a lamp.

The Thief saw the Wise Old Man and spat down in disgust. *The hut of a beggar.* This was not his lucky night.

The Wise Old Man knelt down and caressed the fallen door.

'I was looking at the stars,' he said apologetically.

The Thief pushed him aside and walked out without uttering a word.

'Wait!' cried the Wise Old Man.

The Thief stopped but did not turn around.

'You came here to rob me and found nothing. I can't let you go like this.'

The Thief made a half turn, his face questioning the beggar with the corner of his eye.

*A beggar who was taking off his rags and who stood in front of him as naked as he'd appeared from his mother's womb.*

'Here, take these,' said the Wise Old Man. 'Take my clothes. They're the only things I've got.'

The Thief stood there watching the sorry collection of skin and bones that stood in front of him, his lower lip trembling.

'TAKE THEM!' This time the voice of the Wise Old Man was masterful, commanding.

Part afraid, part curious, but always – always – respectful, the Thief took the Wise Old Man's rags and bowed down deeply until his elbows touched his knees. And then, with a swift gait, he left in the direction he had arrived.

The Wise Old Man's eyes followed the Thief's shadow as it slowly fused with the farthest darkness. Then, when there was no movement left to follow, he sat down and stared at the silver disk up in the sky.

'Poor man,' he whispered. 'How I wish I could have given him this moon.'

### - 26 -

'A combination of egos and too long in power. A whole generation has grown up not knowing any alternative. It no longer occurs to anyone to speak out of turn.'

I'm back at the Raffles, having a coffee at the Empire Café and doing the unthinkable: talking politics with Singapore's most distinguished human rights activist, Alex Au, who has just characterised Singapore's leaders.

'Now, this is not really serious research. But I've noticed that one-party governments whether elected or not, tend to last for seventy years at most. It's some king of magic number. The Soviet Union. The PRI in Mexico. The Kuomintang in China, then Taiwan.'

So when is Singapore due a change?

He thinks for a second and he bursts out laughing: 'Good God, 2030.'

I expected someone who corresponded to *Private Eye*'s image of 'Spart': one-issued, tunnel-visioned, humourless. I had not bargained for an individual who is warm, witty and very intensely human.

'You can't take life too seriously,' he responds.

Although middle-aged, he can convincingly cut two decades off his age; I tell him that. He chooses to ignore it.

'Lee Kuan Yew – how old is he now? He had his eightieth birthday a few years ago and,' he pauses ominously, 'his father died around the age of a hundred. But physically he is frail. The change is visible. Of course, that doesn't mean people are not *frightened* of him.'

I wonder how many streets are they going to name after him when he dies.

Alex laughs. 'People will be confused! Look at how many Raffles places we have. The airport will go first.'

The jokes underline one fact. For someone whose personal signature is all over Singapore, Lee Kuan Yew has kept a remarkably low profile: not even a stamp bears his portrait. Those who call him a dictator don't know enough about dictatorships.

Although now dubbed a 'human rights activist' by *The Straits Times*, Alex started as a gay activist. He is the intrepid Yawning Bread, the author of the website I discovered at Changi airport, who has been criticising the government for more than a decade: like my Singapore Paranormal Investigators, he's another online character whom I just had to meet in person.

I tell him that his blogs are extremely well-written.

He thanks me with that permanent disarming smile. 'I know the government reads them. And *The Straits Times*. To get story ideas.'

I admire him. Not only because of his incisive commentary, but also because of his courage; this is Singapore, not Sydney.

'It doesn't take much courage,' he says. 'In the beginning my blog was more involved with gay issues. Over time, I have become more political. How many times can you write about gay marriage? After a while you've lost the public. But I suppose I've also changed myself. The entries were shorter in the beginning. They are longer now: more serious, less partisan.'

Is he not afraid?

'After ten years I think I know very well where the lines are. And because I think I know where the lines are, I feel safe that I won't trip myself up. The most gratifying thing is that it's not just me. Other people in the gay community watch what I do and use me as an example of what *they* can do. They say: if Alex can write that, then I can, too, *lah*. I hope that I function as some kind of catalyst, because the most vulnerable position for any community to be in is to have only one leader. If that leader disappears, then that's it. In Singapore's gay community there are many leaders now doing different things – though not necessarily in sync with each other.'

He laughs again.

'Singapore can be a fascinating little place. When I look around South East Asia, this bloody little city seems to be in the lead. Everybody wants to form his own gay group. We even have a gay, non-denominational church. They have no money, of course, so they operate out of a large room near a cinema that regularly screens low-brow sexually-titillating films. Halfway through their Sunday services if you excuse yourself to go to the loo, you are cruised.'

Alex has long been the face of People Like Us, the country's first – though not last – gay organisation. Unlike SPI they are unregistered. Singapore's bureaucrats may be ready to embrace the paranormal but are terrified to regularise the habitual.

'We applied twice for registration, but the authorities turned the application down. And in Singapore it is a criminal offence to be a member of an illegal organisation, a law from the time of the secret societies. But now with the AIDS epidemic, they need us. So a minister invited me – and others – for an informal chat. The day before, his PA called me to ask me what my name tag should say, so I told her. And when I arrived, there it was: "Alex Au, People Like Us". There I was, a member of an organisation that is not supposed to exist, discussing AIDS measures with a minister. What do you call that?'

Absurd?

'I call it pragmatic. When they need us, they don't care about the rules.'

But the rules are there to catch them out, if ever the authorities want to.

Alex nods sagely. 'I'll tell you something really absurd. I had organised a public poetry reading once, and we had to submit every word of every poem for vetting. Now, poets being flurry creatures, in the last minute some went, "I don't want to read *this* poem, I'll read *another*" or they changed the order or whatever. So we were concerned, because there were two persons at the back checking what was being recited. But did anything happen? No.'

I abhor censorship.

'You'll like this, then. As you know Singapore retains the death penalty for several offences. Someone organised a play in December 2005 about the death penalty. They had the permit, they had weeks of rehearsals, everything. Just by chance, the opening night was the day after a very high-visibility hanging. I think it was a Vietnamese Australian who was caught smuggling drugs. So the MDA – Media

Development Authority, how Orwellian is that? – withdrew the licence. But – and here the fun starts – they also tried to be helpful and expedited the approval of a new play that was written hastily, two days before it was scheduled to be performed.'

*Two days.* Was that enough time?

'That's the point. They couldn't. And they had sold tickets, they had committed themselves to renting the theatre space and so on. The playwright wrote a play about a father–son relationship within 48 hours but they had no time to rehearse it.'

I fall over laughing – it sounds so comical.

'Yes, it was funny. Every single line was whispered from the sides and the actors repeated it. Which served a different purpose: it was as if some unseen power was telling them what to say and what not to, which is what had happened in reality. So, a play about the death penalty was turned into another play about censorship.'

How very Ionesco.

'This was truly absurd, yes. But normally they are pragmatic in the way they do things. For instance, there was a case once of HIV transmission from mother to baby during pregnancy. Now, there is evidence from clinical studies that if HIV drugs are administered to a pregnant woman early on, there is a very good chance that the baby will be born virus-free. So they passed a law that every woman who shows up in a maternal clinic *must* be tested for HIV.'

*The means justify the ends?*

'Do you know how they dealt with the SARS epidemic? With a surveillance camera mounted in your home! It worked like this: I serve you a notice of quarantine that you must stay in your room for seven days. How do I check on you? Answer: I install a video camera in your living-room and, on unexpected moments, an officer who sits in an air-conditioned office miles away, dials you number: "Mrs Lim, please tell all six members of your family to come and smile." They all parade in front of the camera. "Thank you Mrs Lim. Sorry for the disturbance." Now the officer can call at any time. If you think the UK is bad with all these CCTV cameras on the streets, what do you say to that?'

I don't know. What does one do?

'I don't know either whether to defend it or not, but it worked. We were free from SARS.'

*The Singapore way.*

### - 27 -

The waiter has arrived and I can't help noticing that fried carrot cake is on the menu. I chuckle: 'It sounds like something the Scots could have concocted,' I say to Alex and proceed to explain the toe-curling concept of deep-fried Mars Bars. I can tell he is bewildered.

'It's nothing like that,' he protests. 'It's not sweet and there's no carrots. It's like a pancake with shrimps and radish. Quite tasty'

I am feeling brave, so I order it, along with *char kway teow*, a local dish of fried flat noodles with soy, chilli and prawns. The search for the perfect *char kway teow* in Singapore is akin with the one for the Holy Grail, what with everyone recommending this hawker stall and that; let's give Raffles a try.

Like two conspirators, we wait for the waiter to leave before we continue talking about Singapore's reputation. 'Singapore deserves a *mixed* reputation, and it gets a *bad* reputation,' Alex says.

I agree that it's grossly undeserved. Some unfortunate decisions like banning the importation of chewing gum, were picked up heavily by the media. Guess what – we now have similar laws in London regarding littering streets with chewing gum: penalty £1000. Is Singapore leading the way? I ask in jest.

Alex jumps on my comment. 'Yes! Where did your mayor get the idea about electronic road pricing? Your Oyster Card – isn't it based on our ez-link card? And didn't Tony Blair introduce detention without trial?'

Singapore has been branded as a preserve of intolerance, but what I see is different; there is a lot of tolerance in the city-state judging by its people *and* its leadership.

'The problem here,' he says 'is that the PAP treats its direct opponents very badly. They were detained without trial, they have no voice in the mainstream media, they are hit with defamation suits... But it doesn't mean that the government treats its *citizens* badly. The distinction is too fine for the Western media and it sells no papers. "Lee Kuan Yew as a tyrant" sells.'

I agree. I have read a university thesis positing that Raffles is being brandied as the creator of Singapore and its previous Malay past expunged, because it makes it easier for the people to accept a one-man-leadership in modern times: Lee Kuan Yew's. The idea might appeal in the confines of an academic ivory tower, but it makes no sense on the field. Just a short walk in town will demonstrate that Singaporeans have not averted their gaze from their pre-Raffles past – the opposite is true: excavations, exhibitions and plaques seek to shed light on its pre-colonial history, obsessively one might say.

Alex looks at his hands which he keeps binding and unbinding together.

'People email me and ask me "What shall I do at customs when I arrive in Singapore. What can I bring? What CDs? What DVDs?"'

I snigger. I have seen my own books displayed in bookshops. I have seen some dissidents' books, too. Travel guides warn you that if customs find any books in your luggage, they can charge you $75 – the administrative cost for the censors to read them for approval. Then, when you arrive, they wave you through.

'Exactly. The point is, the laws are there and can be used to threaten you so you exercise self-control. They're not really after you. They want the penalty to be there, so that you worry about it. They want you to control yourself so that they don't have to control you, but the moment you free yourself from that worry, you are a lot more liberated.'

There is one thing that can enhance Singapore's reputation: its multicultural character and the success it has in race relations. Lee Kuan Yew tried hard to forge a sense of nationhood after the riots and the split with Malaysia, what with competitions to find a national flower and all, but he succeeded.

'They tried very hard. There was a time – I would think something like the late 1970s early 1980s – when they decided they had to invent a National Costume.' Alex falls back laughing. 'The Malays had one, the Indians had one, the Scots had one, why the Greeks have one don't they? So they decided that Singapore must have its own National Costume. And they came up with this Hawaiian shirt with orchids all over the place: utterly gaudy – so effeminate looking. It was sold in shops all over town. No one bought it. They all went bust.'

I chortle.

'They were trying very hard. I remember: the competition for the national flower and then came the national floral shirt. More like the great national embarrassment. Not one of their better ideas.'

## - 28 -

The waiter arrives with our orders. I check the fried carrot cake. It looks like an omelette with prawns and white radish. It tastes fantastic and I'm a little disappointed; the only food whose reputation is deserved, must surely be the durian.

I move to the subject of nationhood: Singapore seems to have succeeded where others failed dismally. Look at the Balkans and former Yugoslavia. They couldn't stand each other –

'...although they had to live together.'

How very true. They were forced to choose, they had to *belong*. I mean, what makes a country? Can it be manufactured? Before partition Pakistan didn't think of itself as separate from India.

'You know the origin of the name Pakistan?'

I thought it was the Land of the Pure.

'Not quite. It is an acronym. They put together the initials of the Muslim provinces. "P" for Punjab, "a" for the Afghan areas of the region, "k" for Kashmir, "s" for Sind and "tan" for Baluchistan, thus forming "Pakstan". The "i" was added in the English rendition of the name. The word also captured in the Persian language the concepts of "pak", meaning "pure", and "stan", meaning "land" thus giving it indirectly the meaning "Land of the Pure".'

Alex sits back smugly.

'They invented it! And you know what? Do you know there are Muslim Indians here in Singapore?'

There are, in Farrer Park, around the Mustafa Centre.

'Correct. Some of them are from South India and they still identify as Tamil, but most of them are from Northern India and their forefathers migrated before the break-up. But now they are starting to say: I'm Pakistani. How can that be? Your forefathers didn't come from Pakistan 'cos Pakistan didn't exist when your forefathers disembarked from the boat. That notion of Pakistani/Singaporean: where did it come from? The concept would have been alien to their grandfather who came from "India".'

People are forced to identify.

'Exactly.'

Still, I come to Singapore and I observe how people of different races exist side by side in harmony. In order to make this explosive mixture – mainly the Malays and the Chinese – live together, an identity had to be forged – and was. How did they do it? By force? Did economic success bind communities? What will happen in a slump?

Alex writhes in his seat.

'We are generally *civil* to each other,' he corrects me. 'I don't know if we live in harmony, but we are civil to each other. Have you tried to get a seat on an MRT train? Civility there goes out of the window!'

I know, but by hook or by crook, the PAP have achieved something.

'It is a question of practicalities, and yes there are many things that are wrong. But there are things that are very good,' he concedes.

I want to hear about those Singapore successes; maybe there are lessons to be learned for us in Britain. Many immigrants have arrived and very suddenly. We have a second generation of Muslims, some of whom are rejecting the values of the country they were born in. Plus we are crammed. Not as much as Singapore, but we are becoming more crammed, nevertheless. So guess what? The government is starting to micromanage the social relations – just like Singapore does. Has Alex heard of ASBOs?

'What's that?'

They are Antisocial Behaviour Orders. If someone is behaving 'antisocially' then a magistrates' court can order them not to approach a specific area. They impose a curfew. Some are extreme; one 17-year-old in Wales has been banned from the very street he lives in. So he can't use his front door and is only allowed to use a footpath leading to the back of his house.

Alex laughs. 'That's new to me. We haven't gone that far yet.'

I lean back, my mind spinning with theories. The more we grow in population and diversity, the more we seem to be imitating the ways of a country the Western press used to deride. Maybe there is no other way forward, but Singapore's.

Alex sits up. 'It may be politically incorrect to say that, but the reality is that people are not naturally nice to each other. Some degree of management has to be put in place until people learn to see the other person as the same kind as them. And I can tell you that we have such an example in Singapore's history. When the Chinese migrants came here in large numbers – that would have been the latter decades of the nineteenth century, the early decades of the twentieth – people didn't come here as Chinese. They came here as Cantonese, as Hokkien, Teochew and so on, because they spoke mutually unintelligible languages. They couldn't even call a dish the same name. The city itself was ghettoised. There was a Cantonese area, a Hokkien area – here from the corner up was the Hainanese area – settlers from the island of Hainan. And if you were a Teochew straying into the Hainanese ghetto you were an alien. People used to identify themselves by the province.'

He stops to drink some water. Alex doesn't drink alcohol. He is not a teetotaller, but he's not a great liquor fan either, avoiding it whenever he can.

'After the overthrow of the last emperor, there was a surge of Chinese nationalism. The Chinese intellectuals said: "In order to make ourselves a country we need to unify these various provinces" – we are now talking mainland China. So they created the national language out of nowhere. The Mandarin you hear is a created language. It is based on the Peking high dialect. But it wasn't spoken elsewhere like that – it was imposed. Because in the old days, when there was no technology, the Chinese communicated by letters, by script. People could read the words and they were the same everywhere. But if I read a letter aloud to you and I was Cantonese and you were Hokkien, you would not understand. Chinese script was perfect for running an empire: we don't have to speak the same language as long as the same written character means the same to you and me. But to create a nation, they had to create a unified pronunciation – and they chose the Mandarin pronunciation of Peking – *Beijing*, see?'

Like Israel and Hebrew.

'Here in Singapore we were swept up in this wave of Chinese republicanism and nationalism and the community leaders – the Hokkien community, the Cantonese community, the Teochew community – changed their schools *on their own* from being dialect-teaching to Mandarin-teaching. This happened in the 1930s. Starting from that period, there was a melting down of the barriers between the various communities. Once you have a Hainanese boy who is able to speak Mandarin and a Hokkien girl who is also able to speak Mandarin, they start falling in love. They intermarry and the barriers between the communities break down. And because the only communication they can have between each other is in Mandarin, the children are raised as Mandarin-speaking. Three generations later, people do not identify themselves as Hokkien or as Cantonese but as Chinese. That change has happened.'

So it wasn't the PAP that imposed Mandarin as part of its great nation-building exercise?

'No, the Mandarin schools preceded government action. There was some official intervention: the PAP government banned dialect-teaching altogether. Much later, in the 1980s –'

*The period of forging nationhood...*

' – they changed the Mandarin schools to English schools. I'm talking to you in English, am I not? How did that happen? The PAP killed the Mandarin schools because it needed to create a country that went beyond the Chinese community. Just blending the Chinese provinces was not enough. They had to include the Indians and the Malays and the Arabs and the Thais and the Europeans. It had to be English.'

In England we allow faith schools, we allow instruction, court interpreters, social security leaflets in other languages...

'When you are dealing with first generation immigrants you have no choice. But you need to know when not to overdo it; it would be foolish to encourage it into the second and third generation. I'll tell you something else. People in Little India, Chinatown, Kampong Glam, they don't live there. They go there to work. They go there to shop because they can buy the spices and all. Singaporeans live in public housing – the vast majority anyway. Do you know we have race quotas for public housing?'

*What?*

'Race quotas. In any given block you have to have 75 per cent Chinese and so on, to reflect at neighbourhood level the country's ethnic mix. You are not allowed as an individual to choose too much, because they know that people like to live among their own kind. And this is the way to create ghettos. You don't want a situation when, during some unrest, you can clamp down and barricade the streets.'

We had riots in Bradford, we had riots in Brixton…

'Or in France? In Singapore, they don't allow this situation to occur. Living with racial quotas is easier for the majority than the minority of course. But I am not sure that there are any other, softer ways of achieving the same thing. It is very illiberal: "you can not live there, there's far too many of you there," kind of thing, but I would be hard pressed to offer an alternative myself.'

That Singaporean way again.

'And we have not had any riots. Whereas in Europe where there were separate Serb and Croat villages and areas in town, there was a descent to barbarism. Everyone was behaving like animals when, as you say, they were forced to identify. So maybe there is something to be said for micromanagement of social relations. The question is of course, where you stop. At what depth you go with this.'

So the lessons are that we should acquiesce to ASBOs, break up any ghettos and promote English as a unifier?

Alex grins in anticipation. 'Not always. I overheard something in town today. There was a massage parlour. I saw this doorman doing business with a tourist and the tourist was a difficult customer to sell to. He wasn't so interested and the doorman was trying to entice him. Now, what he meant to say was, "I will give you a 30-minute massage for 20 dollars," which we all understand and makes sense. But it came out wrong. What he actually said was, "If you take the 30-minute massage, I give you 20 dollars."'

Hehe.

'This is also what happens in multicultural societies. People speak in a broken language all the time. Misunderstandings are waiting to happen.'

What about Muslim fundamentalist extremism, I wonder.

'It is one thing that is worrying this government – the Christian–Muslim, hmm, *chasm* if you like.'

They can't do much there. Unless they invent a new religion.

'Don't give them ideas! You know we have three prime ministers in government? The actual prime minister, Lee Kuan Yew's son, Senior Minister Goh Chok Tong and the Minister Mentor Lee Kuan Yew himself. We already have a political trinity. They're on their way.'

I cringe. *The Father, the Son and the Holy Goh.*

'We have political humour even here, you know.'

What about the PAP itself? In the 1950s and the 1960s they were a very progressive force. At some point what was progressive became the establishment and as a result, repressive. When did they lose their direction?

'They haven't lost their direction! I think you are underestimating their ability to adapt to change. The direction is different now than it was ten years ago and certainly twenty years ago. They are evolving. They maybe evolving in a direction we don't like, but they are. They could not keep their grip on power if they were as monolithic and as unyielding as, say, the Brezhnev-era Soviets. Certain things are non-negotiable but many others are.'

What are the non-negotiables?

'You should not insult their ego. You should not cause offence to their sense of honour and reputation. Do not ever accuse them of corruption or nepotism. But what appears non-negotiable now might appear negotiable five years from now. For instance, control of the media. They had no choice there – because of the Internet they had to have a re-think.'

And gay rights?

'Well, they are in the process now of updating the penal code. They had an item there which criminalised any kind of non vaginal sex including oral sex: if it doesn't produce babies it was criminal. So they decided that times have changed, and they will repeal that section. But only if it is a female that is sucking your cock. The gay equivalent, which they call gross indecency between males, they will retain as a criminal act. But they said they will not be enforcing it. You see, they want to have their cake and eat it. They give you enough so that you are partly satisfied, but they won't make you happy at the expense of another lobby group.'

The other lobby group being?

'The American evangelical churches. Christians have much too much power in Singapore.'

Of yes, the humble servants of God. If, like Raffles' parish priest, they could quote from the Bible to judge the emancipation of slaves 'unchristian', what are the chances they are now infallible towards homosexuality? I shake my head. Pity. The government could lead the way. They have done in other areas.

'You are right. It is lack of leadership. What are they afraid of?'

Who else is there except the PAP?

'Absolutely. They would win any election. On their record, they deserve to win, and I would not begrudge them this. But because they haven't seriously contested any, they have lost the knack of persuasion – to go out there and win people over for their manifesto. They have sued and contained the opposition, so they have not had to justify what they're doing and come clean. There's a lot of spin and little transparency and this, in my opinion, degrades the honesty and integrity of public discourse.'

They just have to open up and trust the electorate.

'Exactly. Because we are a little hypocritical in Singapore. On one hand we don't like the government, we don't like the laws, but on the other hand we appreciate the passport when we are on the fast lane abroad. The Singaporean passport is very valuable. Because everyone knows that our laws are very strict, when I cross borders they never check my luggage. They know I would never smuggle anything not just drugs. But if I had a Thai passport I would get inconvenienced at airports. With the Singaporean passport I sail through: UK, Australia, everywhere. We dress well, we look middle class, we have the air of Australian Chinese; there is a certain confidence. So the customs officers think that if they are going to spend time, they had better spend it checking the guy from Indonesia or Thailand.'

As we prepare to leave – and hopefully warm our bones that have been frozen stiff like ramrods from the air con – Alex sees a couple he knows who are eating at a table on the way out. He goes over and greets them.

'Do you know everyone in this town?' I needle him afterwards.

'Singapore is a small city,' he says, 'and I have a high public profile. But sometimes I wonder. Some years ago I went to Bangkok on holiday with a friend who wasn't 'out' at the time. I took him to a gay bar and, as we came in, there were cries of "Alex! Hey! Hi Alex" from every corner. My friend was shocked. "I'm not going on holiday with you again," he complained. "Might as well have come out publicly at Raffles Place."'

Not for the first time during the night, I burst out laughing.

# CHAPTER ELEVEN

# THE MISSING PIECE

Let's have a story with mindless violence and no deep message for a change.

Sultan Mahmud Shah was lying on a sofa in his veranda listening to the melodious airs of his *merbok*. The mullahs in his court alleged that some of these birds recite whole suras from the Qur'an, but in all his time listening to his prize-winning bird he had not been able to make any out.

He rolled over and picked a rambutan from his fruit tray. A lot of things were on his mind. His sultanate of Johore-Riau was being attacked by pirates and his faithful admiral, the Laksamana, was dealing with the problem, but he had been away from the capital, Kota Tinggi, for three months with no news. The Sultan couldn't make up his mind whether no news was good news or not. He leaned on his side and picked on a large *nangka* fruit, when suddenly a piece fell off.

The Sultan examined it carefully. A square portion had been cut and patched back in place, but underneath the flesh had been eaten.

*Was it poison?*

The Sultan clapped his hands and asked for his Bendahara. He, in turn, called for the kitchen master who ate the fruit trembling but survived, so it was quickly established that no poison was involved.

The royal gardener was next to be summoned.

The Sultan and the Bendahara had no doubts as to the identity of the culprit when the gardener entered the audience room on his knees and looked up ashen-faced.

'Forgive me, Your Majesty,' the poor wretch said. 'I was only being kind to a pregnant lady from your harem. She asked me to cut a piece and give it to her because she had a craving for *nangka*.'

The Sultan and the Bendahara exchanged glances. There was no pregnant wife or concubine in the Sultan's harem; the lack of an heir was one of the problems that taxed the Sultan's mind.

'Search the palace for a pregnant woman,' ordered the Bendahara, second-guessing the Sultan, 'and have her confront the gardener.' Within an hour, a well-heeled gentlewoman in an advanced state of pregnancy was forcibly thrown at their feet crying and begging for mercy.

'She has confessed Your Majesty,' said the one of the guards. 'She was the one who ate the fruit.'

Mahmud Shah rose. He was furious at being fed leftovers from his own garden.

'Have the gardener beheaded,' he said, 'and as for this woman: slice her open and retrieve the missing piece of *nangka* from her belly.'

In spite of protestations at his harsh pronouncement – some arising from the appalled Bendahara himself – Mahmud Shah retreated to his veranda to listen to the song of his favourite *merbok* wondering again what the fate of his Laksamana was.

Not long after, he received the news: his admiral's ship had arrived and initial reports were positive, speaking of a routing of pirates around the islands of Bintan and Temasek. A jubilant Sultan gave notice that he would be holding a formal audience with his brave naval commander in three days' time and lay on the sofa in his veranda, occupying himself with thoughts, while listening to his *merbok* –

His *merbok*?

The bird was silent.

Mahmud Shah stood up and approached the cage with trepidation. The bird, was lying on its back, no breath disturbing the tiger-like stripes on its belly. A piece of *nangka* lay half-pecked by his side.

*Was it poison?*

He clapped his hands, but instead of his servants, his Laksamana appeared. Alone. He was holding a long *kris* that had seen recent action in the South Seas.

Mahmud Shah fell back on his sofa, in shock. He clapped his hands more loudly. 'Guards!' he shouted. 'GUARDS!'

'They will not hear you,' said the Laksamana. 'They are all dead. Killed by my men who are standing watch around the palace.'

'In the name of Allah,' cried Mahmud Shah, 'rising against your ruler is blasphemy! Cursed be your children to the seventh generation – if they ever set foot on Kota Tinggi, let them die vomiting blood!'

The *Laksamana* moved closer and stuck his *kris* into Mahmud Shah's stomach.

'My children?' he shouted, as he worked the dagger's curves all the way to the Sultan's belly and below. 'That's for my wife and unborn child that you killed on a whim.'

The last thing Mahmud Shah saw before he died screaming were his intestines, pulled out and smeared with the flesh of *nangka* fruit.

- 29 -

Ah, what a hoot!

The one-hour catamaran journey from the lateritic cliffs of Tanah Merah to the scenic island of Bintan was at best choppy, at worst gut-chundering. The monsoon was blowing on our side and the waves were devouring our stem. I was at the front with three Australians enjoying this unexpected bronco ride in spite of repeated motion sickness checks by the crew, but as far as we were concerned they could charge extra for the roller coaster fun. One of the Aussies was man enough to drink a couple of tinnies without spilling the contents from the can, let alone once they had disappeared down his gullet. Only when we arrived at Bintan and got up unsteadily did we realise that about two dozen rows divided us from the rest of the groggy passengers who had squeezed pell-mell into the back.

*But that's in the past*, I think blithely, and the jolly smile on my lips seems summarily ill-placed, as I am confronted with Indonesian passport control who are most certainly not laughing. They are working in threes. The first studies your picture and looks at you, the second stamps your visa, and the last one interrogates you.

'Born in Athens, Sir?'

'Yes.' (It's best to be as monosyllabic as possible at borders).

'And your British passport was issued in *La Paz*?'

'Yes.' (Don't ask, dear reader, don't ask).

I offer no further explanation and they frown.

'Where are you staying in Bintan?'

'Banyan Tree Resort.'

'Expensive isn't it?'

I shrug my shoulders. I am a guest there.

After what appears to be an interminable interval, the officer stamps my passport with a surly grimace, and I enter Indonesia.

Bintan Island – about the same size and shape as Lesbos in Greece – was one of the main centres of the Johore-Riau sultanate, being considered as an alternative to Singapore until the Dutch moved in. Even its subsequent history is fascinating: it became a centre of Muslim learning and scholars published a grammar of the local language which, for this reason, is considered as the 'purest' Malay in the whole of the archipelago. Its position has led to a constant flow of Singaporean investment in the north, where a resort section has been cordoned off from the rest of the island. Ironically it was in this part, facing Singapore, that artillery was based during the Konfrontasi; what a difference four decades make. The extent of the island division hits me when my Nissan 4WD stops at a private checkpoint and the security guards use a mirror to check for bombs underneath the car. Once inside the guarded perimeter the luxury surrounding me is unreal. I pass through a magnificent 18-hole golf course, designed by none other than Greg Norman, that can double as a birdwatching site. I catch a glimpse of a yellow bittern before a silver leaf monkey nonchalantly crosses the road and monopolises my attention.

A German girl on work experience is dealing with my passports, my rides, my maps and my visas. She welcomes me with a sweet, fermented ginger-and-lime drink. 'Until I came here, I hadn't heard anything about Bintan,' she admits. 'It's the best-kept secret in Asia.'

If the Germans haven't discovered this island, then it is very exclusive, indeed.

'The clientele is mostly Singaporeans, but somehow we also have a lot of Koreans and quite a few Japanese. Some Russian millionaires, too.'

*It is Western Europe's loss,* I think, as I am being driven to my villa in an electric golf-cart. The sun setting over the South China Sea through the palm trees and the tall, thick banyans is spectacular. I nearly swallow my tongue when I see my villa. It is perched on a hill and shaped like an Indonesian longhouse. It is set well apart, so that I can fill my open-air jacuzzi and swim in it naked, scandalising no one but the roosting birds. I could live here forever. I have a four-poster bed with mosquito netting with a spray of orchids spread on my sheets; a DVD player and satellite TV; and a large teak wardrobe with 'his and hers' kimonos. In the bathroom a tub is chiselled into the marble floor with various shampoos, soaps and conditioners in Laura-Ashley inspired and Thai-manufactured ceramic urns. Packets of tissues, toilet paper, even joss sticks are wrapped in floral, embroidered pouches. I take a shower and ask myself why the soap bar isn't foaming until I realise that it is cellophane-wrapped so tightly, I didn't notice. I dry myself in towels that are large enough to serve as queen-size duvets and speculate whether they have been individually pre-fluffed by an army of maids. (I am not too far off: next morning I count three persons working on my room plus, of course, the gardener). I open the window to catch the last, limpid rays of the sunset and admit to myself that this must be the most honeymoony place I know. No wonder the waiters at the restaurant – one of three tending me – keep asking whether my wife will join me later.

As I lie on the bed, I reflect on a line from the Venezuelan film *Secuestro Express* where a kidnapped well-off woman asks one of her captors: 'Why me? I volunteer in a hospital for poor children. I'm one of the good guys,' and he answers back promptly: 'Half of this city is starving and you go about driving a flashy car and you expect that people won't hate you for that?'

Let the pangs commence tomorrow when I venture out.

## - 30 -

Deva is a slim, intelligent 23-year-old Sumatran who is so thin that, had he been born in Milan or Paris, he would be making a career on the catwalk. Instead, an accident of birth has determined that he should live on Bintan to make his fortune in the tourist business. He needs to: although his scraggy, undeveloped body still looks that of a teenager's, he has a Javanese wife and two babies to feed in a village outside the resort perimeter. Once we pass the guards, the contrast is immediate; gone are the lush, first-class villas and in come the long, faceless bungalows of Pasar Oleh Oleh, some of them dormitories of the resort's staff.

Deva is driving me to Tanjung Pinang about one-and-half hours down the island; his eight hour day including car hire and petrol costs me 30 quid. I find out later that this is the average income of the locals per month.

Deva's English is passable – did he learn it from school? No, from his brother who works here, I manage to understand.

His father sent him to a religious school to study the Qur'an. For three hours a day, they had to speak only Arabic. He tells me this and slaps his thigh.

'But in hotel, tourist no speak Arabic! Tourist speak English, Japanese, Korean. My brother speak Korean. A lot of money, Korean,' he says laughing with his tongue against his teeth.

It was then we hit our first hole in the road. The road within the resort confines and over to the dormitory village of Pasar Oleh Oleh is excellent; beyond there, it becomes narrower and windier like a god-forsaken country lane in the Scottish Highlands. The landscape changes from thick forest to plantation – pineapple, banana or rubber tree – to scattered bush as we travel south. The only constant in the horizon is the outline of Gunung Bintan, the 1,000-foot high mountain surrounded by primary rainforest. Local companies offer a trek up to the summit, where climbers are rewarded with a 360-degree view all the way to Singapore. Much that I try to imagine the splendour, the state of the tarmac monopolises my attention. Most of the other road users travel on scooters and swerve around the road holes; we don't and as a result, our suspension and bone cartilage take a beating. The occasional motorbike balancing timber in the back pannier also becomes a major obstacle as the surrounding vegetation reduces the visibility. And all this time I am contemplating the alternative. Is this what Singapore would be like, if Raffles had chosen Bintan as his base?

We pass several Chinese factories. Until recently the Chinese had kept a very low profile in Indonesia. During Suharto's 32 years in power, their organisations, schools and language were banned. The great communist purge in that 'Year of Living Dangerously' resulted in hundreds of thousands of Chinese being murdered: in the sixties almost all communists were Chinese, though certainly the reverse wasn't true. Post-Suharto, there has been a flourishing of Chinese culture but they are still considered as foreigners by the locals.

'Chinese good in business, no?' Deva says. 'Many Chinese in Bintan.'

'How many?'

'Mmm, sixty per cent,' he replies without thinking. 'Tanjung Pinang more.'

I checked Indonesia's 2000 census later. The province with the largest number of Chinese is Bangka-Belitung with 11.5 per cent. The Chinese in the Riau Islands comprise less than 5 per cent of the population, although, of course, they are concentrated in the cities like Tanjung Pinang. Singapore's apprehension was not generated in a vacuum.

The road is becoming monotonous with little to see except the odd humble dwelling. Yet even if the people are poor, the houses we pass are well-tended and clean, and schools have spacious playgrounds where children are running around boisterously. They are all dressed in a uniform matching the national colours: white and red – red like the earth we see more of as we go south.

'*Boxit*,' says Deva, pointing at the entrance of a mine.

'Bauxite,' I translate. Its extraction on Bintan is another source of employment for the locals, although the deposits are now getting depleted. What is still in operation, is the granite quarry in Kijang that underpinned the building craze in Singapore – ever wondered where all the stone and gravel came from? Only recently Indonesia mysteriously banned such exports 'for strategic reasons', throwing Singapore's perpetual construction boom into turmoil. I'm sure there are other countries – Australia? – that will happily step in.

Sometimes, it takes a look from afar to understand a country, and my short sojourn on Bintan made me understand Singapore better than weeks of roaming its streets. If nothing else proves the city-state's First World status, Bintan does. Their economies are interdependent in a manner than can only be described as imperialistic – if the export of surplus capital defines the 'ism'. And it's not just in Bintan. The Thailand dealings of Singapore's state investment company Temasek (headed by a member of the Lee family) under the Thaksin government caused a political earthquake and resulted in the latest Thai coup. Singaporeans are starting to discover what Americans and Europeans have warily accepted long ago: prosperity brings resentment. The country has been accused by its neighbours of the most preposterous things: eavesdropping on mobile communications in Thailand (through owning part of the biggest network); cheating at football (it won the ASEAN Cup in 2007 with a disputed penalty); even causing the killer Johore floods (via a construction project across the straits). The government and the press seem at a loss as to how to respond to all these charges and they very wisely keep a low profile.

'*Bol*,' Deva says now, pointing to our right.

I try to make out the ball – or the ballgame – and it takes me a while to realise what he means. 'Rubber,' I explain. 'These are rubber trees.'

But by then he is pointing at a gated entrance. '*Prostitut*,' he utters with giggles that require no translation.

Yes, the rich neighbour's presence is everywhere: there are the honeymoon couples bathing in the beauty of the developed north whose natural competitors are Phuket, Seychelles or the Maldives; and there are sex tourists in the poorer south who frequent the prostitute retreats that compete with the lorongs in Geylang. Frankly, if sex tourism is not an indication of affluence, I don't know what is. Deva is pointing at the infamous Batu 24. Along with Batu 16 they are the distances in miles outside the capital where the girls are gathered in cheap hotels and rooms by the hour, costing as little at $5–$6 a session. Geylang prices are reserved for the high-class hookers in Tanjong Pinang's karaoke clubs who offer to Singaporean men the extra excitement of legal, non-procreative penetration.

The irony is that it was moneyed, prosperous Singapore that bore one of the world's prime porn stars. Step forward Annabel Chong, the woman who starred in the world's most famous gang-bang, where she had sex with 251 men in ten hours back in January 1995. ('*No different from having sex with one man for ten hours*,' she revealed.) Born Grace Quek into a well-off, middle-class family – her mother was a TV presenter – she was a convent-educated, piano-playing Singapore sweetheart. Scholarship material, she studied Law in London and then Art in Los Angeles in the early 1990s. It was then she answered an *LA Weekly* ad for nude modelling that catapulted her to porn stardom, but it was her short time in London that seems to have marked her indelibly: she was notoriously gang-raped on a council estate. It is hard to assess the impact this incident had on this innocent, cutesy girl, but it is easier to detect an unconscious desire to claim back that nightmarish experience as a willing seductress in that ultimate movie of hers, the World's Biggest Gang-Bang.

This film became one of the biggest sellers in the industry, but Annabel never received from the producer the $10,000 (US) she was owed. In one of those twists of fate, the ensuing documentary, *Sex: The Annabel Chong Story*, shot by cinema student Gough Lewis, became an art house favourite and was nominated for the Grand Jury Award in the 1999 Sundance Film Festival. Watching it can be an ordeal because of its unrelenting sadness; by the time Annabel Chong returns to Singapore as Grace Quek to 'come out' to her family who know nothing about her notorious career, all hankies in the house will have disappeared (and by that I mean to wipe tears).

The jury is out on Annabel/Grace, who has now eschewed all publicity and is working as a database developer and web designer. Was she an articulate pioneer who retaliated on behalf of every subservient woman in South East Asia by turning the tables on the male sex and taking control of her sexuality or was she simply manipulated by the porn business? One thing is certain: a society's sexual mores beget extreme sexual exemplars. Just like Kenneth Williams's campness, frigidity and hatred of his own sexuality could only have originated in the homophobic Britain of the 1950s, Annabel Chong's radical, over-the-top succubus persona can only be comprehended as a defiant rebellion against Grace Quek's strict Confucian upbringing in twentieth-century Singapore.

*TOOT! TOOT!*

The hooting of the *ojek*, motorbikes and scooters – an existential declaration from every motorist to another – tells me that we have finally reached Tanjong Pinang.

I am astounded. Who says time travel is impossible?

Deva drives me straight to the wharf where the tide is at an ebb exposing all kinds of unsavoury matter under the *pelantars* which are hardscrabble houses built on stilts and separated by narrow, plank walkways. Their curved wing-walls remind one of traditional ship's bows; legend has it that the original *pelantars* were docked boats secured onto foundations.

The pervading smell is overwhelmingly of fish whether fresh, barbecued, charcoaled, grilled or dried. In the *Pasar Ikan*, the Marine Market, anchovies, scallops, prawns and seaweed are sold in open sacks. One can easily get lost in the labyrinth of alleys and cul-de-sacs. I turn right and discover a fruit market with the malodorous smell of over-ripe durians and a consignment of ginger; I turn left and catch a glimpse of a Chinese temple celebrating the God of Fortune. I watch fascinated, as a Chinese boy follows his father in kneeling barefoot in front of the weathered scrolls and statues and bends his back to touch his head on the floor – *like a Muslim*.

Deva pulls my sleeve and takes me to a large cage. Through the wooden bars I can see a huge python and three panic-stricken chickens. The snake is asleep – or digesting – but that does not make the chickens any calmer; their terrified cackling has attracted the attentions of the street-kids in the harbour who peek in curiously through the slits. I feel nauseous.

'Let's order a *sampan* for Penyengat,' I tell Deva. After reading about Singapore's sole mode of sea transport for centuries, I have to come to Bintan to experience it.

The wind is strong and the boat's owner is holding on to the wharf steps with a thick rope as the pointed stem is bobbing up and down. Despite his Indonesian blood and slightness of figure, Deva is much less at ease climbing aboard the flat-bottomed skiff than me. I am more comfortable stepping on its narrow wobbling front; I must have a lower centre of gravity. Once inside, we move on under cover and sit on planks that are almost level with the water. The even, horizontal bottom means that we can run aground or be mired in a tidal shore and not heel over – it looks designed especially for this eventuality. As we start on our way, the wind brings sea-foam from the starboard and our captain brings down a tarpaulin to keep us dry. During the crossing to the pancake of an island that is Penyengat, I look back at Tanjung Pinang to solve one of my questions: yes, Singapore's river port had the edge. Raffles did well there.

'Penyengat not like Bintan,' Deva informs me. 'In Peneyengat many Malays.'

The long Penyengat pier has a traditional entrance – a gentle, straight sweep of a roof which changes half way to a 30-degree angle. This is a fairy-tale island perfectly preserved, with no means of motor transport other than a scooter-rickshaw with a wooden, covered passenger-car which is supposed to hold two people – but only if they are slim, archipelago, *orang laut*. That rules me out, so Deva does the honourable thing and rides pillion with the driver. The first place we visit is the mausoleum of the Queen Rajah Hamidah; her grave, full of votive ribbons, is considered a miracle-working *keramat*. The tomb is painted in royal yellow and religious green, combining the traditional Riau pyramidal roof with round domes, a possible Arab influence, or maybe Portuguese.

*This is where it all began.*

The more you delve into history the more fractal it becomes and the more human the protagonists appear, so let's revisit Singapore's birth. When that last sultan, Mahmud III, of the combined Johore-Riau passed away in 1812, his wife, Queen Raja Hamidah, had borne him only one daughter who died soon after her birth. The Sultan himself had left the question of succession open: his two sons, Hussein and Abdul Rahman were illegitimate; the first had a Malay mother and the second was born from a Bugis concubine. At the time of Mahmud's death the elder son, Hussein, was away getting married; the Bugis faction usurped the throne and installed Abdul Rahman. The feud between the Bugis and the Malays had been boiling for over a century, ever since the Malay Sultan Mahmud Shah was assassinated by his Bugis *Laksamana* at Kota Tinggi. When he died, he cursed his admiral's descendants who, even today, will not set foot in eastern Johore.

After the Dutch arrived in Bintan closing the Riau door to Raffles, he covertly came to Penyengat to negotiate with Hussein, after he had clinched the more meaningful deal with the Temenggong on Singapore itself. The reason Raffles could still grope for some semblance of constitutional legality is precisely because of the woman buried in front of me. Queen Raja Hamidah, the stepmother of both pretenders, was holding jealously on to the *nobat*, the percussive and wind instruments that make up the royal orchestra used during a coronation, so not even Abdul Rahman could claim he had been legally enthroned. Hussein left Bintan in February 1819 and was declared sultan in Singapore. One year later, his son Ali attempted to bring over Raja Hamidah and the tools of kingship, but failed. The conundrum was ended by the Dutch who seized the regalia by force in 1822 and legitimised Abdul Rahman's occupation of the throne. The whole affair only mattered for two years: the Treaty of London that divided the colonial possessions between Britain and Holland also split the hyphenated sultanate of Johore-Riau into its two constituents. That was the nightmare the Queen was trying to prevent.

Abdul Rahman himself is buried behind the mosque he commissioned, the Masjid Raya in front of me, or the 'egg mosque' as it has been dubbed, painted as it is with a mixture of egg white and lime to strengthen the cement. After the withering of the power of the Riau part of the sultanate, it became a centre of Islamic learning. The remarkable, later figure of the learned Sultan Raja Ali Haji left a history of the Malay people – for once, from the local point of view – a collection of moral-guiding verses, that first grammar of the Malay language, and an encyclopaedia of Malay customs.

*This is where it all began, and this is where it all ended.*

Or maybe not. Geographical coherence is stronger than artificial borders and so a shadow of the Johore-Riau sultanate has been economically recreated by the governments of Malaysia, Singapore and Indonesia. It is termed the 'growth triangle' and it encompasses, Singapore, Johore and Riau with the shorthand acronym of SiJoRi. The island of Bantam, next to Bintam, and Johore itself became Singapore's industrial hinterland, whereas Bintan is being developed as Singapore's international beach resort, an upmarket alternative to Bali. After two centuries of living apart, the peoples of the archipelago – Malay, Bugis and Chinese – are re-learning how to live together.

Perhaps Queen Raja Hamidah did have the last laugh in the end.

- 31 -

'How was Bintan?' asks Jacky puffing on her cigarette, as I squeeze myself next to her on a sofa in Tantric's courtyard.

I talk to her about the golf courses, the jacuzzis, the *sampans* and the mosques. It's midnight on a weekday and the place is relatively quiet; we both prefer it so.

'I missed you, my sweet,' she says.

'I missed you, too.'

'I need to talk to you about something,' she says.

'Me, too.'

We look at each other.

'You first,' she says.

*Right.*

'Remember when you called earlier, and I said I had a date?' I start.

'Yes.'

'There was someone else who was kind of pestering me. Met him online, but I was after Richard at the time. His name is Andy.'

'Chinese?'

'Yep. Mad about the gym. I arranged to see him today after I arrived from Bintan.'

'And?'

I shake my head. 'Let me show you,' I say. 'This was my first text to him tonight.'

*'Sorry just arrived from Bintan and must dash into town. Can u make it? Like 9ish?'*

'Now that's him.'

*'How about after 10pm so u could rest a bit.'*

I switch between 'Inbox' and 'Sent'.

*'9pm is OK, unless u want l8er. U come over to me?'*

*'Ok, will come. I would like to go to gym first if thats cool? Is after 10 cool w u?'*

*'Yes its OK, say 10pm. Text me when u r by the hotel.'*

I stop. 'See, I texted him "10 p.m.", that's what we agreed. It's important. I just arrived from Bintan, I was tired, and it's only a blind bloody date, after all.

'A blind date? Surely you'd seen his picture before.'

I sigh. 'Have you never heard of PhotoShop? It's still a blind date. Alright?'

'Alright,' replies Jacky.

'Let's continue,' I say. 'That's him.'

*'Ok sure what would we do?'*

*'Lets see if we like each other 1st IRL'*

*'Cool text u later when i m on my way'*

Jacky looks at me. 'So what?'

'Hold on! Now that was eight o'clock. So I wait and wait, until ten to ten when I text him again.'

*'Hi r u on ur way? Im falling asleep here...'*

*'Just stepped out of gym on my way home now'*

*'So when r we meeting if at all?'*

'Were you annoyed?' asks Jacky.

'Yes! And you had texted me by then that you wanted to see me about something, so I was quite impatient.'

I show her the next text I received.

*'Rushin home now to get changed, we ll meet for sure, I wont play u out john'*

*'Sorry, its just too late, maybe it was not meant to be. If u couldnt make it u should say so.'*

*'I thought we agree on after 10 I could b there at half past if u still wanna meet'*

'What's this all about?' she says. 'He's only half an hour late.'

'Hold on,' I tell her. 'We're supposed to meet at ten and he's still in the gym?'

'You know these gym-bunnies, they are crazy.'

'On a first date?'

'Oh well.'

'Anyway, this is me breaking it off.'

*'Forget it. I hope the workout was worth it.'*

'But look how he replied.'

*'Sure no worries I didnt hold it against u b4 when u said u would call but didn't, so much for grace I may b runnin late but at least I would turn up, guess u have a backup, hope its a disappointment'*

'That *really* pissed me off. Thinking that I had a 'backup'. Now, I shouldn't have answered him, but I did.'

'*U r paranoid. Im tired wanted 9 OK'd 10, but 10:30 is too late!! Stop dissing me. Bye!*'

'And then he sends me this!'

'*Oh I forget this is the white rule if its the white's fault point to the nonwhite, dont try turnin the table w me, I dont give in, so everything is about u now, because u r white? U have a business n work to do, while I sit around waitin for ur return? I m not chocho san, n we r not in an opera, u r d one whos a paranoid that i m jerkin u around that started all these unwanted textin*'

'Chocho San?' asks Jacky.

'A character from *Madame Butterfly*,' I explain. 'And look, immediately he sent another.'

'*N BTW dont give me attitudes like we ll meet up first to c if we like each other, u r no better then me, n u r no longer the superior breed, wake up n get ur ideas clear, other Asians might kiss ur feet like Ghandi, this one will have no difficulties fuckin u up*'

'Bloody hell!' exclaims Jacky.

'Yes. I was mightily pissed off.'

'He can't say things like that!'

'I know. He's got a chip on his shoulder – no, make that a fucking wardrobe.'

'You're better off without him.'

'That's what I thought, too.'

'I presume you didn't answer these texts!'

'You must be joking.'

Jacky stubs her cigarette and lights another.

'It's your turn,' I say. 'What happened?'

She looks me in the eye.

'Well, my sweet, while you've been away, I went out with Tim. We met here, we drank and talked. We found we had so much in common. Films, music. Loads. Then he invited me home. He lives not far from here. He said he mixed the best lychee Martini so I took him up on his word. He cooked me dinner. We watched *Tampopo*. We both love this film. He talked about his ex-girlfriends and I talked about my ex-husband. We stayed up talking up till 3 a.m. Then the discussion turned to fuckbuddies and no-strings sex.'

'It doesn't work between a man and a woman,' I say. 'It's a myth. The woman always falls in love.'

'I don't know. I think it may be possible. Anyway, I think he made a pass at me.'

'Glad to hear it. And?'

'I was shocked, so I told him it it's not going to happen tonight. That I like him as a friend. That is the truth. I really, really like Tim, but –'

'It was unexpected and you were caught off guard.'

'Exactly.'

'Did you say "it's not going to happen *tonight*" implying that it might happen some other night?'

Jacky tries to remember. 'I don't know… what I meant was, let's be friends and if it happens, it happens.'

'Would you like something to happen?'

'I don't know.'

Jacky lowers her eyes.

'He texted me next day saying how he enjoyed our meet. But he hasn't contacted me since. It's been a week now.'

I look at her and try to gauge her feelings. 'You miss him.'

'I do.'

'Well, maybe you have to do all the work. Maybe he feels rejected, and men are generally not good with rejection. I mean look at those texts I received today! Plus straight men notoriously don't understand women; maybe you gave conflicting signs.'

'So what do I do?'

'Text him. Text him now. Say that I'm back and that you are with me at Tantric and does he want to pop over?'

She thinks for a moment and picks up her mobile.

'I'll buy you a drink,' I say to leave her alone.

I was hoping that Richard would be happy to see me but no, surprise is the only thing he registers; he thought I'd gone back to London. For once I am not interested in him or his reaction because sitting inside, laughing with his mates, is none other than Dan.

This time I pat him nervously on the shoulder.

'Hi,' I say, 'Dan isn't it? Remember me? This is John. From London? We, ermm, *met* a few years back?'

Dan narrows his eyes. *He does remember.*

'John. Nice to see you.'

'Nice to see *you*.'

'How are you?' he asks. 'Back in Singapore?'

'For all my sins.'

I'm not sure what to say next, but I want to *know*.

'How are you – really? I mean your health. Last time someone told me you were very ill. That you had –' I know I have to name the disease in case the wrong one is surmised, '– *cancer*.'

Dan looks me straight in the eye and touches me on the small of my back.

'That was a long time ago. I'm fine, now, John,' he says. 'Thank you.'

'And your sleep?' I ask. 'Still uneasy?'

Dan doesn't answer. 'You're still a very sexy man,' he says instead with a rueful shade in his voice, as he walks back to his friends.

Outside Jacky is grinning like the cat that found the milk. 'He replied! He is too tired to come out now, but that's not the point. He replied!'

'You are a very strange woman,' I say to Jacky.

'I know.' She goes quiet. 'Sometimes I think I am abnormal. Here in Singapore people don't kiss, don't embrace so easily and I am so tactile. Then, I go out all the time. I know some people who wait for a birthday or an office function to go out because their husband or their wife don't let them. I have never placed such shackles on my husband. He doesn't own me, and I don't own him. I only tell him where I will be out of politeness. I just don't want to hurt his feelings.'

*Something does not compute.*

'I thought you were separated with your husband,' I say. 'You always refer to him as your ex.'

'He is. We *are* separated. But we still live together.'

'You do?'

'Oh, yes. Why are you laughing?'

'It's just that this is so un-Confucian,' I say. 'Here is a city that is supposedly basing itself on a traditional moral code and gay men are coming out in droves. Couples separate but still cohabit. There is strict censorship but prostitution is thriving. Bloody hell, I'm having the same discussion I had with a guy called Chang when I was here last.'

'What discussion?'

'About the globalisation of values and ideas.'

'Globalisation of *what*?'

I'm too tired to explain and take a sip from my drink instead.

## CHAPTER TWELVE

# DREAMLAND

Dim and Xim, the twins, and every other boy in the school knew they could go wild after lunch since their teacher, Master Ho, used to take a short nap and left them to their own devices. They tiptoed away from the ancient banyan tree under whose long lianas their teacher snored obliviously and into the nearby forest where they played hide-and-seek among the bushes, the trees and the fallen branches.

One day Dim and Xim started fighting with some other boys; this wasn't news, for the twins always got in a scrap. What was different this time was that the brawl was noisy and the ear-splitting ruckus woke up Master Ho. He separated the quarrelling parties, imposed penalties and asked where the rest of the boys were.

'Playing in the forest, Master,' answered Dim truthfully.

Master Ho was incandescent. 'In the forest? How many times have I told you that the woods are dangerous? That you should not even go near the place? Have you done this before?'

The boys lowered their heads.

'We don't go too far in, Master,' said Xim – and he was also telling the truth. 'We're always back before you wake up.'

Master Ho slapped Xim in the face.

'I am not *asleep*,' he said angrily. 'I am in Dreamland, communicating with the old sages! Getting tips on how to deal with you scoundrels! Don't you ever dare say that I fall asleep during the day! Now run and tell your friends to come back! The whole class will stay here after school to copy the first fifty analects! Ten times! In proper calligraphy!'

And so it came to pass; the boys were punished and stayed back in class copying lines from Confucius. It had been a long, hot day, and by the time the boys started the sixth or seventh reproduction they felt sleepy. Dim and Xim were the first to doze off.

Master Ho was up like a jack-in-the-box to beat the twins' arms with his ruler. 'What's this?' he said. 'Falling asleep during detention? Do you want to copy more lines?'

Dim was quick to retort: 'We were not asleep, Master. We were in Dreamland, getting the benefit of the sages' wisdom like yourself.'

Master Ho felt a flush of anger. 'Oh, you were, were you? And what, pray tell, did the elders impart to you?'

This time it was Xim who replied. 'We asked them to give us some of the insights they gave to Master Ho. But, they claimed, they had never met such an individual.'

- 32 -

I am standing outside McDonalds at Clementi Station playing spot-the-paranormal-investigator. There are several people sitting on the outside benches, and not all of them seem devotees of the junk fare on offer. Why, if they have a camera, they have been positively identified: who carries their Sony Cybershot to immortalise their Big Mac Meal for posterity? No, they – we – are waiting for the SPI team and, when they eventually arrive, they look most impressive; one could certainly remark *chic*, donning as they are SPI-logo T-shirts, black boots and combats, plus army-style bum-bags stuffed with torches and isotonic fluids. We're certainly prepared enough to invade Johore single-handed: look, Uranium has even tucked his combats into his army boots.

'It's to prevent mosquito bites,' he says to me, as poker-faced as ever.

I laugh. Mosquitoes? In Singapore? I thought the local variety had been sprayed to extinction and the foreign pests couldn't get visas.

'We're going to swamp areas,' he clarifies, this time rather ominously.

Sunkist has taken our names, collected the subscriptions and called the mobile number of every absentee to double-check. All in all, we are a party of forty-plus and a bus has been hired for the occasion. Wherever we are going, it is a big production.

'By the way, don't expect to see anything paranormal,' Uranium warns me. 'This is a special, educational tour compared to the ones we did before.'

My heart sinks: being scared shitless will have to wait. My disappointment must have been visible, because Uranium is quick to utter the S-word: 'Educational but also *spoo-ky*.'

Once on the bus, MJ MCs the show. 'My name is MJ Chow,' he says into a mike. 'If you can't hear in the back, put up your hand! Geddit, geddit? *If you can't hear put up your hand*. Right?'

*Right.*

'I don't know how many people know about me. If you don't know anything about me – *good*. Anyway, I am the vice president of SPI. On my left here we have Wisely and over here I have Sunkist and right over here we have Uranium. You won't find him on the website; he's our Secret Agent.'

I giggle.

'And right at the end of the bus we have AK47. During the tour if there is anything you need to ask, you may approach any one of us.'

Uranium takes over: 'If you are not sure what SPI is, we are a non-profit organisation which means that we all have our own jobs, our own professions. That's why we normally go out at night, not only because it is spoo-ky but also because we have to work in the daytime. We do sleep. But we sleep at odd times.'

He sits down while MJ continues.

'Before I go further, does anybody here remember the Japanese invasion?'

No hands are up.

'This means that most of you were born after that. John what about you?'

'No!' I reply. *Bitch.*

'Quite a few people asked us why we organise this tour near the Chinese New Year. Well, there is a reason behind that. Singapore was surrendered to the Japanese on the first day of the Chinese New Year, 1942.'

Oh, no, not World War Two, *again.* It must weigh down on the Singaporean psyche as much as on the British. Even more so, if you think that it is still alive in the minds of current, politically active personalities: Lee Kuan Yew famously saw the British prisoners march to Changi as an 18-year-old student. The Queen and the Duke of Edinburgh excepted, there have been no memories of the war in the higher echelons of Britain's governing class since the time of Margaret Thatcher.

We pass a cemetery and Uranium takes over in what seems like a double act.

'This is the famous Choa Chu Kan Cemetery,' he says. 'This is where we conducted one of our most daring experiments. Sunkist combed her hair at midnight. We do crazy things like that.'

Nobody laughed, so I didn't either. It is an old Chinese legend that if you comb your hair at midnight, you will see a ghost in the mirror. I suppose, you need a hairdresser with balls for that, and they aren't easy to find, *dahlings*, so maybe it was truly daring, after all.

'Our first destination tonight is Sarimbun Beach,' MJ informs us. 'As you know, it is located in the north-west of Singapore and is officially the first place the Japanese landed on the island. So where was the "unofficial" place?'

I know! It was none other than Pulau Ubin. The Imperial Guards mounted a diversionary tactic early on 8 February by landing on this idyllic island to the northeast of Singapore. They fooled Percival, who was easily conned, anyway. The north-west corner was left to the Australians who were pummelled by artillery for 24 hours – you'd have thought that Percival might have taken the hint, but he was never the sharpest blade in the toolbox.

'Why did the Japanese forces choose Sarimbun beach as their place of landing? Reason number one is that the allied forces were rather weak compared to other areas in Singapore and the Japanese knew that. Reason number two is that this is the closest point to the Malayan peninsula and is opposite to the palace of the Sultan of Johore which is built on a big hill – the highest point in the surrounding area. From there General Yamashita could observe the progress of the landing.'

The bus stops and outside it's blacker than the hair Sunkist was combing at Choa Chu Kan.

'I hope you all have torches,' says Uranium.

Erm, no we don't, so he gives us the next best thing: glowsticks – to make the ambience more 'spoo-ky' or to provide some light, I know not, but we end up looking like a party of ravers in search of a warehouse.

'Try not to follow the wrong light, 'cos it may be something else,' he continues. 'The worst case we've had is one couple when something followed them home. No casualties so far, but we hope that there are no more repeats.'

He says all this with a straight face, and we all nod in agreement with an even straighter one.

'Also, since so many people died on the beaches around us, I am asking all of you to take photos. Sometimes objects appear as orbs or electromagnetic fields on camera. You show us the images, we look at the orbs, and we can tell you what is paranormal and what is dust.'

The moon is full, and we can make out the flat hill opposite, the Sultan of Johore's palace and erstwhile Japanese army HQ.

'This is how it was during the night of 8 February 1942,' says MJ.

Well, sort of. The mangrove swamp to our right where the fighting took place, has been drained and dejungled and, as the landing was a week before the Chinese New Year, the moon must have been at a quarter waning.

'Last year we conducted an experiment here. We got one of our members to dress like a Japanese lady with a kimono dancing to a Japanese folk song.'

I'd like to have seen *that*.

'Suddenly she felt very depressed – and I tell you, she's not psychologically unstable. Then we set up the offering and one

SPI member who spoke Japanese said: "We are here, we have an offering for you, come and collect it." Suddenly the tide surged in very fast and the waves came through like a tsunami and all our offerings were under water. Now the tide should not have been coming 'cos we had checked, so afterwards we went to the meteorological station and they said, "Oh no this is not supposed to happen, possibly a ship was passing by." But there's no harbour around the vicinity, and it's a dead end: the Singapore–Malaysia Causeway is further down. If it was a ship, it must have been a fairly big one.'

*Like a landing craft, maybe...*

'A ship can cause a swell, but not so big as to have our offerings swept away like that. We didn't have time to collect our nice Japanese engraved cups! And all the time, the lady kept crying and crying. The rest of us were rather pissed off 'cos it was obvious that the Japanese had come and collected the offerings very abruptly.'

*Brutes.*

But brave brutes, nonetheless. It was here that 4,000 Japanese of the 5th and 18th Division landed in small, collapsible – but motorised – landing crafts holding about a dozen people each. The Australians were spread thinly, lacked proper defences and were demoralised because of the relentless bombardment. The barrage had cut the telephone lines and orders to turn on the searchlights over the straits never arrived. Australian artillery cover was inadequate, communications were dismal, and the soldiers had confusing orders to defend *or withdraw* to a line further in. Within hours, the Australian lines started disintegrating to retreat and regroup. One of the soldiers whose headstones I surveyed in Kranji – that R. Currey of the 2/20 Infantry Battalion – was almost certainly killed during the retreat from this very position; the dates and the battalions match.

'What is that fence structure?' I ask MJ pointing at the huge wall erected near the jetty we are standing on.

'It is to prevent the illegal immigrants,' he replies. 'They come swimming from Johore. During high tide all this will be covered and part of the mangrove forest as well.'

'This small wall? Can't they swim around it?'

'No. Can you not see it going all the way round the beach? In both directions?'

I squint in the dark. 'Oh yes. OK then – can't they climb over it?'

'No, look, the top of the wall slopes back towards the sea and you can't climb it if you are swimming. It goes on for kilometres all the way to the other end of the island. We call it the Great Wall of Singapore.'

Just like that legendary Cape of Stakes: a wall to prevent not an attack of flying swordfish, but maybe an attack by pirate *praus*. Has anyone thought of that?

'What about conditions like now? The tide is well on the ebb.'

'It's dangerous. They would get caught in the mud.'

I think of the Chinese cockle-pickers at Morecambe Bay and agree that MJ is right. You don't want to wade here at low tide.

'There are also infrared cameras and movement detectors further on among the trees. The border guards will quickly get to them. Do you see that light? It is a police patrol boat coming to check on us.'

Nice to see that the north part of the island is well-defended for once.

## - 33 -

It takes us hardly any time to reach our next destination, the famous Kranji beach, which was the second landing site of none other than the Emperor's elite troops, the Imperial Guards.

'This is where the invasion force suffered some of their greatest losses,' MJ tells us. 'Why? Because the Woodlands fuel depot is very near to this place. The Imperial Guards landed on the night of the ninth and found it very difficult to walk in the mud. The Australians started to release the fuel and set fire to it. Many of the Japanese were burned to death. There's been a folk belief since that whenever someone starts a fire here, a Japanese spirit appears in their vicinity.'

Astonishingly, and despite the casualties they were inflicting on the enemy, the Australians again withdrew under the orders of Brigadier Duncan Maxwell who overrode Bennett's contrary instructions. Afraid that he might be outflanked, Maxwell wanted to face the enemy behind the Kranji river that was running north/south. It was most definitely an operational error, possibly the biggest in the defence of Singapore – especially since he didn't tell anybody else about it, like the Gurkha Regiment to his right who found themselves suddenly under attack.

I stop daydreaming while my nostrils pick out the acrid smell of burning flesh. *Is it my imagination?* I think, but then I see the flames, then the shadows...

'There are a lot of people having barbecues here so there must be a lot of Japanese spirits around,' I hear MJ say in his deadpan voice. 'I suggest you take a lot of pictures and let us examine them afterwards.' He's right. The orbs I will pick up in my night images afterwards can keep SPI in business for a year.

I peer through the tall palm trees and the scattered, flickering barbecue sparks into the distant, captivating lights of Johore.

The city looks very pretty, its skyline curvier than Singapore's, like Kate Winslet posing next to Nicole Kidman. MJ approaches to absorb the vibe. I want to say something memorable in this warm and pleasant night, but I end up with just 'Full moon.'

'Yes,' says MJ, 'full moon. Somebody feeling werewolf?'

Uranium might be, since he's turning creepy: 'A family of four were killed over there including a mother and two of her kids. They were wandering along the low tide area in the vicinity of the reservoir release zone. Then the reservoir overflow opened because of heavy rain, and water suddenly flooded the area. Somehow, they didn't hear the warning siren and everyone was swept away. Drowned,' he says in a tone partly-concerned, partly-horrified and most certainly fascinated.

I retire to the bus.

We have driven quite some time before Uranium again takes the mike: 'A small clue for our destination number three: during the attack on Singapore, it saw the most intense fighting. We've been ourselves there before and we know this fighting has not stopped. But it's not between the Allies and the Japanese. It's between the monkeys!'

'Bukit Timah,' I hear some voices shout.

'I'm sure many people have heard about the Kranji war memorial over the junction, but hardly anyone knows about the Bukit Batok War Memorial in the Bukit Timah Nature Reserve, a Shinto shrine built *during* the occupation.'

So far we've travelled up through Choa Chu Kang to Sarimbun and are now driving down from Kranji to Bukit Timah. This is, this is –

'We're following the routes of the Japanese invasion force,' I tell MJ.

'That's the point,' he replies.

As it's a long way to Bukit Batok, Uranium tells us a story to pass the time. 'There used to be this Indian temple in Sungei Tengah that was demolished for some reason. It has since been occupied by a makeshift prayer altar with a number of Chinese deities. One day – some of you may have heard this story – a worshipper smelled something bad. He looked around. There was a small bundle by the statue of Tua Peh Gong, the Hokkien god of wealth. He opened it layer by layer. The cloth was covered by inscriptions and inside the cloth was a dead baby!'

He pauses for emphasis.

'So we went there to investigate whether this was a real "child spirit" having been offered to the gods. When we arrived, we set our equipment to measure humidity and any breezes, the infrared cameras and all. At twelve midnight, MJ's alarm watch went off. Now, he never sets his alarm. In fact, he didn't think it was him. He was quite surprised – we caught his look on video. Only in the end did he realise it was him. Everyone stopped and there was a bad smell like rotten eggs. One of our members, Yellobie, was at the bottom of the hill and he didn't know anything about what was happening with us. He said afterwards independently that, at midnight, he saw a shadow going past, but when we reviewed the tape we saw nothing on camera. Now listen to this: on a *second* visit to the same hill, our founder and president Kenny noticed that his watch had also stopped at twelve midnight! Coincidence or what? Some of you here were there on that trip and you know I'm not bluffing.'

The bus plunges into silence. I look at the Chinese faces around me; if they were scared, impressed or nonplussed, they didn't show it, as they wouldn't.

'This is the *spookiest* place we will visit today, and since it is
the *spookiest* place we will do the *spookiest* thing,' says Uranium
whose range of adjectives is rather limited tonight. 'We will
make an offering. Anyone know about Japanese culture? To
help us with the offerings?'

*Karaoke. Sushi. Hara-kiri.*

I must have thought aloud, because my neighbour – with
whom I haven't spoken during this period – gives me a 'you-
are-not-taking-this-seriously' look. I am, I just want to see a
ghost, and I don't think my wish will be fulfilled tonight.

'During the offering we will invite you to take as many
photos as you can and check the environment. Avoid doing
crazy things – unless you want something to follow you back.'

A tape of old Japanese songs starts playing on the radio 'to
create an atmosphere' and I can't help thinking that they sound
so vampishly Western. I am also wondering what those crazy
things are. Those I shouldn't do.

The first sight that greets us as we climb out of the bus at
Bukit Batok is a sign with a monkey face, a hand holding
a banana and a red, diagonal prohibition stripe across both.
'Don't disturb the monkeys; they are extremely aggressive,'
Uranium keeps warning us. I examine the surroundings
anxiously but I see none, and I am hardly listening anyway. I
am soaking up the mood of this place.

The Bukit Batok War Memorial was a plan of Yamashita's
that was executed after he had fallen out of favour with
Tokyo and had been semi-exiled to Manchuria to put the
frighteners on the Russians. The Yokohama Engineering

Regiment and 20,000 POWs worked for six months to build it. Once it was completed in early 1943, those same POWs would be sent to die in Burma on the notorious Death Railway. A plaque shows us how it looked: set in two large platforms with wide, steep steps, it was a Far-Eastern rendition of the Mesoamerican Aztec pyramids of the Sun and the Moon. A long obelisk on top, more than seven metres tall, towered over the remains of the Japanese soldiers; in a rare display of chivalry, a large wooden cross commemorated the Allied dead a short distance behind. It must have been the most short-lived of all grandiose structures: just before the surrender in August 1945, the Japanese Army razed it to the ground.

That's where I catch MJ again.

'Today everything is demolished,' he is saying. 'When the Japanese leave a place, they take everything with them and that includes their soldiers' remains. The only original item left behind are these two concrete structures that stood at the bottom of the staircase on either side of the gate.'

He takes a breath to ask one of his rhetorical questions.

'Why did they choose this spot for a war memorial? Because it overlooks that site which saw the most intense fight in Singapore between the Japanese and the Allied Forces.'

I run up with Uranium and Wisely who are setting up the offering: sake, sweets, incense, four candles. It's windy and the candles won't light. The two short red ones are OK, but the two tall white ones are impossible. If Uranium tries to light the right one, the left one goes out. If the left one lights up, the red one goes. This is beginning to look like a failed experiment. But then MJ's young son places a small Japanese flag in front of the sweets and, magically, both candles light up with no problem.

'Did you see that?' asks Uranium. 'When the boy brought the flag –'

'Yes. I saw it.'

'Coincidence?'

*Of course.*

As the rest of the group comes up, the snap of cameras eclipses the sound of crickets. We watch the candles intensely, waiting for something to happen. Someone takes a picture of me. Just watch out, in case he tries to pass me off as an apparition. I don't think SPI will be fooled; one thing I'm not is ethereal.

'Look,' Sunkist whispers to me.

The white candles burst into a large flame that is then suddenly reduced to a small bright point at the end of the wick. The candles are almost blown away, but then they flare up again. Sunkist looks at me and than at the flames that are still oscillating from zero to max with an unnerving regularity. 'What do you think?' she says.

I say nothing. It was, of course, the wind – but if, purely for the sake of argument, this were a signal from outer space picked up by that panoply of NASA radars, we'd be talking 'Intelligent Life Exists' headlines by tomorrow.

- 34 -

Our last stop is the most spectacular: it is the hilly reserve of Kent Ridge Park, the scene of the battle of Pasir Panjang that produced some of the most heroic acts of the week-long siege. It overlooks the south-western coast where the illuminated maze of the oil refineries at Pulau Bukom glow in the night horizon. Our arrival disturbs several courting couples in the car park and, as I climb up to the highest observation point, I upset another one that sits up dishevelled in a gazebo. Our glances cross; their amorosity has gone rather far. I swallow hard as I realise that I have my digital camera all cocked and ready. The girl's eyes shout 'pervert' and the boy's eyes cry murder. I decide to walk down back to safety.

'By 14 February 1942 the Japanese had fought all way south towards here,' says MJ. 'Look down and you can see how strategic this place was and why, after it fell, Percival surrendered.'

Even before the surrender, Singapore was steeped in a cloud of capitulation. The previous day – Friday the thirteenth – bottles of alcohol were being smashed at Raffles Hotel, so that the Japanese troops would find nothing to drink and stay sober. In Keppel Harbour, the naval base was being dynamited and Australian deserters were storming ships carrying civilians to Jakarta. Like his troops, Gordon Bennett was the only high-ranking officer who left Singapore. He faced censure for abandoning his command and never held another commission. As for that popular expression that bears his name: although some etymologists claim that it precedes his appearance in history, the first written record we have is from the 1960s, so it could well be attributed to the general's existence.

I walk around in the park which has been subject to a heavy dose of reforestation. The National Parks Board is fighting a constant war against invasive plant species such as the bearded smilax, an aggressive local vine you can see all over Singapore and Koster's curse, a perennial shrub that forms dense thickets that shade out all other vegetation. But next to the local flora such as the thorny kapok trees, the short-stumped silverbacks and sweet-smelling tembusu, they seem to have left intact the Australian wattles, one of the fastest-growing trees known to Man that has become a pest almost everywhere else. Never mind, they will soon learn.

I reach the edge of the car park.

The last stand of the 1st Malay Regiment took place just down from here. It was the Battle of Opium Hill, named after a fully-fledged opium factory that was based there. The Malays had not been used earlier because no one knew the strength of their fighting spirit; Percival need not have worried: the regiment didn't believe in surrender. Thinking them green and unbloodied – which they were – the Japanese dressed like Punjabis and started marching in formation in order to deceive them. But the Malays were sharp: these soldiers were marching in fours and the British-drilled troops marched in threes. The Japanese troops were slaughtered, and it was because of those heavy losses that their comrades ran in a rage towards Alexandra hospital a few hundred yards away when the battle was finally over.

As it would be, for Yamashita concentrated the last remnants of his artillery on Opium Hill. After a 48-hour struggle, the Malays fought down to the last man led by the Second Lieutenant Adnan Saidi of 'D' Company. He was caught alive by the Japanese, put in a sack, hung upside down from a tree and used for bayonet practice. After a few days, the Japanese took him down and burned his body, knowing that for Muslims this was the worst fate that can befall their remains. The corpses of many Malay soldiers who fell on Opium Hill were never found which is why their names, including that of Adnan Saidi, are inscribed on the Kranji Memorial. I know, I saw them there.

'So why was it the Japanese won the war? I'm sure John here knows about it.'

Know about it? The greatest defeat of the British Army, maybe *ever*, has been the subject of analysis and counter-analysis by armchair strategists for decades. It has recently become fashionable to blame the Australians for allowing the

Japanese to get a foothold on the island. While they bear some of the blame, the fish starts stinking from the head. Within 48 hours Yamashita was on the island himself; Percival remained in the underground bunkers of Fort Canning. Nuff said.

So long after the event, the whole sorry episode seems like an exercise in the punishment of hubris: the haughtiness of the bungling, buck-toothed Brits and the overconfidence of the Australians who believed their own propaganda deserved to be pricked. On the other hand, the jaw-dropping cruelty of the Japanese who committed so many atrocities just had to be avenged. It is the details that hurt. When one English couple – Charles and Kathleen Stapledon – lost their housekeeper during the bombing, they received a message that he had been knocked off his bicycle by a shell but was recovering in hospital and wanted to see them. It was then they realised they couldn't find him, because they didn't know his name; he had always been 'Boy' to them, like every other Chinese servant. Then again, how could the Japanese ever be the good guys when the punishment for those who listened to Allied broadcasts was to hammer sharpened pencils into their ears – to quote from the Kempeitai's official torture manual? The fall of Singapore and the subsequent horror of the nuclear bombings look like justified divine censures for two different styles of imperialism, especially since the Japanese divisions who carried out the massacres were mostly recruited from the cities of Hiroshima and Nagasaki. It's enough to make you believe in collective karma.

Still, that it was a momentous event there is no doubt: the speed of the collapse of the British presence in Malaya cast a shadow which never quite left. It is 800 kilometres from the top of Malaysia at Kota Bahru to Singapore. The Japanese plan allowed for 90 days to completion. They did it in 70; if only IT projects could run half as well. The shambolic manner of the retreat down the peninsula was deeply shameful: the *tuans* and the *mems* leaving their plantations and houses without regard for their servants; the implementation of a scorched earth policy with no heed for the native population; the way the army abandoned Penang, Kuala Lumpur, Malacca and their Chinese communities to their fate. If you lose face in Asia, you lose it forever.

The rest follows from that, really.

The Chinese resistance fighters in the jungles of Malaya trained by British Special Operations tried to wrest control after the war, in the manner of the Yugoslav and Greek partisans in Europe. Malaya was created as a barrier to the tide of communism. Security Acts involving detention without trial were passed in Singapore which still mire the statutes now. Without a European war, Britain concentrated its troops on Malaya and won the insurgency. Singapore benefited immensely as the headquarters of an army that reached, at its peak, 60,000 men. It profited further when another war started in neighbouring Indochina; it was American troops this time that came to Singapore to recuperate. At a time when developing countries begged for foreign capital, Singapore didn't need to advertise. As any estate agent will tell you, all that matters is location, location, location.

Uranium interrupts my thoughts. 'How did you like the trip?' he asks.

'Good,' I say laconically.

The truth is that the choice of theme surprised me. The Japanese seem to be haunting Singapore in more ways than one.

'Hope you enjoyed it,' Sunkist says as we say goodbye.

'I did,' I say and I'm telling the truth.

Uranium takes her by the hand.

'She's my girlfriend,' he explains in answer to my questioning looks. And then, he adds with a wide grin: 'SPI is not a social club – but people do socialise.'

Tired from the trip, but still sober on a Saturday night, I am contemplating whether to go out or not, until I receive a text from Jacky: '*In Taboo come str8 away*'; I simply can't refuse such summons.

When I arrive, it is well past midnight and Jacky is well past drunk. Not the best time to make a call to Tim.

'Call him over,' she demands.

'Me? Why? You call him.'

'No, you do it.' She is insistent.

'I'll do it,' says a member of Jacky's entourage, takes her mobile and walks to a more quiet corner.

By the time I bring back the drinks, Jacky is jubilant. Tim is coming and she has put him down on the guest list to make sure he gets in past the long queue.

'He's coming,' she says. 'We'll patch up now – as friends.'

'Him sober, you drunk, not the best combination.'

'That's why you must stay with me all the time,' she says.

Tim arrives after about half an hour. He looks restrained, as sober people do and Jacky is more exuberantly touchy-feelie than usual.

'Can I get you a drink?' I ask him.

'Get me a coke, thanks,' he replies.

'Are you sure?'

'Very sure. I'm sober for the whole of February. Detox.'

I look at Jacky. I don't care about the next month, it is tonight I am concerned about. The coupling is well unbalanced.

'I normally have January off. After Christmas,' I tell him.

'February is shorter,' he replies with a wink.

So we sit in the chillout room and I bore everyone with stories about Bintan and the ghostbusting tour that wasn't, until just me, Jacky and Tim are left.

'I'm leaving next week,' I tell Tim. 'Are you coming for a last supper?'

'I don't know,' he says. 'I'm leaving next week, too.'

Jacky sits up.

'You're leaving? Where to?'

'I'm off to the US for a project. For about two or three months.'

Jacky is silent.

'That's my job. I go on short assignments abroad. Three months here, six months there.'

'And you like this life?' she asks with a quivering voice.

'Yes, I do,' he replies. 'This is me.'

This was getting a bit personal; despite this, I decide to stay. Like a proper chaperone, I know that my presence puts a lid on the expression of any strong feelings and that's how it should be.

Except that I'm getting slowly drunk. And there is also Dan.

*Who?*

'Hello sexy,' he says to me, and for a minute, I too, am younger, my arm in a sling, confronting and misunderstanding the Orient. Just for a minute, mind you, for now I have got under its skin and what you learn you can't unlearn.

*But you can have a second go at things left unfinished.*

Dan waves me over. I look at Tim and Jacky and decide that it's about time they sort out whatever they have to sort out.

I stand up.

'See you later, guys,' I say and follow Dan downstairs.

# CHAPTER THIRTEEN

# THE QUESTION

The Hindu Monk couldn't sleep; an awkward, metaphysical query had formed in his head and would not let him rest. He meditated for hours, then days, then weeks, and finally reached such a state of concentration that he approached the Four Great Kings of the Four Directions through his spirit and asked them his question:

'Oh, Sages, where do the four elements, Fire, Earth, Air and Water cease to exist?'

The Four Great Kings looked at each other and shrugged their shoulders. 'We don't know,' they said. 'But you should appeal to the Thirty-three Gods of the retinue of Brahma who are higher and more sublime than us; they are the Keepers of all Knowledge.' And they showed him the Way.

The Monk now advanced towards most sublime of spirits: the gods of Yamma and Nimmarati, the Sakka, the Santusita and everybody tending the Brahma Himself. He asked with utmost respect: 'Oh, Sages, where do the four elements, Fire, Earth, Air and Water cease to exist?'

The Thirty-three shrugged their shoulders. 'We don't know,' they said. 'But you can question the Great Brahma Himself. He will know. Just go to the place where light shines forth, and a radiance appears and He will come.'

And they led the way.

It was with the utmost trepidation that the Monk who was following the Thirty-three met the Great Brahma and asked him, 'O Lord and Teacher, where do the four elements, Fire, Earth, Air and Water cease to exist?'

The Brahma said to the Monk: 'I am the Great Brahma, the Conqueror, the Unconquered, the All-Seeing, All-Powerful, the Sovereign Lord, the Maker, Creator, Chief, Appointer and Ruler, Father of All That Have Been and Shall Be.'

The Monk fell silent. 'Yes, Lord, you are all that, but where do the four elements, Fire, Earth, Air and Water cease to exist?'

The Brahma dismissed the Thirty-three with His hand and took the Monk to one side.

'The Thirty-three Gods of my retinue believe that there is nothing I can not see; that there is nothing I don't understand; there is nothing that my consciousness has not realised. But even I, the Great Brahma, do not know where the four elements cease to exist. Why did you come to me and bypass your Venerable Master?'

And with that, the Brahma and his Kingdom disappeared and the Monk found himself back to his monastery facing his teacher. Shamed and perturbed, he asked him the same question: 'Master, where do the four elements, Fire, Earth, Air and Water cease to exist?'

And this is what his Venerable Master told him.

'A company of sea-merchants had a bird in their possession that could always find the nearest shore from far away in the sea. When they lost their way, they let the bird free. It then flew upwards and then to a direction that they followed. If it did not see the shore in any direction, it flew back to the ship. It is thus that you have flown to the domain of the Brahma in search of an answer to your question, and you have returned to me.'

The Monk respectfully bowed his head.

- 35 -

For a moment I stand still, my senses stunned: the Leong Sang Temple is so much more ornate and more harmoniously balanced than I recall, its gratifying round bends fighting the tyranny of straight lines, considered evil spirits with no feeling for opulence. That black roof with its wavy tiles is a real stormy sea with serpents and ships; the giant pearl shines in the middle like an exploding supernova; dragons engarland the parapets like multi-coloured gargoyles. Last time I hadn't noticed the majolica tile line below the ramparts nor the left handed swastikas nor the bevelled paintings of the Eight Immortals.

Today the temple is also exploding in the acoustic dimension. Five Buddhist monks are chanting in front of a throng of black-clothed women. Their syllables are uttered in a nasal staccato rising and falling like two tape loops running at different speeds that reinforce each other in a positive feedback when they occasionally step in sync. I stand there absorbed, hypnotised. There is a trance-like, revelatory quality to the music, its effect mesmerising and soothing like a Brian Eno album – is there a *Music for Monasteries*? Occasionally the reed-like sound of the *so-na*, a wind instrument consisting of a tapered wooden seven-hole pipe ending in a flared brass horn, cuts sharply and brings you back down with an earthly shriek. This is more in the tradition of Byzantine liturgical hymnody or the Sufi's *qawwali* harmonising tradition than either of them would admit. The Orient may well start in Vienna, after all.

In the midst of this, a mobile rings. I check frantically. Phew, it isn't mine. It's the Resident Monk's – and it is the same one who asked me about my sling last time who runs outside to take the call that cut our mental threads so inappropriately.

I slip in the back where heaps of food are stacked in front of the ancestor tablets of the departed on tables ceremonially covered in heavily embroidered decorations of red, black and gold. There are flowers, oranges, pears and pomelos; tea and rose water; and a mind-boggling array of stir-fries, biscuits and rice clouded in pungent incense fumes. On either side of the Veneration Hall whole families sit and consume some of the foods which I now know to be sacrifices dedicated to the spirits of the ancestors.

I hear a solo voice and a smash of cymbals behind me. The ceremony is about to end. The monks have stopped chanting while the swish of cymbals is left to ring, sizzle and fade. I return to the main temple where the Resident Monk is back at his favourite spot, standing next to the statue of Confucius. With his small John Lennon glasses, shaved head and shiny demeanour, he looks more and more like the Dalai Lama. I approach him to ask what kind of service this was.

'A ceremony paying homage to the ancestors,' he says. 'We perform that three times a year.'

I point at the food in front of the altar, served as meticulously as it has been decorated. What was going to happen to all this?

'It will stay there until about five in the afternoon and then we're going to clear it.'

Are they going to eat it?

'No. This is food for the deities; it will be thrown away,' he says and points at the statues of Buddha and Guan Yin. 'The food at the back – have you been at the back? – that is for people like you and me and we can eat it afterwards.'

*I wonder if the food is less tasty after the offering.*

I tell him that I have been here before and that we have talked together. He doesn't remember me, I didn't expect he would.

'Although the Leong San is not on the main tourist routes, there are many who keep coming here. I don't know why,' he says.

I don't know why either. Maybe it's the sheer beauty of the temple, stuck as it is in a residential neighbourhood, maybe the fact that it is a living, breathing entity and not a museum piece.

'Oh, we certainly are busy,' he agrees. 'Many people come here for funerals and other rites. Even those who are Christian want to honour their ancestors the traditional Chinese way.'

He takes me aside.

'What's your name?' he asks me and when I tell him, he laughs heartily.

'My name is Shi Miaodao,' he says. 'Every monk is given the surname, title, call it what you like Shi. But my previous name was John, too. I went to a Catholic school.'

It is clear he wants to talk more, and I encourage him by listening.

'But the concept of Karma and awakening led me to Buddhism. It is the cause and effect of your own doings. Karma means that nothing is accidental. It is you who sows the seeds and eventually reaps the harvest. So don't blame anyone and don't fear anything. Everything that comes your way, embrace it. It is part of you. All your acts in your current life and your previous lives count towards your circumstances in this one. You can atone for your sinful acts and your punishment may be lessened, but you will still have to pay. In this connection, Buddha's teachings help to guide one to self-salvation.'

*There are many ways to the top of the mountain.*

'Absolutely! And it's up to you to find your own.'

I point questioningly at the statue of the White Tiger. And *this*?

'It's all symbolism. That represents the wildness of the human soul. The stone bell is supposed to suppress this savage tendency innate in human beings. The ceremony, the chanting – we put on a show. What is important is what is in your heart. People come and ask me. How does my ancestor know what I'm offering? I tell them, if you offer it sincerely – that is what matters.'

He pauses.

'Even a Muslim businessman came to see me, you know. He wanted to know Buddha's doctrine because he wondered why the Chinese are so good in business. His friend told him to pray to Buddha and to draw divining-sticks which could predict his fate. So he comes here and asks to light some sticks and pray for good fortune. But I stop him. I tell him that his fortune does not depend on the sticks. I tell him that we all have a life force in us and, like a battery, it gets weak with usage over time. So we pray to the Buddha for enlightenment and blessings. This is the way devout Buddhists recharge their batteries. Luck comes only to those who help themselves. So I tell him you have to take more interest in your business than simply sit back and pay the salaries.'

I listen nodding with my head.

'This other businessman comes to me. Chinese. He was retired. He was rich. His business was tended by his sons. He had been faithful to his wife all this time. And, shortly after he retired *bam* he started an affair with a 29-year-old woman. He was in his sixties. So he comes to me and wants my advice. He says he wants to break his affair. I ask him how sure he is. He says 80 per cent sure. I turn to him and say, no, to me you are only 20 per cent sure. It is either 100 per cent or nothing. Then comes an SMS – from *her*. I tell him not to reply. But I am sure he did afterwards, don't you? It's like eating durian.'

*Eating durian?*

'Once you have tasted the fruit, you can not give up. You have to have another one and another one.'

I let this pass.

'Chances are he'll have another affair. And another one. It was that 80 per cent that convinced me. People are not sure about anything any more. Their business, their love life, their religion. So they come to us monks, because we *are* sure. They like that.'

I look across to the Temple of 1,000 Lights.

'They are different from us,' the monk says following my gaze. 'They are Thai, closer to India and they keep some very old traditions. Them, and the Cambodians. And

Burmese. There are a few differences between them and us. Now, we are vegetarian as you know…'

I interrupt him by pointing at the sumptuous god-feast at the altar.

'All of them vegetarian dishes. Strictly. If you believe in reincarnation how can you eat chicken or duck, they could be your forefathers!'

He turns towards the Thai temple.

'But they eat anything. This is, because in the old times monks used to wander around being dependent on alms. They didn't expect people to cook for them, so they had to eat anything they were offered to keep themselves alive. So the Thai monks, they eat everything. But until noon.'

*Noon?*

'Yes. From noon until sunrise next day, they eat nothing.'

*How Ramadan,* I tell myself. The Thais and Burmese are not only close to India, they are also close to the Middle East. I remember the Chinese worshipping like Muslims in the Bintan temple and wonder if the Orient is not a continuum of beliefs and variations of practices, after all.

'They also tell you your fortune. Is this why you have come?'

I hate to say no, but yes, but no, but yes, he's right.

Promising that I will keep in touch, I say good-bye to the Venerable Miaodao and make my way across to the Thai temple which is like I remember it: mostly empty. This time I ask for the exact number of lights – they are 989 – and go directly to the Wheel of Fortune where I pay my 50 cents, take a deep breath and spin the wheel.

The caretaker picks up the prediction:

*'The Wheel of Fortune says fate is like a little boat in the middle of a storm in a wide rough sea. You shall toil and sweat before*

*you gain anything you wish but persevere and you will win help*
*from a kind-hearted person and you will enjoy threefold happiness*
*namely Marriage, Luck and a Healthy Son. But if you should*
*institute any form of litigation you will have no success. Your fate*
*is comparable to the time when the Lord Buddha was incarnated*
*as Maha Janaka who went to trade on the high seas and whose*
*ship with cargo was wrecked and all was lost but he, himself who*
*swam safely to shore with the help and guidance of Mekala, the*
*angel of light.'*

I liked the first one better.

## - 36 -

I stop Richard before he goes to mix me a vodka and tonic
which by now he does on auto.

'Is the birthday boy here?' I ask him and I have to repeat it,
because the DJ at the back has pumped up the volume tonight.

Before he can answer, a round, rouged-up face with long, false
eyelashes that could be construed as a deadly weapon kisses me
on the cheek.

'I'm he-*ere*!' he pouts and shouts. 'Thanks for coming, *dah-*
*ling*, mwah, mwah.'

I hardly recognise Dan. Jackie Chan was never his model in
the masculinity stakes, but, but...

'You are in drag,' I tell him, feeling stupid for stating the
obvious.

'Not yet *dah-ling*, not yet,' he says, blowing me kisses as he
disappears in the crowd and a good crowd it is, too: for a Sunday
night the place is full. What happened to the Asian work ethic?

It's early and I am not drunk and, as I sit in Tantric's oh-
so-familiar forecourt to escape that accursed Singaporean
air conditioning, my mind wanders off on its own.

The city-state is only forty-something and, like a grand Hollywood actress, she is at the peak of her beauty. She is rich, successful but also wiser and more experienced. No wrinkles, double-chins or bags under the eyes detract from her perfect aspect and any contemplation of future facelifts is fanciful, remote. More than ever, our diva is also at the peak of her professional prowess: she can dictate her own terms, choose the scripts carefully, and start directing films herself. The PAP government, like a dutiful husband who has managed her from her poor beginnings, sits back and watches her achievements with pride. Hollywood being Hollywood, of course, the tongues are wagging lethally. They wonder how the couple have stuck it together for so long and, instead of admiring their resilience, they claim that she wants a divorce, but her husband is using dirty tricks to keep her from running to the lawyers. Some decry her husband's unscrupulous business techniques: producing new blockbusters is not enough – he wants to grind the competition to the ground as well. But then, what do you expect from Hollywood?

'Vodka jellies?'

Richard is going around offering customers these lethal concoctions. They are free and they are perfect. 'So difficult to get them right,' he says, and I have never seen him so proud. 'You can't use too much vodka 'cos they won't set. You have to get the balance exactly right.'

It's all a question of balance, yes, and it hurts the liberal in me to admit that on balance Singapore has got it more right than wrong and that its version of democracy deserves to be examined rather than dismissed out of hand. Take detention without trial, where the normal response is the knee-jerk 'can't condone it': like Singapore itself, it deserves a second look. The Internal Security Act was set up in 1948 by the British during the communist insurgency in Malaya. Post-independence, it's been invoked only twice for threats against the state, more recently against the terrorists of Jemaah Islamiyah to prevent a Bali-like atrocity. Even then things are not so black-and-white: under the Act each case is reviewed every two years and detainees are discharged when *they do not pose a significant security threat*. One of them has already been released for *responding positively to religious counselling*: Ali Ridhaa bin Abdullah, a Muslim convert whose original name was Andrew Gerald. There is a criminal variant of this act that broke the back of the Chinese secret societies which operate as clandestinely as terrorist cells; Lee Kuan Yew himself has said that this was the most difficult task he faced after independence. Singapore must be the only place in the world – including London where Triad gangsterism has been routed.

It's easy to dismiss such laws with a specious sense of European superiority. But keep in mind our reaction to our own anti-terrorism acts: once threatened, did we not readily accept an erosion of our rights to prevent a greater disaster? Do we not clap and cheer for the hero in Hollywood films when he steals a car in order to prevent a lethal explosion? In Singapore, the conundrum 'does the end justify the means' has been answered with a resounding 'yes' whereas we, in the West, are still wrestling in the dark with the dilemma.

The racket inside draws me back in. A spotlight hits a makeshift stage and a tarted up Dan, complete in a black bouffant, tight red dress and false boobs, starts mouthing the lyrics to One Night Only – more Jennifer Hudson than Ricky Martin. The whole bar is whistling approvingly, and someone next to me asks me whether I know the name of the act. Certainly Dan looks professional enough: he is strutting about confidently with the right dose of camp and competence. It's all, as we agreed, a question of balance.

But hey, *a change of costume*! That black bouffant lasts only for the slow part of the song; Dan disappears for a second and *wa lao,* he's back with a tighter white dress and a platinum blond wig – it's Madonna! He finishes with an up-tempo Beyoncé mix of the song and, as we applaud rowdily, I can't help thinking that such death-defeating exuberance can only emerge from a death-defying experience.

The DJ asks us if we want an encore. We cry 'Yes' and Dan steps into a gymnastically perfect 'Vogue'. His timing is perfect: how long does he spend miming to Madonna videos? I am rendered speechless as he swings his hips and moves his arms around his head with perfect panache. He is so larger-than-life that when he takes a bow the girl next to me shakes her head.

'Is that all?' she says. 'Is that the show?'

I turn to her, explain the situation and she's impressed. She is Japanese, from Tokyo. There is a mixed party of them here. They look a bit demure.

'We went to the Powerhouse, but they wouldn't let us in. Private party.'

Oh, no! This is my last Sunday in Singapore and I really, really want to go to the superclub by the Harbourfront, a converted power station that's become the hottest night in town. Damn! Why did I wait until today?

I help Dan down, abuzz with the excitement of his triumph, and kiss him. 'You were *fabulous,*' I say and mean it. 'Is this the beginning of a second career or what?'

'Don' be silly,' he laughs. 'You come with us to Powerhouse later? Goes on till fo' in the morning.'

I point at the Japanese. 'The guys there have been already. There is a private party tonight.'

Dan winks at me: 'They say that to people they don' wan' in.'

*Oh.*

'Come outside, we have a bottle of champagne and then we go to the club.'

I hate this American teen word but I will use it anyway: the Powerhouse was *awesome*.

Of course, being let in to any venue that has just barred a party of younger and more beautiful people would be enough for me to sing its praises, but the Powerhouse really is the Godzilla of all clubs. A cross between a warehouse and a grand arena, the place oozes presence; imagine a rave at Battersea Power Station and you get the picture. Dozens of illuminated structures and a beehive of lighted squares on our left compete with the abstract back-projections on our right. The tribal house sound is as clean and as technically perfect as can be outside the digital showrooms of the Funan Centre. Eight-hundred-odd punters are crammed on the dancefloor, on the overlooking balconies, in its various nooks and corners. To top it all, we don't have go-go dancers; we have go-go trapeze artists who display their aerial acrobatics above us without a safety net – I suppose we are it. You'd expect this in LA or Tokyo but not in an unfashionable corner of South East Asia. It doesn't look like it's going to remain like that much longer – someone tell the Beckhams: Singapore is well and truly swinging.

I lose Dan almost immediately and roam around drunk.
Cocktails, coke, beer: everything is cheaper in pitchers and,
this being Singapore, nobody says no to a bargain. Well, I
do: like hell I am going to hold one of those monsters on
the dancefloor, so I order a normal-size vodka and tonic. I
am served reasonably quickly but wait interminably for my
change; by the time it arrives I have almost finished my drink
and I haven't moved away from the bar. Instead of working
myself into a fit, I sigh with resigned sentimentality. There
is always a place in Singapore where some choreography is
attached to ordering. Here, the barman puts your dollars in
a leather folder and hands them to a cashier at the end of the
bar, along with your order sheet. It is the cashier – always a
woman, why? – who handles the payment. It makes some
sort of sense until you realise that, in practice, the folders
stack upwards and the queuing is 'first in, last out': if too
many people use the bar after you, you've had it.

Clumsily, I turn and spill what's left of my drink onto a
guy's shirt by accident. I apologise. He nods unperturbed
and continues talking to his mate.

I squint. *It can't be… Yes, it can!*

'Excuse me,' I say, knowing in advance my question will
sound stupid, 'you are chewing gum.'

They look at each other. 'Yeah,' says the culprit who is
sporting a goatee.

'But I was told you can't buy gum in Singapore.'

The guy picks up a packet of Wrigley's from his top pocket
and draws back the silver foil to offer me a piece.

'Thanks, I'm drinking alcohol,' I excuse myself, slurring
my words. 'I will only swallow it and it will get stuck in
a corner of my bowels where it can only be flushed with
a colonic.'

They both look at me suspiciously and leave. I wonder if they were dealers. They certainly tried to push their gear.

Jimmy James' 'Fashionista' hits the decks and I can't believe it; people on the podiums are mouthing the words with the ease Dan mimed Madonna: '*New York, London, Paris, Milan/Tokyo, I think it's in Japan.*' These dancing girls and boys have known nothing but the PAP and nothing but prosperity, and I wonder what's going on in their heads that are woggling weakly to the rhythm: '*Asia, Malaysia, Las Vegas to play/LA, if you pay my way.*' Do they care about politics or have they given up altogether because it's not advisable to raise their heads above the parapet? The West has been scorned by the Asian tiger economies for caring more about abstract human rights than real, concrete ones like poverty and hunger: get the people fed first and free them later, they counter in unison. Alright, fine. So what happens now that the only hungry souls in Singapore are ghosts wandering aimlessly during the seventh lunar month?

I always leave Singapore with a question more subtle than the last one.

## - 37 -

South Boat Quay's godowns are so Disney-drawn that they feel like an urban planner's folly, set as they are against the glass-and-metal skymonsters of the CBD. Yet they have been there forever – well, since Raffles reclaimed the unhealthy swampland that covered that tract of the rivermouth. For half a century about three quarters of Singapore's freight business was transacted through this small strip of land, until the late 1860s when Keppel

Harbour started handling the new Suez Canal traffic. Nowadays, I wouldn't blink if I learned that Boat Quay might well be responsible for three quarters of the tourist restaurant turnover. There is many a museum that a three-day-tourist en route to Australia may miss, but everyone is sure to dine al fresco at Boat Quay.

I meet Jacky at Harry's Bar, which became internationally famous as Nick Leeson's favourite watering hole, although his most legendary escapade (mooning at a party of Singapore Airlines' stewardesses) occurred at Off Quay, a few doors up.

Ah, the Leeson case; it has become part of Singapore folklore. What with *Rogue Trader*, the book and subsequent movie starring Ewan McGregor, everyone knows how historic Barings – bankers to the Queen and fund managers of the 1803 Louisiana Purchase – collapsed in 1995 after Nick Leeson lost millions and diverted the losses to a clandestine account. Leeson fled Singapore in order not to face charges here and was arrested in Germany hoping to be tried in the UK. But being a rogue trader means exactly that: the boys in the city didn't try too hard for his extradition and let him sweat it out in Singapore where he was sent down for six-and-a-half years. After serving just over half his sentence, Leeson – suffering from colon cancer and having lost his wife who divorced him – was let free; on the night of his release, a party was held at Harry's Bar which he, unsurprisingly, did not attend. Having survived the disease, he remarried and moved to Ireland, where he is now general manager of Galway United and enjoys his status as an after-dinner speaker. In a recent interview, he said he is considering going back to trading full-time. You've been warned.

Still, he is one of the most iconic figures associated with Singapore. He represents not only the greedy face of unfettered capitalism that encompassed the island and the whole of Asia in the 1990s, but also the maturing of Singapore's financial structures. It was the local regulator that eventually discovered Leeson's scam and it was Singapore's not the Bank of England's report into the scandal that was more highly rated more among the City eggheads – including Nick Leeson himself. The whole sorry episode, if anything, strengthened the reputation of the city-state as a place to do business.

Harry's Bar is another winner from this sordid affair. Busy and important, with a website, a newssheet and several new offshoots all over town, it stands in a modest, two-storey old warehouse at the end of Boat Quay. It's a difficult joint to pigeonhole. On one hand, it is decorated with pictures of BB King, Art Blakey and Grover Washington and offers live jazz, but on the other, it serves Heineken beer on tap, Premiership football on TV and fish and chips to its patrons. The decor downstairs is modern with aluminium-frame chairs and tall, iron bar stools, but the more exclusive upstairs bar is more akin to a Mayfair Gentlemen's Club: the furniture is teak and leather rather than rattan; sofas and poufs replace the chairs and stools; and a pool table makes an appearance instead of a sports widescreen. Like the Raffles of times past, it is creating a new urban narrative for the city in the twenty-first century. It doesn't yet have its own Singapore Sling, but it's working on it. May I suggest the Madame Butterfly for your delectation – although, lest we forget Nick Leeson, there is the Bank Breaker, too.

That's what I'm drinking now with Jacky.

'Tim couldn't make it?' I ask.

'I didn't tell him,' she answers. 'I fucked up.'

I wait patiently to hear the whole story.

'After you left us at Taboo, I thought I'd clear the air. "About that awkward episode in your flat last week," I said to him. "Do you remember?" He said he didn't.'

'Good.'

'So I reminded him.'

*Oh, no.*

'I told him what happened. Or what I understood happened. And what I meant.'

She lights a cigarette.

'And then I snogged him.'

*I should not have left her alone.*

'But Tim was not interested. He was stand-offish. He said I was too forward.'

'He was sober and you were drunk,' I reminded her. 'What could he do? If he made a move he'd be accused of taking advantage of you. Tim is too much of a gentleman for that.'

'Now I don't even have his number. I deleted it, embarrassed, this morning.'

'You overcompensated.'

She looks at me downcast.

'John, I've been married for too long, I don't know how to date anymore.'

I look at her and realise there is more to it.

'This has happened before, hasn't it?'

There is a long pause while Jacky finishes her Martini.

'Well, yes, it has,' she says. 'There was this ex-boyfriend of mine. He was the first man I ever loved. We went out for a few years when I was a teenager and then we split.'

'Why?'

'He had another girlfriend. I asked him to choose between me and her but he couldn't make up his mind. I was younger than her. Maybe he thought I was less mature. Anyway, I split with him and never saw him again.'

She takes a big puff from her cigarette.

'Until a few years ago.'

She talks softly, taking a long time between the sentences.

'Do you remember the tsunami? I suppose no one has forgotten it. He was in Thailand then and lived through it. As his life flashed in front of his eyes, he realised that he still loved me, that I was the only one who mattered to him. Or so he said. A month later he sent me an e-mail out of the blue.'

'How did he find you?'

'It's not too difficult. Let's say, I have a high profile.'

I order more drinks.

'I didn't reply at first. I said to myself, "God, not another tsunami rebirth experience." But he persisted. I thought that if he says he loves me after all this time, it must be genuine. So I agreed and after twenty years we met again. I took two gay friends and one girlfriend with me. I dressed in my grungiest gear in order not to encourage him. I was frightened. And the reason I was frightened is that I was still in love with him.'

'And?'

'We met.'

'And?'

'He's got a wife and two kids.'

'*And?*'

'Like the first time, it wasn't meant to be,' she says and stubs out her cigarette.

'History repeats itself,' I mumble.

'I still think of him. But he is someone unattainable, someone I think of and it hurts. We talked a lot. I asked him: "How did you choose this woman to marry? How did you know she was the one?" He replied with platitudes. "First I thought she would make a good wife, then she would make a good mother."'

'Confucian crap.'

'Precisely. That's what they've brainwashed him with. That's why he comes back twenty years later and realises he's made a mistake and wants to correct it. What *I* think of is: can I grow together with this man? Do we have the same interests? Can we communicate? Can we be friends? 'Cos after a while, the sex and the passion diminish.'

I look at Jacky's pretty face for a long time. Sometimes the more you learn about a person, the less you like them. In Jacky's case the opposite is true.

*Like this city itself.*

'Is this why you are so confused about Tim?' I ask her.

She nods. 'I don't want to make the same mistakes again, but I do.'

We stop talking, but Harry's Bar is far from silent.

'You know what Jacky?' I finally blurt. 'Do you know why I really, really like you?'

'Why?'

'Because we come from completely different backgrounds, our experiences are so different, – you live in Singapore and I in London – but our minds can meet. We click. And I find this comforting.'

She leans over and kisses me on the cheek. We remain silent for some time; we don't need to speak to communicate.

'Will you come to London to see me?' I ask her eventually.

'I come to fashion shows in Europe once a year.'

We sit back contemplating our parting.

'If I come, can I stay with you?' she asks.

'Sure. Anytime,' I say and squeeze her hand.

'Will you let me smoke in your house?' she asks with a smirk.

I smile. 'You can smoke in the kitchen.'

She giggles involuntarily but quickly turns quiet.

'When is the best time to come?'

'For me, the autumn. It's cool, but not cold. The trees shed their leaves and the colours look beautiful. It's the only time when you expect rain, so it doesn't bother you. And when a shower does come, the leaves become musty and a mild, sweet smell is in the air. It's the only time when London smells sweet.'

She sits back, immersed in her thoughts.

'You know what?' she asks after a while.

'What?'

'I'll file for divorce. It's about time.'

'I thought people here didn't divorce'.

She looks at me perplexed.

'Who told you that?'

I shrug my shoulders.

'Never mind.' I reply.

## - 38 -

I get off the metro at Raffles Place, but I don't lose my bearings any more. It still feels like a giant Broadgate development stretched to infinity, but now the skyscrapers are familiar, have names and are as such less threatening. To my left stands my favourite: the Caltex-Hitachi Tower, its steel and glass ring-shaped structure providing a visual alternative to the linear geometry around me. As a homage to the currency-exchange hawkers of old when ships and sailors descended on the river in droves, it stands protectively over Change Alley that leads to Collyer Quay. Behind me rises the grey UOB Plaza, part of the curtain of granite and glass that began to define the global city of the nineties: two octagonal towers, linked by an office bridge hanging over the gateway to Boat Quay. But the octagons are not complete: the floors are stacked on top of each other, some aligned properly, some rotated at 45-degree angles like a giant corkscrew made out of cleaving cubes. This is a landmark that can be seen from the Padang, from the Esplanade, and during that fleeting moment over the bridge coming from the airport on the ECP Expressway.

The post-modern, flashy fabric of the rest of the buildings – HSBC at Ocean Towers, the UCO Bank, the Indian Bank – are stitched together between these two architectural tours de force. Except for one much older structure that stands on the other side of the UOB Plaza: the 18-storey Bank of China. Completed in the mid-fifties, it is the granddaddy of them all. Not only was it the first skyscraper to stand near Raffles Place, but it was also the first centrally air-conditioned building in Singapore – if it only knew the terrible trend it started. But its transgression is forgiven, for it is beautiful, combining the elements of modernism with subtle Chinese ornamentation under its façade.

I walk across to the Padang for a last stroll. Everywhere I look is a reminder that this is a city which changes and mutates, as if standing still is a transgression. The old Legislative Council in front of me, a genteel, Georgian building, is now housing the Asian Civilisations Museum. That wonderful, domed Supreme Court has become an empty shell; the functionaries have moved to a new address on North Bridge Road. The City Hall next door that saw all the important events in Singapore's History is vacant, too. A sign says that, along with the Supreme Court, it will house Singapore's National Art collection by 2012. That leaves enough time for the censors to veto the nudes, I suppose.

I walk up the river to the gaudily-coloured MICA building; this is where the MDA is based, easily my least favourite institution, and one of those niggling questions forms in my mind: how can you aim for a grand art collection with such strict censorship laws? Whom are they supposed to protect, anyway? There are few countries whose citizens are as educated and mature as Singapore's.

I am about to turn right, but something catches my eye. I walk to the bottom of Fort Canning, the old Forbidden Hill, and look over to the River Valley Swimming Pool. It is fenced off, the pools are empty and the tiles are being ripped up. Opposite, on the other side of the river, a new hotel development is being erected. These baths are far too central and the land they occupy too valuable. Except that their demise is also that of a legend; that of Forbidden Hill and the sultan's harem that used to bathe in the springs on this very spot. The River Valley Complex may well have been underused but it kept the myth alive.

Here is Hill Street with its Armenian church. Her orchid garden may have given way to a mall, but in this graveyard the headstone of Agnes Joaquim is commemorated with a plaque. This city can be mawkish when regretful.

I walk past Bras Basah Road up Victoria Street towards Arab Street and I tell myself that there much less to regret (censorship? gay rights? punishments?) than to admire in Singapore: its tranquillity, its mindset, its material success. And I always get a buzz from its amalgam of cultures that manifests itself wherever you stand to look, smell or listen: the mix of architectural styles, the range of food in the hawker stalls, the multilingual chatter on the pavements. As I tread on the steps of the procession that on 21 July 1964 led to the Singapore riots, I know that these people have finally got it right where it matters: living together with mutual respect. That date is now celebrated in the city's schools but not as one of division: it is Racial Harmony Day, when pupils learn to appreciate each other's cultural background. It takes courage and guts to take the blackest day in your history and turn it into one of reconciliation. Could we designate 7 July as a day to celebrate our own diversity?

There is a small Asian country that can show us the way.

I am back at Raffles Place where everything is so familiar and it is this very familiarity that I carry as a burden. You are never sorry to leave a place as a tourist because by definition you have kept aloof. You are not affected by its life or its rhythm because you have put on a protective suit with goggles and a face mask. But when you learn enough and crave to know more – ah, it is that knowledge that hurts. I wish I were a typical tourist, one leaving tomorrow after a two-day break en route to Australia. I wish I could wear my sling again and use it as an excuse not to go out, not to meet people, not to be involved, but it's not possible any more, for now I know and I care.

# NOTES

## THE MYTHS

I have compiled the myths from several sources, but I have rewritten them extensively in this book: for instance, I have made up a complete story around Shushan's famous *koan* about the most valuable thing in the world in chapter three. *The Buddha's Message Is Eternal* comes from that classic of Chinese literature by Wu Ch'êng-ên, *Journey to the West*, which appears in the references as *Monkey*; *The Immortal* is a parable which I found in Percival Yetts' article on The Eight Immortals; *The Favourite* is a well-known story quoted by Hinsch that you can read at Fordham University's website along with others; *The Dutiful Son* is a fable on filial piety that I first noticed in the Haw-Par Villa; *What the Eyes Don't See* is from *The Book of Mencius* written by Ke Meng during the Warring States period (around 300 BCE); *Ghost For Sale* and *The Rabbit's Sacrifice* both come from the book *Mooncakes and Hungry Ghosts: Festivals of China*; *The Missing Piece* is a traditional folk legend from the island of Bintan that tries to make sense of the historical event of the assassination of Sultan Mahmud Shah II in 1699 CE.

*The Question* is actually part of the Buddhist canon, the Tipitaka – which was allegedly brought to China by Xuán Zàng as described in the first chapter – so I have kept it closer to the original than everything else. It appears in the *Kevatta Sutta* and the version I have read has been translated from Pali by Thanissaro Bhikkhu. Unlike my rendition, the question *does* get answered in the Buddhist text, and you are all urged to go to the website in the references and read it.

Every Singaporean will recognise the tale of the swordfish plague which appears in the *Malay Annals* (as translated by Raffles' friend Dr John Leyden) but I should make clear that in the *Annals* it was the Sultan's advisors who prompted him to assassinate the boy. But, hey, was anyone present during the discussions? And he did give the order, didn't he?

Finally, I admit that I have cheated and I have added three Japanese Zen stories, but I have justified it to myself by the fact that they are timeless, they are Buddhist and, well, if a Japanese team can play in Singapore's football league (it does) then I can put some of their tales in my book. They are *The Wise Old Man* and *Dreamland* from that wonderful volume *Zen Flesh, Zen Bones* and the other is, of course, Shushan's *koan* about the head of the dead cat in *On Inns and Valuables*.

## CURRENCY

Unless explicitly shown otherwise, all prices given are in Singapore dollars whose exchange rate is about three to the British pound at the time of writing.

# GLOSSARY

**Ah:** A particle appended at the end of a sentence implying a question and requiring confirmation, something like our 'innit?' as in: 'You English, *ah*?'

**Ang moh:** A slightly derogatory term in Singlish, meaning a Westerner (literally 'red-haired' in Hokkien).

**Atap (or attap):** Malay for roof/shelter, denoting the palm-leaf thatched houses common in the old kampongs.

**Bendahara:** In the classical Malay sultanates this was the title given to the sultan's prime minister, who was also the treasurer and chief executive of the kingdom.

**Batu:** Malay unit of distance equal to a mile also used to refer to sections of the motorway.

**Box-wallah:** Anglo-Indian term denoting a businessman.

**Char kway teow:** A popular dish in Singapore made with flat rice noodles fried together in pork fat with prawns, fish, egg and other seafood. The word is of Hokkien origin and it means unsurprisingly 'fried flat noodles'.

**Godown:** A warehouse.

**Keramat:** The tomb of a Muslim holy person, normally with miraculous properties.

**Koan:** A brief question, story or saying that appears impenetrable by reason but can be understood by intuition. It forms part of the teachings of the Zen school of Buddhism.

**Kris:** A dagger with a sinuous blade used by the Malays and other people in the South Seas.

**Lah:** A particle appended at the end of an exclamation for emphasis – it is similar to our 'hey' or 'oi' even the American 'yo' at the beginning of a sentence. 'Oi, go home!' would be 'go home, *lah*!'

**Lai dat:** A Singlish expression at the end of a sentence, meaning 'like that'.

**Laksamana:** The commander of the fleet in the classical Malay sultanates, a position equivalent to an admiral.

**Leh:** A particle similar to lah, but slightly pleading – 'Go home, *leh*!' implies 'please go home, don't be so bloody difficult!'

**Li:** A traditional Chinese unit of distance equivalent to 500 metres.

**Lor:** A particle like *lah* or *leh*, carrying an air of resignation. 'Go home, *lor*' would be appropriate talking to a drunk or a truant kid.

**Mak nyah:** The preferred expression for Malaysian male-to-female transsexuals.

**Mee:** This Hokkien word also means noodles, but these are fat noodles made of dough, not the rice noodles used in *char kway teow*. They are called 'mein' in Cantonese which is where our 'chow mein' comes from.

**Merlion:** A mythical creature with the upper body of a lion and the lower body of a fish, the symbol of Singapore.

**Nangka:** A jackfruit.

**Nanyang:** South East Asia as known throughout China, literally 'the South Seas'.

**Ojek:** An Indonesian motorcycle-taxi where the paying passenger rides pillion.

**Orang laut:** Literally meaning 'sea-person'. A Malay term that is used to describe the people of the archipelago who literally live on their boats, eking an existence from the sea. Some writers freely translate it as 'sea-gypsy' which is rather apt.

**Prau or prahu:** A long, narrow Malay boat with a triangular sail. In Raffles' time they were decked and up to sixty feet in length, but modern *praus* tend to be open and much smaller.

**Punkah-wallah:** A boy who was employed to keep moving a large piece of cloth, used as a fan, by pulling the end of a rope with his hand, or more usually with his foot.

**Sagga:** The domain of Buddhist paradise populated by worthy beings who are still subject to reincarnation and rebirth.

**Tuan/Mem:** A respectful title meaning Sir/Madam in Imperial Malaya and Singapore.

**Wa:** A Japanese word, meaning social harmony.

**Wa lao:** A Singlish expression equivalent to 'goodness gracious', or 'Oh My God'. It actually means 'I'm old' in Mandarin – the sentiment expressed being equivalent to someone so befuddled that he or she feels suddenly aged.

**Wang:** (i) 'Lucky' as in 'Lucky' Wang (ii) a corruption of *wén*, a unit of payment that was used in China and amongst the Chinese diaspora until the late nineteeth century when it was replaced by the *yuan*.

# REFERENCES

Allen, Charles *Tales from the South China Seas* (Abacus, 1983)

Anthony, Rachel *Singapore* (Lonely Planet, 2002)

Beng Huat, Chua *Life Is Not Complete Without Shopping: Consumption Culture in Singapore* (Singapore University Press, 2003)

Bravo-Bhasin, Marión *Culture Shock! Singapore: A Survival Guide to Customs and Etiquette* (Marshall-Cavendish, 2006)

Ch'êng-ên, Wu *Monkey* (translated by Arthur Waley, Allen and Unwin, 1942)

Collis, Maurice *Raffles* (Graham Brash, 1982)

Dalby, Andrew *Dictionary of Languages* (Bloomsbury, 1998)

Dawson, Raymond *The Chinese Experience* (Phoenix Press, 2005)

Dobbs, Stephen *The Singapore River: A Social History, 1819–2002* (Singapore University Press, 2003)

George, Cherian *Singapore: The Air-Conditioned Nation: essays on the politics of comfort and control, 1990–2000* (Landmark Books, 2000)

Hinsch, Brett *Passions of the Cut Sleeve: The Male Homosexual Tradition in China* (University of California Press, 1990)

Humphreys, Neil *Notes from an Even Smaller Island* (Times Media Private Ltd, 2001)

Kah Choon, Ban *Absent History: The Untold Story of Special Branch Operations in Singapore, 1915–1942* (Horizon Books, 2001)

Keay, John *The Honourable Company: A History of the English East India Company* (HarperCollins, 1991)

Lau, Albert *A Moment of Anguish: Singapore in Malaysia and the Politics of Disengagement* (Times Media Private Ltd, 2003)

Leeson, Nick *Rogue Trader* (Little Brown,1996)

Leyden, John *Malay Annals* (Longman, Hurst, Rees, Orme and Brown, 1821)

Lim, Gerrie *Invisible Trade: High-class sex for sale in Singapore* (Monsoon Books, 2004)

Modder, Ralph *The Singapore Chinese Massacre* (Horizon, 2004)

Nurvidya-Arifin, Evi; Ananta, Aris and Suryadinata, Leo *Indonesia's Population: ethnicity and religion in a changing political landscape* (Institute of East Asian studies, 2003)

Powell, Robert *Singapore Architecture: A Short History* (Periplus Editions HK Ltd, 2004)

Reps, Paul *Zen Flesh, Zen Bones* (Penguin, 1957)

Savage, Victor R. and Yeoh, Brenda S. A. *Toponymics: A study of Singapore Street Names* (Eastern Universities Press, 2004)

Smith, Colin *Singapore Burning: Heroism and Surrender in World War II* (Penguin, 2006)

Somers Heidhues, Mary *Southeast Asia; A Concise History* (Thames and Hudson, 2000)

Stepanchuk, Carol and Wong, Charles *Mooncakes and Hungry Ghosts: Festivals of China* (China Books, 1991)

Tannahil, Reay *Sex In History* (Sphere Books, 1989)

Thai Ker, Liu (Chairman) *Report Of The Censorship Review Committee 2003* (Ministry of Information, Communications and the Arts, Singapore, 2003)

Wise, Michael and Him Wise, Mun (editors) *Travellers' Tales Of Old Singapore* (Times Books International, 1996)

Yetts, W. Percival, 'The Eight Immortals' *The Journal Of The Royal Asiatic Society*, V36 (1916)

Young, Gavin *In Search Of Conrad* (Penguin, 1991)

# GUIDES

Augustin, Andreas *The Raffles Treasury: Secrets of a Grand Old Lady* (Kin Yiap Press, 1988)

Masjid Sultan – Brief History, leaflet

The National Heritage Board: *Discover Singapore: Heritage Trails* (National Heritage Board, 2004)

Unknown, *Haw-Par Villa: The Original Tiger Balm Gardens: A Guide* (undated)

# WEBSITES

http://www.scroll.demon.co.uk/spaver.htm
Firstly, of course, my own website with some pictures of the places described here, as well as the poem that inspired the title:

http://www.yawningbread.org/
Alex's weblog as Yawning Bread

http://www.paranormal.org.sg/
Singapore Paranormal Investigators

http://www.etymonline.com
Dictionary of languages

http://www.nesa.org.uk/html/alexandra_massacre.htm
Alexandra Hospital Massacre

http://hinduwebsite.com/buddhism/essays/buddhist_heaven.asp
Buddhism: Philosophy and Concepts

http://tinyurl.com/ywf4og
In case you don't believe my ASBO story, read: 'Yob banned from his own front door' by Paul Carey, *Western Mail*, 20 January 2005

http://www.corpun.com/awfay9405.htm
An account of Michael Fay's crime and punishment by Alejandro Reyes ('A Caning in Singapore Stirs Up a Fierce Debate About Crime and Punishment', *Asiaweek*, Hong Kong, 25 May 1994)

http://infopedia.nlb.gov.sg/
Official collection of essays on Singapore's heritage

http://www.elibraryhub.com
The *Malay Annals* available online

http://www.fordham.edu/halsall/pwh/china-gaytexts.html
The story of Mi-zi Xia

http://china.tyfo.com/int/literature/fables/20000221literature.htm
Tales from Meng Ke's *The Book of Mencius*

http://www.accesstoinsight.org/tipitaka/dn/dn.11.0.than.html#gods
The answer to *The Question*

http://www.ashidakim.com/zenkoans/
Zen *koans*

**Brazil**
**Life, Blood, Soul**

John Malathronas

£8.99

P/B

ISBN: 1 84024 350 3
ISBN 13: 978 1 84024 350 5

'*In Brazil the motto seems to be: if you've got it, flaunt it, and if you don't, flaunt it even more...*'

Brazil: an eclectic nation that evokes images of vibrant carnivals, crowded shanty towns and football on the beach. Shaped by its many cultures, the Portuguese, African, Indian and European communities have ensured the evolution of a colourful, diverse population.

**John Malathronas** fell prey to Brazil's seductive allure in the early nineties, a fascination that continues to this day. His odyssey through the adrenaline-fuelled, chaotic city bars, the extravagant and exotic Carnaval, the lush vegetation of the Amazon rainforest and the destitute shanty towns reveals the throbbing heartbeat of this remarkable country.

'*... An intimate and articulate account of life – in all its multifaceted glory*'                          A Place in the Sun magazine

'*... One of the most telling accounts of contemporary South America I have read*'                          Errol Uys, author

'*... An amazing book that truly captures the heart of this vibrant country, and will make you want to book that flight to Rio sooner rather than later*'                          Palatinate News

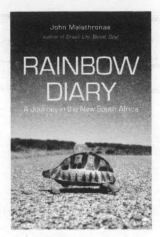

**Rainbow Diary**
**A Journey in the New South Africa**

John Malathronas

£8.99

P/B

ISBN: 1 84024 445 3
ISBN 13: 978 1 84024 445 8

From the stillness of the Karoo savannah to the warmth of the Indian Ocean, and from the exclusive white neighbourhoods of Pretoria to the destitution of the black townships, **John Malathronas** chronicles a journey in one of the most beautiful countries on Earth.

Whether dancing the night away in a club, mountain-biking down a hair-raising incline or looking out for leopards on a safari, the author is full of sharp observations – be they social, historical, political or even botanical. A gifted storyteller, he draws fascinating portraits of the many Afrikaner, Xhosa, Zulu, Indian and Swazi characters he encounters, all of whom make up the tapestry of the new South Africa.

'... South Africans will learn something about themselves by reading this travelogue; it takes a stranger to shine a light on our country'
Johannesburg Star

'Follow this gifted story-teller as he journeys through South Africa. A compelling read, with insightful glimpses of the nation and its people'
Travel Africa

'An ambitious book that sees him flit between nightclub, township and safari in an attempt to reach the heart of the African nation'       TNT magazine

'Insightful'                                         The Lonely Planet: South Africa

www.summersdale.com